STUDIES IN ENGLISH LITERATURES

Edited by Koray Melikoğlu

Shafquat Towheed (ed.)

New Readings in the Literature of British India, c.1780-1947

STUDIES IN ENGLISH LITERATURES

Edited by Koray Melikoğlu

ISSN 1614-4651

1. *Özden Sözalan*
   The Staged Encounter
   Contemporary Feminism and Women's Drama
   2nd, revised editon
   ISBN 3-89821-367-6

2. *Paul Fox (ed.)*
   Decadences
   Morality and Aesthetics in British Literature
   ISBN 3-89821-573-3

3. *Daniel M. Shea*
   James Joyce and the Mythology of Modernism
   ISBN 3-89821-574-1

4. *Paul Fox and Koray Melikoğlu (eds.)*
   Formal Investigations
   Aesthetic Style in Late-Victorian and Edwardian Detective Fiction
   ISBN 978-3-89821-593-0

5. *David Ellis*
   Writing Home
   Black Writing in Britain Since the War
   ISBN 978-3-89821-591-6

6. *Wei H. Kao*
   The Formation of an Irish Literary Canon in the Mid-Twentieth Century
   ISBN 978-3-89821-545-9

7. *Bianca Del Villano*
   Ghostly Alterities
   Spectrality and Contemporary Literatures in English
   ISBN 978-3-89821-714-9

8. *Melanie Ann Hanson*
   Decapitation and Disgorgement
   The Female Body's Text in Early Modern English Drama and Poetry
   ISBN 978-3-89821-605-5

9. *Shafquat Towheed (ed.)*
   New Readings in the Literature of British India, c.1780-1947
   ISBN 978-3-89821-673-9

Shafquat Towheed (ed.)

New Readings in the Literature of British India, c.1780-1947

ibidem-Verlag
Stuttgart

Bibliografische Information der Deutschen Nationalbibliothek
Die Deutsche Nationalbibliothek verzeichnet diese Publikation in der
Deutschen Nationalbibliografie; detaillierte bibliografische Daten sind im
Internet über http://dnb.d-nb.de abrufbar.

Bibliographic information published by the Deutsche Nationalbibliothek
Die Deutsche Nationalbibliothek lists this publication in the Deutsche Nationalbibliografie;
detailed bibliographic data are available in the Internet at http://dnb.d-nb.de.

Cover illustration:
Photograph of Vishwanath Singh, the Maharajah of Chhatarpur, by Lala Deen Dayal, c.1882, reproduced
with the permission of the Prints, Drawings and Photographs Section of the Asia, Pacific and African
Collection, The British Library.

∞

Gedruckt auf alterungsbeständigem, säurefreien Papier
Printed on acid-free paper

ISSN: 1614-4651

ISBN-10: 3-89821-673-X
ISBN-13: 978-3-89821-673-9

© *ibidem*-Verlag
Stuttgart 2007

Alle Rechte vorbehalten

Das Werk einschließlich aller seiner Teile ist urheberrechtlich geschützt. Jede Verwertung
außerhalb der engen Grenzen des Urheberrechtsgesetzes ist ohne Zustimmung des Verlages
unzulässig und strafbar. Dies gilt insbesondere für Vervielfältigungen,
Übersetzungen, Mikroverfilmungen und elektronische Speicherformen sowie die
Einspeicherung und Verarbeitung in elektronischen Systemen.

All rights reserved. No part of this publication may be reproduced, stored in or introduced into a retrieval
system, or transmitted, in any form, or by any means (electronic, mechanical, photocopying, recording or
otherwise) without the prior written permission of the publisher. Any person who does any unauthorized act
in relation to this publication may be liable to criminal prosecution and civil claims for damages.

Printed in Germany

Contents

Introduction   1
Shafquat Towheed

1. Colonialism, Slavery, and Religion on Stage:
Late Eighteenth-Century Women Dramatists,
the Hastings Trial, and the Making of British India   11
Marianna D'Ezio

2. India as Gothic Horror: Maturin's *Melmoth the Wanderer* and Images of Juggernaut in Early
Nineteenth-Century Missionary Writing   41
Andrew Rudd

3. Intrepid Traveller, "She-Merchant," or Colonialist
Historiographer: Reading Eliza Fay's *Original Letters*   65
Nira Gupta-Casale

4. The British Woman Traveller in India: Cultural
Intimacy and Interracial Kinship in Fanny Parks's
Wanderings of a Pilgrim in Search of the Picturesque   93
Nandini Sengupta

5. Inconsequential Lives: *The Voyage Out* and Anglo-Indian Fictions of Voyaging and Domesticity   119
Pia Mukherji

6. Remade Womanhoods, Refashioned Modernities:
The Construction of "Good Womanhood" in *Annisa*,
an Early Twentieth-Century Women's Magazine in
Urdu   147
Rekha Pande, K. C. Bindu, Viqar Atiya

7. Abu'l A'la Mawdudi: British India and the Politics
   of Popular Islamic Texts   173
   Masood Ashraf Raja

8. Memoirs of Maharanis: The Politics of Marriage,
   Companionship, and Love in Late-Colonial Princely
   India   193
   Angma Dey Jhala

9. The Reception of Marie Corelli in India   219
   Prodosh Bhattacharya

10. "The Sahib try to kiss me": The Construction of the
    Queer Subaltern in J. R. Ackerley's *Hindoo Holiday*   245
    Shafquat Towheed

11. Cultural Contestations in the Literary Marketplace:
    Reading Raja Rao's *Kanthapura* and Aubrey Menen's
    The Prevalence of Witches   279
    Ruvani Ranasinha

12. Casualty of War, Casualty of Empire:
    Mulk Raj Anand in England   301
    Kristin Bluemel

Contributors   327

Introduction

Shafquat Towheed
Open University

Emphasising the mutual interdependence of the exchanges, economic, cultural, and otherwise, between Britain and India over the last two centuries, Harish Trivedi has coined the term "colonial transactions" to suggest the "interactive, dialogic, two-way process" of this prolonged engagement (15). Sixty years after independence, the implications of this on-going process of colonial (and postcolonial) transaction are as evident as ever. The twelve contributions to this book amply demonstrate the richness, vitality and complexity of these colonial transactions, and they do so by approaching the topic from a specific perspective: by interpreting the rubric 'new readings' as broadly, creatively and productively as possible. They cover a wide range of literary responses and genres: eighteenth-century drama, the gothic novel, verse, autobiography, history, religious writing, journalism, women's memoirs, travel writing, popular fiction, and the modernist novel. All twelve chapters offer substantially "new" readings of their chosen (and often contested) transactions between Britain and India. Several contributors examine work previously neglected by academic scholarship, such as the reception and translation of Corelli into Indian languages (Bhattacharya), or the importance of Urdu women's magazines in shaping community and gender identity (Pande, Bindu, and Atiya), while others offer trenchant new interpretations of well-known works, such as Woolf's *The Voyage Out* (Mukherji) or Anand's *Across the Black Waters* (Bluemel). Throughout this collection, contributors have paid attention to the mutually interdependent relationship between texts and their consumers and between readers and their reading material, by remaining alert to the complexities of dissemination, reading and reception among disparate reading communities in a colonial society. By opening up a generically diverse range of texts for discussion from a variety of critical and theoretical standpoints, *New Readings in the Literature of British India* urges renewed attention and scrutiny from its readers, asking them to read afresh both the intertextual and the intratextual evidence of nearly two centuries of colonial and textual transactions between Britain and India.

The first two chapters demonstrate the limitations, as well as the possibilities, of attempts to represent and articulate India to a British readership in the Romantic period, through the interactions between seemingly incongruent genres. In the opening chapter, "Colonialism, Slavery, and Religion on Stage: Late Eighteenth-Century Women Dramatists, the Hastings Trial, and the Making of British India," Marianna D'Ezio reads the popular plays and farces of a group of women dramatists – Hannah Cowley, Elizabeth Inchbald, Mariana Starke and Frances Burney – in the light of the protracted impeachment and trial of the overtly Orientalist first Governor of Bengal, Warren Hastings. Sara Suleri has commented that the Hastings trial, while ostensibly offering to expose the excesses of the East India Company, effectively did the opposite: the trial protected "the colonial project from being indicted from the larger ill of which Hastings was simply a herald" (45). In her reading of these contemporary plays by women dramatists, D'Ezio finds evidence of the dramatic material to emerge from this, the most dramatic of trials. Instead of covering up the implications of colonial misrule, the Hastings trial heightened the political awareness of otherwise disparate women playwrights, both conservative and radical, on a number of issues, from the rights of women, to the abolition of slavery, and from miscegenation to the inexorable social mobility of the new *nabobs*, even while they claimed *not* to be writing about politics.

In a similar vein, in his chapter "India as Gothic Horror: Maturin's *Melmoth the Wanderer* and Images of Juggernaut in Early Nineteenth-Century Missionary Writing," Andrew Rudd teases out the symmetry between the exaggerated, often anti-Catholic modes of gothic fiction and the heated anti-Hindu rhetoric of Evangelical Protestant polemic.

Introduction

Rudd closely reads two specific responses, one factual and the other fictional, to the *rath yatra* at the Jagannath Temple at Puri: Claudius Buchanan's first-hand, though extravagantly rhetorically intemperate account in *Colonial Ecclesiastical Establishment* (1813), and Charles Maturin's fictional rendering of the same event (derived, sometimes almost verbatim, from Buchanan), in his gothic masterpiece, *Melmoth the Wanderer* (1820). Rudd's wonderfully insightful analysis demonstrates the extent to which gothic fiction and Evangelical polemic were mutually legitimising discourses, both limning the change in British attitudes towards Indian religions from the enlightened Orientalist benignity of the 1780s, to the crusading intolerance of Lord Teignmouth's sponsorship of the "pious clause" during the East India Company's charter renewal in 1813.

Chapters 3, 4, and 5 all examine a literary genre that more than any other has come to typify the protracted colonial encounter between Britain and India: the British woman's Indian travel narrative. Temporarily emancipated from the physical constrictions of life in nineteenth-century England by the prospect of travelling to, from, and within India, she carried at the same time the almost suffocating cultural baggage of an interventionist (and often overtly supremacist) colonial order. And yet, many of these women refused to act simply as Ruskinian standard bearers for an entrenched colonial and domestic ideology. In "Intrepid Traveller, 'She-Merchant,' or Colonialist Historiographer: Reading Eliza Fay's *Original Letters*," Nira Gupta-Casale's new reading argues that Eliza Fay's correspondence, often seen as a casually sympathetic endorsement of the colonial project from within, offers a surprisingly disobedient, unladylike and unfeminine subtext. Gupta-Casale observes that Fay's writing repeatedly refuses to sit contentedly within inscribed codes of class and gender, a discomforting fact that *all* her British editors, from the Reverend Firminger in 1908, to E. M. Forster in 1925 and M. M. Kaye in 1986, have failed to either contain or adequately explain.

Nandini Sengupta develops the often latent ideological complexity of British women's travel narratives further in her chapter, "The British Woman Traveller in India: Cultural Intimacy and Interracial Kinship in Fanny Parks's *Wanderings of a Pilgrim in Search of the Picturesque*." Examining perhaps the most famous nineteenth-century woman's account of travelling in India, Sengupta's fresh interpretation highlights Parks's cross-cultural identification, as well as her determination to build lasting friendships (with both the culturally and religiously hybrid Gardner household, and the deposed Maratha Queen Baiza Bai of Gwalior) across the often fraught interstices of what Mary Louise Pratt has called the colonial "contact zone" (4). Sengupta draws attention to the cultural inclusiveness of Parks's text, which features both an Islamic blessing and an invocation to Ganesh, reminding us again of what William Dalrymple has celebrated as a world "far more hybrid" and with "far less clearly defined ethnic, national and religious borders, than we have been conditioned to expect" (xxiii).

The last of the three chapters of British women's Indian travel narratives focuses on the home rather than the world. In "Inconsequential Lives: *The Voyage Out* and Anglo-Indian fictions of Voyaging and Domesticity," Pia Mukherji examines the relationship between the explicitly imperative (but equally implicitly conflicted) ideological and linguistic register of Anglo-Indian domestic conduct works by Maud Diver, Sara Duncan, Flora Annie Steel and Constance Sitwell, and the complex negotiations of both public and private tyranny in Virginia Woolf's *The Voyage Out* (1915). Woolf's first full-length exercise in Modernist subjectivity and consciousness, Mukherji argues, draws heavily upon the complicated gendered self-definition found in these Anglo-Indian narratives of the "voyage out." The explicit repudiation in *The Voyage Out* of the conduct books' overt aim (married colonial domesticity) is a determined refusal by Woolf to endorse either the public or the private ideological implications of both patriarchy *and* imperialism.

Introduction

The new readings offered by chapters 6, 7, and 8 examine colonial transactions from a completely different perspective, that of the self-definition of specific Indian reading (and writing) communities through their engagement with the determining exigencies of mass print culture. Anindita Ghosh has persuasively argued that Indian print culture is typified by the "collisions and negotiations on the borders between orality and print," undermining previous interpretations of the arrival of print "clamping its vice-like grip on the colonized imagination" (14). These three chapters find further evidence of the unique (and often unpredictable) use of print culture to articulate, as well as shape, specific reading communities. In "Remade Womanhoods, Refashioned Modernities: The Construction of 'Good Womanhood' in *Annisa*, an Early Twentieth-Century Women's Magazine in Urdu," Rekha Pande, K. C. Bindu, and Viqar Atiya examine the construction of a specific Deccani Muslim female (and largely elite) identity through the pages of the Urdu language journal, *Annisa*. Edited by Begum Sughra Humayun Mirza, a leading member of Hyderabad's Nizami nobility, *Annisa*, Pande et al. note, was more than merely a conduct journal (although that was its explicit aim), for it engaged in the debate over the construction of a modern Muslim identity raging across the country in the first quarter of the twentieth century. *Annisa* did not uncritically absorb, translate, and disseminate progressive (or Western) ideas in Urdu, but actively engaged with such thinking and sometimes refuted it; its curious silence on the issue of equal rights for women is perhaps the most notable example of this autonomous and indigenous process of selection and self-definition.

Mass print opened up channels for united resistance to colonial rule, but at the same time it offered the possibility of shaping new, essentialist identities for reading communities defined by language, religion, or caste. In "Abu'l A'la Mawdudi: British India and the Politics of Popular Islamic Texts," Masood Ashraf Raja examines the counter-hegemonic writing of one of India's leading (and most popular) early twentieth-century Muslim religious writers. Access to popular print allowed Mawdudi to further his advocacy of a Muslim identity that was both modern (especially in its engagement with Western thought) and essential (he wanted to remove the dependence of Indian Islam on schools of interpretation). Raja's chapter provides a incisive reminder that Benedict Anderson's "imagined communities" did not always see themselves as putative nation-states; the ambivalent nature of print gave expression to reading communities that were potentially supra-, non-, or even anti-national.

In "Memoirs of Maharanis: The Politics of Marriage, Companionship and Love in Late-Colonial Princely India," Angma Dey Jhala offers an impressive reading of the memoirs of five Hindu Maharanis, and provides a fascinating demonstration of the first engagements of these educated, princely, Indian women in the world of print, the genre of autobiography, and their own self-identification through their use of the English language. While publishing these autobiographies in English cemented these ladies' sense of autonomous selfhood (as progressive and educated upholders of a princely tradition), it also documented the active intervention of the British in supporting favourable alliances between princely states: another expression of the determining influence of Imperial hegemony. Jhala teases out the complexities of these acts of self-assertion, which had to negotiate both indigenous and imported social codes, nowhere more so than in the issue of marriage. In all three of these chapters, literary activity determines the self-selecting identity of a specific religious, caste, or gender group; in the case of last of the three, Jhala's reading of the memoirs of Maharanis, the literary activity itself serves as a validating (and valedictory) marker of a former royal status and esteem that has been increasingly marginalised in independent India.

Returning to the centrality of fiction in articulating the cultural transactions between Britain and India, chapters 9 and 10 provide detailed, culturally specific new readings of two particular and extremely divergent authors, Marie Corelli and J. R. Ackerley, by using interpretive approaches from book history and critical theory respectively. In

Introduction

"The Reception of Marie Corelli in India," Prodosh Bhattacharya offers a comprehensive examination of the translation, publication, reading, reception, literary influence, and reprinting of the works of Marie Corelli in India. Productively melding book history with literary criticism, Bhattacharya's analysis maps the cultural footprint of Corelli in Bengal in the last century, and his close reading of successive translations astutely demonstrates the extent to which translated texts can become transformed through an implicit process of cultural assimilation. In Britain, Corelli had been lambasted for writing crassly intemperate and vitiated populist fiction; at the hands of their Bengali translators, many of those very novels became thinly veiled commentaries on issues as divergent as Hindu values, the role of women, the suitability of love matches for the urban middle-class, and so on. Both Corelli and her Bengali translators advocated often contradictory positions on a range of issues, from the rights of women to the importance of religious tradition; but as Bhattacharya demonstrates, it would be a mistake to assume that these were the *same* contradictory positions.

While chapter 9 maps reception and response to offer a new reading, my chapter productively superimposes two models from current critical theory onto a thinly veiled, generically indeterminate travel memoir by J. R. Ackerkley. In "'The Sahib try to kiss me': The Construction of the Queer Subaltern in J. R. Ackerley's *Hindoo Holiday*," I offer a close reading of Ackerley's irrepressibly discursive and sensationally indiscrete book, by investigating the interstices and overlaps between the perspectives offered by queer theory and postcolonial theory. Queer theory has often remained silent about its complicity in discourses of colonial dominance, while postcolonial theory has frequently attempted to present a coherently heteronormative facade, despite clear evidence to the contrary. Ackerley's semi-public, semi-private book, neither wholly novel nor autobiography, a text shaped by both sexual difference and cultural relativism, glosses the totalising impulses of competing discourses, while registering indigenous resistance to it.

The last two chapters bring the colonial transaction full circle by examining the publication and reception of two Indian and one Anglo-Indian (or more precisely, Irish-Indian) novelists in the British marketplace. In "Cultural Contestations in the Literary Marketplace: Reading Raja Rao's *Kanthapura* (1938) and Aubrey Menen's *The Prevalence of Witches* (1947)," Ruvani Ranasinha offers a detailed and entirely original assessment of the often contradictory tensions both these writers faced in the publication and reception of their novels in an increasingly commercial marketplace. Noting the shaping influence of British reviewers, Ranasinha observes that while Rao was accused of being too culturally specific and therefore too hard for his British readers to understand, Menen was viewed as a mediator between two divergent cultures, despite his own protestations to the contrary. Ranasinha's chapter brings another sense to the term 'new readings'; she demonstrates that the reading and presentation of these books by their British reviewers determined their reception for a generation of readers, and in uncovering the articulation of this cultural framing, she recasts the novels in a fresh, revivifying light.

In the final chapter, "Casualty of War, Casualty of Empire: Mulk Raj Anand in England," Kristin Bluemel delivers a new reading of Anand's celebrated First-World-War novel, *Across the Black Waters*. Published at the start of the Second World War, and resolutely deploying a hybrid, Indo-Anglian linguistic register, Bluemel sees Anand's novel, caught in a complex web of sometimes mutually incompatible transactions, as a prime example of both the institutional collaboration and the individual resistance that typified British rule in India. Bluemel opens up a new reading of Anand's novel by showing how the Janus-like text, looking in two directions at once, both memorialises the sacrifice of Indians for the perpetuation of British liberty, while also anticipating their own.

Brought together in one volume, these essays offer a small, but representative sample of the multifaceted literary and cultural traffic between Britain and India in the colonial period. In the richness and diversity of the various contributors' strategies and interpretations, these new readings urge us to return once again to texts that we think we know, as well as to explore those that we do not, with a freshly renewed sense of their complexity, immediacy, and relevance.

Works Cited

Dalrymple, William. *Begums, Thugs & Englishmen: The Journals of Fanny Parkes*. New Delhi: Penguin, 2002.

Ghosh, Anindita. *Power in Print: Popular Publishing and the Politics of Language and Culture in a Colonial Society, 1778-1905*. New Delhi: Oxford University Press, 2006.

Pratt, Mary Louise. *Imperial Eyes: Travel Writing and Transculturation*. London and New York: Routledge, 1992.

Suleri, Sara. *The Rhetoric of English in India*. Chicago: Chicago University Press, 1992.

Trivedi, Harish. *Colonial Transactions: English Literature and India*. Papyrus: Calcutta, 1993.

1. Colonialism, Slavery, and Religion on Stage: Late Eighteenth-Century Women Dramatists, the Hastings Trial, and the Making of British India

Marianna D'Ezio
University of California, Rome Study Center
and the University for Foreigners of Perugia

Following the Hastings trial in London (1787-1795), both public opinion and the literary world in Britain were suspended somewhere between colonial anxiety and imperial guilt. What had previously been seen as the vast but remote Indian territory was now becoming more and more relevant to Britain's economic, political and international power, as well as to Britain's own (mis)perception of a new "Other," neither the servile black slave, nor the picturesque yet proud native American. Many travellers had already undertaken the long journey to India to gather information about the land and its inhabitants and had returned to England with the purpose of narrating their experience in works, which by the end of the century had become very popular.[1] As first governor of British India, Warren Hastings had contributed to the promotion, knowledge and appreciation of India in England by patronizing oriental scholarship and encouraging the translation of Sanskrit literature.[2] A large part of the literary market was thus already dominated by prose, verse, fiction, travel narratives and letters which tried to satisfy the curiosity of British readers regarding the manners and customs of those newly acquired subjects of the Empire.[3] The literary image of British India was inevitably shaped by a persistent ambivalence in the attitude towards exotic (and erotic) cultural practices,

---

[1] See *Travel Literature and India*.
[2] In 1784 he established the Asiatic Society and wrote a memorable preface to Charles Wilkins's translation of the *Bhagavad-Gita* (1785); see Bernstein; Davies; Feiling; and Moon.
[3] See Raza; Singh.

which finally induced British writers to a self-critical perspective. This approach also contributed towards creating and establishing clear distinctions between Western and Eastern cultures, and encouraged the political and public debate about the actual government in the colonies, especially in India.

A few writers, most prominently women writers and dramatists, seemed to have subtly opposed the diffusion of a canonical, one-sided and politically dominated image of the Empire. Despite their own uncertain status (that of women dramatists acting and writing for money) they chose to stage and explore ideas of despotism (Bolton 202). By challenging the censorship often imposed upon the so-called illegitimate theatres (Moody) as well as upon licensed theatres (Drury Lane and Covent Garden during the winter season and Haymarket in the summer) they made their own contribution towards spreading radical ideas about colonialism and abolition. My essay offers an analysis and a close reading of some of the plays, farces and afterpieces by women dramatists of the late eighteenth century, such as Hannah Cowley, Elizabeth Inchbald, Mariana Starke and Frances Burney. It aims to highlight the strategies they used in order to realize their objectives: firstly, that of undermining cultural beliefs and prejudices in order to either condemn or justify British colonization of India (Brown 4), and secondly, their clear intention to participate in the debate on Britain's responsibilities in colonial India, emerging from their interest in the impeachment of Warren Hastings, and in contemporary political and colonial British affairs.[4]

As Governor of Bengal between 1772 and 1785, Warren Hastings contributed to the establishment of a British colonial settlement in India, transforming the East India Company from a mercantile enterprise into a political and military presence, with the power to rule over the

---

[4] I am extremely indebted to the recent volume by O'Quinn (*Staging*).

area.[5] Hastings started his political career in 1757, when he was made British Resident of Murshidabad and then later appointed to the Calcutta council (1761). After governing Bengal, he became the first Governor General in the history of British India (1773-1784). Although he created a complicated system of alliances with Indian rulers through treaties and agreements, Hastings's policy was seen by many in Britain as a way to encourage local rivalries in order to increase British influence over their territories; his own methods were ethically and financially dubious. It was for this reason that he was charged with extortion by Edmund Burke, Sir Philip Francis (wounded by Hastings in a duel), the dramatist Richard Brinsley Sheridan, and the Whig politician Charles James Fox. As Burke and his followers pointed out during the trial, Hastings favoured a corrupted governance of British India, relying on violent means of subjugating the natives as well as the slaves who were brought there from Madagascar and from the Red Sea. Burke was not new to vehement and passionate parliamentary speeches on India. On 1 December 1783, he gave a speech on "Mr Fox's East India Bill," in which he underlined that

> the total silence of [some] gentlemen [i.e. the ministers] concerning the interest and well-being of the people of India, and concerning the interest which this nation has in the commerce and revenues of that country, is a strong indication of the value which they set upon these objects. (2: 359)[6]

By examining the East India Bill, "a charter to establish monopoly and to create power" (362), Burke was already preparing the ground for his next speech, "on the Nabob of Arcot's Debts, 28 February 1785." As Green has pointed out, while pursuing the cause of Indian dignity,

---

[5] See Keay; Lawson; and Sutherland. On the Hastings trial, see Carnall and Nicholson; Musselwhite; O'Toole, especially 224-34; and Marshall, *Impeachment*.

[6] On Burke's involvement in the Hastings trial, see De Bruyn; Franklin ("Accessing" and *Representing*); McCann; and Samet.

he was also issuing a brilliant "rehabilitation of British imperialism, which, he maintains, can still be a civilizing and beneficial force for colonizers and colonized alike" (395).[7] When Warren Hastings was formally impeached on 10 May 1787 and the trial was officially opened before the Lords in Westminster Hall on 13 February 1788, the audience had already been primed for the event. Burney's diary records that Queen Charlotte herself asked Frances (then working as second keeper of the Queen's robes) if she wished to be present at the beginning of the trial, and gave her "six tickets from Sir Peter Burrell, the great chamberlain, for every day; that three were for his box, and three for his gallery" (Burney 95). As if describing a theatre, Burney continues with a narration of the shape of the hall, the boxes and the galleries (96) and then turns to the character of Burke as a "cruel prosecutor [. . .] of an injured and innocent man" (97), finally introducing "the procession" (97-98) of lawyers, peers, bishops, officers, princes, followed by the chancellor and ultimately, by Warren Hastings, who, in fact, opened the public performance of his own trial.

The political and public debate on the authority and the legitimacy of the East India Company was inevitably linked with the current tide of abolitionist thinking. Despite the charges against Hastings, the East India Company "did not prohibit the export of slaves until 1789 and allowed slavery legal status until 1843" (Banaji; qtd. in Moskal 123). William Pitt's India Act (1784) had already tried to reduce the supremacy of the East India Company by restoring military and ruling power back to the Crown and the Parliament:

> all political instructions and dispatches addressed to the Company's offices in India had to be submitted to a supervisory body called the Board of Control, which could amend or reject them as it saw fit. Henceforward (as Hastings had wished), the final voice in the affairs of India was not the Company's board of directors, but the British government,

---

[7] See also Suleri.

1. Late Eighteenth-Century Women Dramatists

exercising its responsibility through an appointed agency of its own making. (Graham 85)

The Society for Effecting the Abolition of the Slave Trade had been founded in London in 1787; as Jeanne Moskal reminds us, "in May 1788 Pitt had persuaded the House of Commons to agree that the slave-trade would be debated in the next session," which led to "the largest petitioning campaign on public matters ever to have been organized in Britain up to this point" (122).

Through hinting at the controversial issue of slavery in their representation of colonial subjects and slaves and the advocacy of their freedom, British women writers' imaginations displaced *their own* anxiety about their place in the literary canon and the marketplace, as well as in society. Their position and status seemed to frequently mirror that of the colonial subjects and even that of the slaves, and it is surely for this reason that much of their writing explores and challenges not only the power relations between *self* and *other*, but, more importantly, between *master* and *slave* (Choudhury 113).

Despite the fact that some of these writers took part in the anti-slavery campaign and the abolitionist movement, their power to give voice to such radical ideas on a theatre stage was limited. The Licensing Act of 1737, which demanded pre-production government censorship of plays, strictly prevented explicit references to controversial social and political matters. Increasingly, dramatists tried to make the audience guess the unsaid, sometimes by indirectly questioning and criticizing slavery itself from a gendered perspective. In light of their potential contribution to antislavery discourse and their involvement in the public debate on the Hastings impeachment, the plays I am going to examine employ a range of differing strategies.[8] Playwrights as

---

[8] The plays I have chosen are: Hannah Cowley's *A Day in Turkey; or, The Russian Slaves. A Comedy, as Acted at the Theatre Royal, in Covent Garden*, first performed at the Theatre Royal, Covent Garden, 3 December 1791; Elizabeth Inchbald's *The Mogul Tale; or, The Descent of a Balloon. A Farce, as it is*

15

disparate as Hannah Cowley, Elizabeth Inchbald, Mariana Starke and Frances Burney, although concerned with the Hastings trial and the debate on slavery, also showed their apprehension about the consequences of British colonial expansion in India.

The fear of an eventual loss of British identity when in contact with Indian culture is expressed through a fervent patriotism and a "nationalist myth-making" (Moskal 112), as evident in Starke and Burney, or by portraying the Indian (the "Other"), through a "set of representative figures, or tropes," and through "style, figures of speech, setting, narrating devices" (Said 21), as in Cowley and Inchbald. In both cases, the playwrights drew upon a developed and accepted cultural code that they implicitly shared with their audience. Rather ironically, the closer they came to 1807, the year of the abolition of the slave trade, the more that nationalism emerged. Burney's *A Busy Day*, datable around 1800, ends with a celebration of London as the "foster-mother of Benevolence and Charity, and the pride of the British Empire" (79), while Starke's *The Sword of Peace*, staging what Jeanne Moskal describes as the "final vision of colonial acclamation" (118), ends with the rejoicing of the British settlement in India over the arrival of a new governor:

Acted at the Theatre-Royal, Smoke-Alley, first performed at the Theatre Royal, Haymarket, 6 July 1784; Elizabeth Inchbald, *Such Things Are; A Play, in Five Acts. As Performed at the Theatre-Royal, Smoke-Alley*, first performed at the Theatre Royal, Covent Garden, 10 February 1787; Mariana Starke's *The Sword of Peace, or, A Voyage of Love; A Comedy, in Five Acts*, first performed at the Theatre Royal in the Haymarket, 9 August 1788; and Frances Burney's *A Busy Day; or, An Arrival from India* (1800-1801), first performed in 1993 at the Hen and Chicken Pub Theatre in Bristol (see Doody 293-300). All quotations from these plays are from the first editions. I have excluded Starke's *The Widow of Malabar* (1791), a true "Indian" play dealing with the issue of the *sati* as seen from a British viewpoint, as it is actually a translation of Antoine Marin Le Mierre's *La Veuve du Malabar, ou, L'Empire des Coutumes* (1780). On *sati*, see Mani.

1. Late Eighteenth-Century Women Dramatists

JEFFREYS. Mr. Northcote made Resident! – the whole place is run wild for joy, Sir – blacks and whites, masters and slaves, half casts and blue casts, Gentoos and Mussulmen, Hindoos and Bramins, officers and soldiers, sailors and captains [. . .]. They do nothing but call him father – they keep blessing him and his *children*; and King George and his children; and their great prophet and his children. (59)

The binary oppositions seen above become even clearer when we look at the settings of some of the plays I mentioned. In Cowley's *A Day in Turkey* and Inchbald's *The Mogul Tale* the setting of the play and its events in a harem or seraglio, a closed and limited space within the colonial area, highlights the necessity to remain separate from a dangerous immersion into the Other's culture, but it also suggests ways in which to enter the Other's world to dominate it. Significantly, the space where the colonizer and the colonized meet is one dominated by women. Male power in the seraglio (except for the Sultan) is in the hands of the eunuchs, whose authority is threatened by the virility of the European men. Furthermore, entering *the harem* did not equate to entering Indians' private spaces in general. India, during the eighteenth century, was a kaleidoscope of religions, languages and customs, but for the British colonial government, it was the Muslim Mughal rulers who caused the greatest inconvenience and, it was this power that the late eighteenth- and early nineteenth-century narratives and travel logs questioned and criticized the most. Once Mughal power had been contained and a new wave of evangelical thinking had reached India, Hinduism and its practises became the new target of scrutiny and criticism.[9]

The second issue, to which all these plays referred, was the anxiety of aristocrats and middle-class society in Britain over the emergence of a new class of people. This new social group was being formed by those (often from the lower classes) who had returned to England

---

[9] On British encounters with Hinduism, see Oddie.

from the colonies with their new imperial wealth, thus destabilizing class hierarchy. The "nabobs," an Anglicization of a Mughal honorific,[10] represented a concrete threat to the domestic balance of power, exacerbating the tensions already existing between aristocrats and an emerging industrious middle class.[11] For this reason, they began to be satirized on stage, becoming a recurrent character in the comedy of the late century, like Samuel Foote's *The Nabob* (1778).

If, as Mita Choudhury observes, "laughter veils the colonialist implications of Orientalism" (111), what strategies did these women dramatists use? They wrote comedies, comic operas and even farces, genres that allowed them to present their political concerns to audiences with a levity and ambiguity that escaped government censorship. Cowley and Starke explicitly underline that they were *not* discussing British politics in their plays: "Not a breath of politics, I vow!" exclaims Mr Palmer in the Prologue of Starke's *The Sword of Peace*; and "I know nothing about politics; [. . .] politics are *unfeminine*, I never in my life could attend to their discussion," Hannah Cowley declares in the advertisement of *A Day in Turkey*. Describing herself as a "comic poet," she cleverly averted any connection with political satire (Choudhury 124). More obviously, as Daniel O'Quinn has pointed out, is the fact that the 1799-printed version of Mariana Starke's play carries a note indicating that "[t]he Lines in inverted Commas, are omitted in Representation." O'Quinn observes "how significant the omitted passages are to the play's politics" ("Long Minuet" 2). Hannah Cowley's *A Day in Turkey* is a comic opera, whose first version was written in 1779 and premiered at Covent Garden in 1792. The whole action takes place within the Other's dominions, which visibly shrink as the play progresses. The scene moves from "a Turkish camp" to the "the Gardens of the Bassa," then "the Palace," "the Court," "a Quadrangle," "the Building," "the Prison," to

---

[10] On Anglicisation of Indian words, see Lewis.

[11] On the nabobs, see Juneja; Lawson and Phillips; Marshall, *East*; Raven; and Spear.

1. Late Eighteenth-Century Women Dramatists

finally "the Harem" and "the Bassa's apartment." The strict organization of space (even the trees in the garden are geometrically organized) suggests that in the Bassa's dominions strict social, sexual and political laws are enforced. This is destabilized by the arrival of the foreigners, who on their part reject and subvert these laws and establish their own. This can be read as Cowley's indirect condemnation of British colonialism in India, which was often justified (as Hastings had done) by the appeal to native despotism.

The action of the play centres on the experiences of four prisoners of war taken to the seraglio of the Turkish Bassa, Ibrahim. They are Orloff, a Russian army officer, and his new bride Alexina, who was captured immediately after the ceremony and before their marriage was consummated. The other prisoners are Paulina, the daughter of Alexina's father's vassal and A La Grecque, a French emigrant who is Orloff's valet. Forced to wear Turkish national dress, Paulina is mistaken by the Bassa for Alexina, whom he is eager to enjoy as a new love. In her anger, Paulina showers contempt on this stranger's claim to love her, but her scorn only increases the Bassa's raptures. Meanwhile Alexina, who has succeeded in avoiding being brought before the Bassa, is put in solitary confinement by the malicious slave Azim. Orloff demands that his bride be restored to him "in the same condition" as when he led her to the altar. On discovering that she is married, the Bassa tries to stop seeing Paulina (still mistaking her for Alexina), who by now has fallen in love with him. A happy ending ensues when Orloff learns that it was Paulina in the Bassa's arms and that Alexina has remained chaste; similarly, the Bassa learns that Paulina is not Orloff's wife and may now love her freely.[12]

Despite her public declaration of disinterest in politics, Cowley cleverly achieves a subtle political criticism through the character of A La Grecque, whose name visibly alludes to Catherine the Great of

---

[12] For a more detailed summary, see Gagen (82-105).

Russia's "Greek Plan."[13] When his master Orloff is imprisoned, A La Grecque talks to him as his "brother slave," subverting the master/slave relationship throughout the play. A La Grecque comments that in Russia "they still continue to believe that a prince is more than a porter, and that a lord is a better gentleman than his slave," adding that "had they but been with me at Versailles, when I help'd to turn those things topsey turvey there!"(18) they would know that this was not true. A La Grecque's political speech is developed by the Turks:

> AZIM. Such a wailing about freedom and liberty! Why the Christians in one of the northern islands have established a slave-trade, and proved by act of parliament that freedom is no blessing at all.
> MUSTAPHA. No, no, they have only proved that it does not suit dark complexions. (10)

Cowley seems to go even further in her condemnation of slavery as an institution; again, a Turk (Mustapha) says that "every country has its fancies, and we are so fond of liberty that we always *buy it* up as a rarity" (35). Even though interest in the Hastings trial had cooled by the time Cowley's play premiered at Covent Garden, much of the action in the comedy hinges on the impeachment. The fact that Cowley intentionally set the play in Turkey and that the foreigners were Russians also links the comedy to the contemporary crisis of the Whigs (especially to Pitt's unpopular attempt to enter a war with Russia), an event which eventually split Edmund Burke and Charles James Fox and condemned the party to dissolution.[14] Cowley's comedy was cer-

---

[13] Having annexed Crimea to Russia, Catherine the Great's secret plan was that of allying with Austria (and France) to drive Turkey back from Europe. This was a plan that obviously excluded Britain from sharing power and influence over the area. See O'Quinn and Bolton for further details.

[14] See O'Quinn's essay on Cowley's *A Day in Turkey*; and Bolton. Both O'Quinn and Bolton deal with the Oczakow affair and Britain's expedient support of the Ottoman Empire against Russia.

1. Late Eighteenth-Century Women Dramatists

tainly political, commenting on domestic political issues and characters that the audience could easily recognize.

There is one point that links this play to other "Indian" or "Oriental" comedies (such as Inchbald's) that has not been debated enough, namely, the marked presence of contrasting religious beliefs and attitudes. Such a contrast is explicit from the very beginning in Cowley's comedy, in the opening cues between an "Old Man" and his "Son," Paulina's father and her brother, who says:

> SON. Come father, lean on me, and let us walk faster, or we shall be pick'd up by some of the *turban'd gentry*. They are out a foraging; and they always consider *christians* as useful cattle. (1-2)

The distance is also created by the two servants, A La Grecque and Azim, who respectively represent an "enlightened West" and a "wicked East," and repeatedly address each other by stressing their religious faiths – "good Mr Mussulman," says A La Grecque; "good Mr Christian," replies Azim. The happy ending is a celebration of Western magnanimity; a pitiful Alexina petitions for Azim's forgiveness, and the Sultan expresses a sudden interest in Western values, especially religion:

> IBRAHIM. [*To Alexina.*] Pronounce, Madam, the fate of the profligate slave, whose villainy had nearly brought about such disastrous events --- shall he perish?
> ALEXINA. Ah, in this hour of felicity, let nothing perish but *misfortune*! Be the benevolent Mustapha rewarded, and let Azim have frank forgiveness.
> IBRAHIM. Charming magnanimity! if it flows from your CHRISTIAN DOCTRINES, such doctrines must be RIGHT, and I will closely study them. (83-84)

In Cowley's play, the foreigners who arrive and upset the balance of power and question the religious creed in the idealized colony are Russians who have been taken captive in Turkey. In Elizabeth Inchbald's farce *The Mogul Tale*, written in 1788 and performed in the same year at Haymarket, however, it is an odd trio of English people who descend in their hot-air balloon directly into the Mughal Sultan's seraglio, an unidentified oriental place in India. Again, as many critics have pointed out, the harem was an ideal dramatic setting because of its association with gender oppression. More importantly, the characters coming from the outside, Western world, grant themselves the freedom to inviolately penetrate spaces and to invade foreign territories. It is true that "images of despotic sultans and desperate slave girls became a central part of an emerging liberal feminist discourse about the condition of women not in the East, but in the West" (Zonana 594). However, the domestic enslavement of women in the seraglio is also a metaphor for the political enslavement of men in the colonies. Inchbald's farce takes a greater step forward in comparison to Cowley's comedy, because it is openly subversive and political. Personally linked to William Godwin and his entourage of radical and revolutionary thinkers and writers, Inchbald provides a more direct approach to political issues.

A Wapping cobbler, Johnny, and his wife Fanny, take off from Hyde Park Corner in a hot-air balloon with an untrained guide and land in the garden of the Great Mogul. They are immediately taken captive by the Great Mogul, who pretends he wants to torture them and put them to death merely to see their reactions. Their outrageous assumed identities (the Pope of Rome and the Ambassador of the King of England) lead to a hilarious trial scene, where the Great Mogul sets them free. The hierarchical order of power relations is completely subverted and the Mughal Sultan turns from being a tyrant and a torturer to an enlightened sovereign, essentially "indistinguishable from contemporary European philosophers" (Bolton 8). By contrast, Christianity and British imperialism become the targets of a witty satire, as tyrannical expressions of political power. To avoid any possible risk of impeachment or sedition, Inchbald's religious satire turns to Roman Catholicism and culminates in an extremely funny scene that may well have shaken the theatre with the audience's laughter,[15] while retaining that powerful opposition between religions already observed in Cowley's *A Day In Turkey*:

> MOGUL. Then who art thou, slave, that dare come into our presence?
> FIRST EUNUCH. He is no slave; know, my most royal master, this is his highness the Pope of Rome.
> JOHNNY. [*Aside* – The Devil I am!] Yes, and please your highness, I am the Pope, at your service.
> MOGUL. A great Pontiff, indeed --- Is that the fashion of his robe?
> FIRST EUNUCH. His travelling dress only.
> JOHNNY. My Air-Balloon jacket, please your honour.
> MOGUL. I want no enumeration of his dignity, I have heard it all.
> JOHNNY. Yes, yes, all the world have heard of the Devil and the Pope.
> MOGUL. Cruel and rapacious. The actions of his predecessors will never be forgotten by the descendant of Mahomet. I rejoice I have him in my power --- his life will but ill repay those crimes with which this monster formerly pestered the plains of Palestina. Who is that female?
> JOHNNY. She does not belong to me, she is a nun, and please your highness, taken from a convent in Italy, and was guilty of some crime, not to be forgiven, but by severe penance, enjoined to accompany us.

---

[15] Donkin has argued that Inchbald's success as a playwright depended on her previous career as an actress (110-19).

> MOGUL. In our country dress she would have charms! ---
> [. . .] Give her another dress, and take her into the Seraglio ---
> [. . .].
> FANNY. Oh Johnny --- [. . .]
> MOGUL. Johnny!
> JOHNNY. Yes, and please your holiness --- I am Pope Johnny the twelfth. Please your Mogulship I will talk to her in private --- perhaps I may persuade her to comply with your princely desires, for we Popes have never any conversation with women, except in private. (12-13)

The Sultan in *The Mogul Tale* is not only enlightened and magnanimous, but he also admits to having learnt, from an inferior "other," how to rule, punish and forgive. He is comically redeemed by the effects of an Oriental interpretation of European and Christian "enlightened" thought:

> THE MOGUL. Keep silence while I pronounce judgement – Tremble for your approaching doom. You are now before the tribunal of a European, a man of your own colour. I am an Indian, a Mahometan, my laws are cruel and my nature savage – You have imposed upon me, and attempted to defraud me, but know that I have been taught mercy and compassion for the sufferings of human nature; however differing in laws, temper and colour from myself. Yes from you Christians whose laws teach charity to all the world, have I learn'd these virtues? For your countrymen's cruelty to the poor Gentoos has shewn me tyranny in so foul a light, that I was determined henceforth to be only mild, just and merciful. (21-22)

Through the Mughal's denunciation of the injustices perpetrated upon his people, Inchbald was also staging the debate on the East India Company's governance on India, and contributing to preparing the ground for Burke's speeches during the Hastings trial. Furthermore, as

1. Late Eighteenth-Century Women Dramatists

O'Quinn noted, the spectacular descending balloon also links the farce with "a series of satirical prints published throughout December 1783 that figured the fate of both the East India Company and Fox's East India Bill as similarly troubled balloons" (*Staging* 20).

The Mogul Tale was Inchbald's debut as a playwright. On 10 February 1787, her five-act comedy *Such Things Are* opened to astounding success.[16] The combination of popular features (an exotic Eastern setting, recognizable characters, and the serious and comic discussions of contemporary issues such as tyranny and the state of prisons) made the comedy extremely enjoyable at a time when the Hastings impeachment was about to begin. Set in the dominions of a tyrannical Sultan – this time in Sumatra – Inchbald borrowed heavily from William Marsden's *The History of Sumatra*, published in 1783.[17] The central character Haswell, described during his visits to the Sultan's prison, is a tribute to the philanthropist John Howard, whose work as a prison reformer was universally praised. The dungeon scenes where Haswell meets, and succeeds in reforming, the would-be thief Zedan, and where he also encounters the Sultan's wife Arabella (who is presumed dead) are regularly contrasted with the lazy English inhabitants of the island. Sir Luke Tremor and his wife, Lord Flint and a prospective nabob, Mr Twineall, are accurate representations of British colonial life (a trope which would be developed further by Mariana Starke's *The Sword of Peace*). These characters embody some of Inchbald's peculiar comic subjects: "the pretence of society, the pretence of dress, the pretence of language" (Jenkins 197). The plot consists of a love story in the Sultan's prison, dependent upon mistaken identity. One such example is the story of a would-be prisoner, Elvirus, who having petitioned the Sultan in vain to take his father's place, asks for Haswell's help. Haswell becomes then the mediator between the two cultures, one of "probability" (the colonizer's) and the other

---

[16] For the reception of Inchbald's plays, see Boaden.
[17] For Inchbald's borrowings from Marsden, see Green (397-98).

one of "uncertainty" (the colonized); this is supported by a rhetorical religious opposition. When Haswell is presented to the Sultan and is asked which reward he would like for restoring the Sultan's troops to health, he launches into a brave and idealistic defence of justice that mirrors Burke's own righteous indignation:

> HASWELL. The prisoner is your subject --- there misery --- more contagious than disease, preys on the lives of hundreds --- sentenced but to confinement, their doom is death. --- Immured in damp and dreary vaults, they daily perish --- and who can tell but that amongst the many hapless sufferers, there may be hearts, bent down with penitence to Heaven and you, for every slight offence --- there may be some amongst the wretched multitude, even innocent victims. --- Let me seek them out --- let me save them, and you.
> SULTAN. Amazement! retract your application --- curb this weak pity; and receive our thanks.
> HASWELL. Curb my pity? --- and what can I receive in recompense for that soft bond, which links me to the wretched? --- and while it sooths their sorrows repay me more, than all the gifts or homage of an empire. --- But if repugnant to your plan of government --- not in the name of pity --- but of justice.
> SULTAN. Justice! ---
> HASWELL. The justice which forbids all but the worst of criminals to be denied that wholesome air the very brute creation freely takes; at least allow them *that*. (33)

Although his eloquence certainly wins the Sultan's curiosity, it does not succeed in changing his mind; Haswell shrewdly turns to a more successful strategy:

> SULTAN. Sir, your sentiments, but much more your character, excite my curiosity. They tell me, in our camps, you vis-

ited each sick man's bed, --- administered yourself the healing draught, --- encouraged our savages with the hope of life, or pointed out their *better* hope in death. --- The widow speaks your charities --- the orphan lisps your bounties --- and the rough Indian melts in tears to bless you. --- I wish to ask *why* you have done all this? --- What is it prompts you thus to befriend the wretched and forlorn?
HASWELL. In vain for me to explain --- the time it wou'd take to tell you why I act thus ---
SULTAN. Send it in writing then.
HASWELL. Nay, if you will *read*, I'll send a book, in which is *already* written why I act thus.
SULTAN. What books? --- What is it called?
HASWELL. "The Christian Doctrine." [*Haswell bows here with the utmost reverence.*] There you will find all I have done was but my duty. (34)

To this, the Sultan is compelled, not without relief, to reveal his painful secret – that he is no Sultan at all, as he converted to Christianity after meeting his (European) wife, and pushed by his thirst of power, secretly became an apostate:

SULTAN. Your words recall reflections that distract me; nor can I bear the pressure on my mind without confessing --- I am a Christian. (34)

This event seems to be much more interesting than Inchbald's recognition (and condemnation) of Britain's imperial politics (Green 411) that emerges in the last few famous cues of the play between Haswell and Zedan:

HASWELL. My Indian friend, have you received your freedom?

ZEDAN. Yes --- and come to bid you farewell --- which I wou'd *never* do, had I not a family in wretchedness till my return --- for you shou'd be my master, and I *wou'd* be your slave. (63)

The closure of the play is in fact a celebration of the ambiguous Burkean approach to fighting the corruption and avarice of Hastings's East India Company, towards gaining justice for the oppressed Indian population, without actually criticising British colonialism itself. This would maintain the image of India as a "tropological repository from which colonial (and postcolonial) imaginations have drawn […] their most basic figures for the anxiety of empire" (Suleri 5). Both the audience and the Sumatrans in the play seem to tacitly consent to leaving an "impostor" on the throne of Sumatra.

In complete contrast, it is the enlightened sovereignty of a British governor that dominates Mariana Starke's *The Sword of Peace*. Set in India, the comedy deals mainly with the British women's marriage market in the East Indies. Unlike Inchbald or Cowley, Starke had actually lived in India (her father was governor of Fort St. George in Madras), and clearly wrote the play with the purpose of reconfirming British imperial power during the Hastings trial. Indeed, *The Sword of Peace* portrays the story of a corrupt governor who is finally replaced by an honest one, David Northcote (played by John Philip Kemble). Amidst the change in political power in the colony is the romantic plot that starts with the journey to India of two young cousins, Louisa and Eliza Moreton. Louisa has come to India on behalf of Sir Thomas Clairville, to buy back the sword of his young nephew, a soldier who died and bequeathed the sword to his friend Lieutenant Dormer, while Eliza's father's will requires her to go to India in order to inherit her fortune. By happy coincidence, she also seeks her faithful admirer Edwards, who had left London for India when his family denied him permission to marry Eliza, thinking her penniless. Around them, a myriad of funny characters portray the situation in British India. These include women who have travelled there in order to get married and gain a social position, corrupt governors and their sycophants, and honest politicians replacing the less honest ones. The insertion of one particular subplot, seemingly unconnected to the main storyline, does undermine Starke's seeming Imperial triumphalism. An English servant, named Jeffreys, buys a black slave's freedom but ironically, freedom to Caesar (the former slave) seems to have no other meaning than the new desire to resemble an Englishman:

> JEFFREYS. Shou'd you like to serve me and go over to England?
> CAESAR. Oh, Massa! yes, yes – [*leaps for joy.*] – me love England, 'cause my old Massa love it – he hate India – so do I. (15)

> JEFFREYS. You are free, Caesar; I make you so. But, you dog, I must make you a lad of spirit, like an Englishman, or else, what's your liberty good for?
> CAESAR. Ah, Massa, I free! I like you! – Am I Englishman? – oh teach me to be Englishman.
> JEFFREYS. That I will, you rogue. – An Englishman – ay, he lives as he likes – lives *where* he likes – *goes* where he likes – *stays* where he likes – *works* if he likes – lets it *alone*, if he likes – starves, if he likes – abuses who he likes – boxes who he likes[18] – thinks what he likes – speaks what he *thinks* – for damme, he fears nothing, and will face the devil. (27-28)

The subplot of a black slave's liberation by a white servant in a colonial settlement was relatively nonconformist. Such a subversion of the master/slave hierarchy, in addition to a social system threatened by the nabobs, or of the traditional family system, menaced by women of un-

---

[18] These last two lines were omitted in representation.

certain origins who ran to India to find the husband they could not have in England, was a potential threat to the whole Indian settlement. In the opinion of the previous Resident (and possibly also Hastings), the newly arrived governor, with his liberal thought, represented an alarming change in the system of the colony:

> RESIDENT. Lookye, Mr. Northcote, if you continue to go on in this stile, Sir, I must write home; there is no going on thus; "for what with your pretended benevolence and generosity, and stuff," Sir, you set the whole settlement in an uproar! There's no governing them – blacks, whites, Gentoos, and Hindoos, all alike running made after you, and your vagaries, truly.
> NORTHCOTE. Yes, Mr. Resident, I feel for human nature, of whatever colour or description; I feel for the name and character of an Englishman. "I feel neither the power of gold, prejudice, nor partiality; and where the lives and properties, or even happiness, of others, are concerned, I have re-garded the impulse of humanity." (52)

Both Green and Moskal underline that the final restoration of "British" order is on the one side dictated by the fact that the colonizers "are masters, not by force of conquest, but by moral deserving" (Green 413), and on the other side by the reduction of the master/slave relation to a parent/child relation, thus "naturalizing the [colonized] submission through the metaphor of the patriarchal family" (Moskal 118). Once the order is re-established, the binary oppositions already mentioned also return; the rhetoric of the happy ending could not have been more celebrative.

A similar strategy, that of submitting the political message to the subplot in order to secure the moral purpose of the play while still celebrating the Empire, is even more evident in Frances Burney's un-performed (until 1993) *A Busy Day*. The comedy is set in London, to where the protagonists have just returned from the East Indies. Eliza

1. Late Eighteenth-Century Women Dramatists

Watts has long been in India with her adopted father, Mr Alderson, who has left her an inheritance of eighty thousand pounds. She returns to London with her fiancé Cleveland (they met in India) who has been recalled home by his uncle Sir Marmaduke to become his heir. Sir Marmaduke and Lady Wilhelmina want him to marry Miss Perceval. Meanwhile, Cleveland's brother Frank meets Eliza by accident and plots to marry her because he needs money to repay his gambling debts. On declaring his real love to Eliza, Miss Perceval and Frank determine to get revenge on Cleveland. They invite Eliza's "vulgar" family to a party with Sir Marmaduke and Lady Wilhelmina with the intention of humiliating both Eliza and Cleveland. When, however, Sir Marmaduke threatens to disinherit Cleveland, Eliza solves her hero's financial problems and her generosity is rewarded by the happy ending. In Burney's opinion, their marriage was based on a "nabob's" wealth, and she gave them (and their imperial wealth) the elevated place she believes they deserve in society. The play has almost nothing to say about slavery and abolition, the colonial issue or the Hastings trial,[19] except that the first act opens with Eliza talking to her maid Deborah and another English servant about the black servant she brought back with her from India:

> ELIZA. [. . .] pray assist my servant in taking care of my trunks.
> 1ST WAITER. What, the Black?
> ELIZA. Yes; be so good as to see if he wants any help.
> 1ST SERVANT. What, the Black?
> ELIZA. Yes. He is the best creature living. I shall be extremely concerned if he should meet with any accident.
> 1ST SERVANT. What, the Black? (22)

Deborah then adds:

---

[19] The Burneys were supporters of Hastings, despite Frances Burney's early friendship with Burke; see Chevalier (36) and Thrale.

> DEBORAH. Why, that's very good of you, my dear young lady, to be so kind to him [. . .]: but, [. . .] after all, a Black's but a Black; and let him hurt himself never so much, it won't shew. It in't like hurting us whites, with our fine skins, all over alabaster. (23)

Curiously, "the Black," whose name is Mungo (one of the most typical names for a black slave) never appears on stage; Africans and Indians as characters were rarely represented on stage, an omission that has only recently been studied and discussed.[20] The few reliable sources we have today are the newspapers and the gazettes of the time, the playbills and the dramatis personae in the published texts. Looking at the printed versions of Cowley's, Inchbald's and Starke's plays, all the Indian and black main character roles were played by (white) British actors and actresses, despite the fact that there must have been actors of colour in London at that time who could also speak good English. Their "presence" is in fact underlined by the fact that many playwrights, and Hannah Cowley was among them, "introduced Negroes [. . .] because of their box-office appeal" (Carlson 2), although we cannot be sure of the authenticity of these negroes' darkskin; they could have been white actors in disguise, as generally happened when there were such roles (such as Othello).[21] Furthermore, the word "black" during the eighteenth century was a generic term, and included Indians, as evident in Burney's play. Characterizations, changes and adaptations could easily be achieved by stereotyping the character and associating him with an unmistakable stage object, such as a turban, a veil, a fake beard and blackening their skin with burnt cork.

 A Busy Day is a reaction (at least an ideological one) to such generalization, for Eliza seems to be willing to mark the difference between the "Black" referred to by both the English servant and Deborah, and

---

[20] See Carlson; Moody; O'Quinn.
[21] See Shyllon; Nussbaum.

the actual Indian servant she brought with her from India, by clarifying his ethnicity throughout the play:

> MISS WATTS. Pray, sister, do the Indins [sic] do much mischief? --- What kind of look have they? Do they let 'em run about wild? Wa'n't you monstrous frightened at first?
> ELIZA. Frightened? The native Gentoos are the mildest and gentlest of human beings.
> MISS WATTS. La, nasty black things! I can't abide the Indins [sic]. (26)

Burney's apparent philanthropy may have referred to things to come (the Bill for the Abolition of the British Slave Trade was finally passed a few years later), but her view of India and the Indians was still influenced by Hastings. The same image of India found in Starke's *The Sword of Peace* and Inchbald's *Such Things Are* is faithfully reproduced in Burney's play. The characters are now in London, at the heart of that Empire still at the beginning of its making. And yet, as Chevalier acutely observes, "the opening action immediately suggests London as a place of danger – far greater danger, in fact, than the Calcutta that Eliza has left" (31). London is thus to Eliza the "foreign, exotic landscape" that India must have appeared to be to the eyes of the adventurers who travelled in the opposite direction. Burney's comedy proceeds with the expansion of its main theme, i.e. the acquisition of Eliza's inheritance and her rise in social class. Such social mobility as Eliza enjoys in London, as well as a new economy of the social system itself, derives directly from the wealth of the whole Empire overseas, and especially from British India, which begins to be perceived also as an "emporium."[22] The idealized, traditional and *ancien régime* perception of British India (represented by Hastings) had

---

[22] For this idea of "Empire" as an "emporium" I am indebted to Joseph W. Childers, in a paper delivered at the International Conference on Travel Literature and India, University of Delhi, 20-21 Feb. 2007.

waned, opening the way to a modern colonization, relying more and more on the trade in luxury goods for consumption in the heart of the Empire. Other protagonists would take Hastings'splace in celebrating the glories of British India, this time, however, by looking at it through an evangelical and utilitarian lens. The exploitation and subjugation of the natives remains, still today, one of the darkest sides in the process of colonial expansion that was just at its beginning. Other authors would later react, this time by learning how to speak out and back their contempt, anger and indignation, finally achieving the freedom of self-definition, confidence and expression of which the women dramatists of the late eighteenth century were deprived.

Works Cited

Banaji, D. R. *Slavery in British India*. Bombay: D. B. Taraporevala, 1933.

Bernstein, Jeremy. *Dawning of the Raj: The Life and Trials of Warren Hastings*. Chicago: Ivan D. Ree, 2000.

Boaden, James. *Memoirs of Mrs Inchbald: Including Her Familiar Correspondence with the Most Distinguished Persons of Her Time*. 2 vols. London: Richard Bentley, 1833.

Bolton, Betsy. *Women, Nationalism and the Romantic Stage: Theatre and Politics in Britain, 1780-1800*. Cambridge: Cambridge University Press, 2001.

Brown, Laura. *Fables of Modernity: Literature and Culture in the English Eighteenth Century*. Ithaca: Cornell University Press, 2001.

Burke, Edmund. "Speech (December 1, 1783) Upon the Question for the Speaker's Leaving the Chair in Order for the House to Resolve Itself into a Committee on Mr. Fox's India Bill." *The Works of the Right Honourable Edmund Burke. In Twelve Volumes*. Vol. 2. London: John C. Nimmo, 1887: 357-447.

1. Late Eighteenth-Century Women Dramatists

Burney, Frances. *A Busy Day; or, An Arrival from India*. Ed. Tara Ghoshal Wallace. New Brunswick, NJ: Rutgers University Press, 1984.

___. *The Diaries and Letters of Madame D'Arblay, Edited by her Niece* [Charlotte Barrett]. 7 vols. London: Henry Colburn, 1854.

Carlson, Julia. "New Lows in Eighteenth-Century Theater: The Rise of Mungo." Romantic and Victorian Theatre Workshop, NASSR/NAVSA Conference, 31 Aug.-3 Sept. 2006. Purdue University, West Lafayette, Indiana, USA.

___. "Race and Profit in English Theatre." Forthcoming in *The Cambridge Companion to Eighteenth Century Theatre*. Eds. Jane Moody and Daniel O'Quinn.

Carnall, Geoffrey, and Colin Nicholson, eds. *The Impeachment of Warren Hastings: Papers from a Bicentenary Commemoration*. Edinburgh: Edinburgh University Press, 1989.

Chevalier, Noel. "Redeeming the Nabob: Frances Burney, Warren Hastings and the Cultural Construction of British India in *A Busy Day*." *The Burney Journal* 2 (1999): 24-39.

Choudhury, Mita. *Interculturalism and Resistance in the London Theater, 1660-1800. Identity, Performance, Empire*. Lewisburg: Bucknell University Press, 2000.

Cowley, Hannah. *A Day in Turkey; or, The Russian Slaves. A Comedy, as Acted at the Theatre Royal, in Covent Garden*. London: G. G. J. and J. Robinson, 1792.

Davies, A. Mervyn. *Strange Destiny: A Biography of Warren Hastings*. New York: Putnam's Sons, 1935.

De Bruyn, Frans. "Edmund Burke's Gothic Romance: The Portrayal of Warren Hastings in Burke's Writings and Speeches on India." *Criticism* 29 (1987): 415-38.

Donkin, Ellen. *Getting into the Act: Women Playwrights in London, 1776-1829*. New York: Routledge, 1995.

Doody, Margaret Ann. *Frances Burney. The Life in the Works*. New Brunswick, NJ: Rutgers University Press, 1988.

Feiling, Keith. *Warren Hastings*. London: Macmillan, 1954.

Foote, Samuel. *The Nabob; A Comedy, in Three Acts. As it is Performed at the Theatre-Royal in the Haymarket*. London: Printed for T. Cadell *et al.*, 1778.

Franklin, Michael J. "Accessing India: Orientalism, Anti-"Indianism", and the Rhetoric of Jones and Burke." *Romanticism and Colonialism: Writing Empire 1780-1830*. Ed. Tim Fulford and Peter J. Kitson. Cambridge: Cambridge University Press, 1998.

___. *Representing India: Indian Culture and Imperial Control in Eighteenth-Century British Orientalist Discourse*. 9 vols. London: Routledge, 2000.

Gagen, Jean. "Hannah Cowley." *Dictionary of Literary Biography*. Vol. 89 (1989): 82-105.

Graham, Gerald S. *A Concise History of the British Empire*. London: Thames and Hudson, 1970.

Green, Katherine S. ""You Should Be My Master": Imperial Recognition Politics in Elizabeth Inchbald's *Such Things Are*." *Clio* 27.3 (1998): 387-414.

Inchbald, Elizabeth. *Such Things Are; A Play, in Five Acts. As Performed at the Theatre-Royal, Smoke-Alley*. London: Printed for G. G. J and J. Robinson, 1788.

___. *The Mogul Tale; or, The Descent of a Balloon. A Farce, as it is Acted at the Theatre-Royal, Smoke-Alley*. London: F. Powell, 1796.

Jenkins, Annibel. *I'll Tell You What. The Life of Elizabeth Inchbald*. Lexington: University Press of Kentucky, 2003.

Juneja, Renu. "The Native and the Nabob: Representations of the Indian Experience in Eighteenth-Century Literature." *Journal of Commonwealth Literature* 27.1 (1992): 183-98.

Keay, John. *The Honourable Company: A History of the English East India Company*. London: Harper Collins, 1993.

Lawson, Philip. *The East India Company: A History*. London: Longman, 1993.

___, and J. Phillips. "'Our Execrable Banditti': Perceptions of Nabobs in Mid-Eighteenth Century Britain." *Albion* 16 (1984): 225-41.

Lewis, Ivor. *Sahibs, Nabobs and Boxwallahs: A Dictionary of the Words of Anglo-India*. Delhi: Oxford University Press, 1998.

Mani, Lata. *Contentious Traditions: The Debate on Sati in Colonial India*. Berkeley: University of California Press, 1998.

Marsden, William. *The History of Sumatra, Containing an Account of the Government, Laws, Customs, and Manner of the Native Inhabitants, with a Description of the Natural Productions, and a Relation of the Ancient Political State of that Island*. 1783. New York: Oxford University Press, 1966.

Marshall, P. J. *East Indian Fortunes: The British in Bengal in the Eighteenth Century*. Oxford: Oxford University Press, 1976.

___. *The Impeachment of Warren Hastings*. London: Oxford University Press, 1965.

McCann, Andrew. "Edmund Burke's Immortal Law: Reading the Impeachment of Warren Hastings, 1788." *Cultural Politics in the 1790s: Literature, Radicalism, and the Public Sphere*. Houndsmill: Macmillan, 1999. 33-58.

Moody, Jane. *Illegitimate Theatre in London, 1787-1843*. Cambridge: Cambridge University Press, 2000.

Moon, Penderel. *Warren Hastings and British India*. New York: Collier, 1962.

Moskal, Jeanne. "English National Identity in Mariana Starke's 'The Sword of Peace': India, Abolition, and the Rights of Women." *Women in British Romantic Theatre. Drama, Performance, and Society, 1790-1840*. Ed. Catherine Burroughs. Cambridge: Cambridge University Press, 2000. 102-31.

Musselwhite, David. "The Trial of Warren Hastings." *Literature, Politics, and Theory: Papers from the Essex Conference, 1976-84*. Ed. F. Barker et al. London: Methuen, 1986. 77-103.

Nussbaum, Felicity. *The Limits of the Human: Fictions of Anomaly, Race, and Gender in the Long Eighteenth Century*. Cambridge: Cambridge University Press, 2003.

Oddie, Geoffrey A. *Imagined Hinduism: British Protestant Missionary Constructions of Hinduism, 1793-1900*. London: Sage, 2006.

O'Quinn, Daniel. "Hannah Cowley's *A Day in Turkey* and the Political Efficacy of Charles James Fox." *European Romantic Review* 14 (2003): 17-30.

___. *Staging Governance. Theatrical Imperialism in London, 1770-1800*. Baltimore: The Johns Hopkins University Press, 2006.

___. "The Long Minuet as Danced at Coromandel: Character and the Colonial Translation of Class Anxiety in Mariana Starke's *The Sword of Peace*." *British Women Playwrights around 1800*. 1 Sept. 2000 <http://www.etang.umontreal.ca/bwp1800/essays/oquinn_sword.html>

O'Toole, Fintan. *A Traitor's Kiss: The Life of Richard Brinsley Sheridan, 1751-1816*. New York: Farrar, Straus, and Giroux, 1998.

Raven, James. *Judging New Wealth*. Oxford: Clarendon Press, 1992.

Raza, Rosemary. *In Their Own Words. British Women Writers and India 1740-1857*. Delhi: Oxford University Press, 2006.

Said, Edward. *Orientalism*. Harmondsworth: Penguin, 1978.

Samet, Elizabeth D. "A Prosecutor and a Gentleman: Edmund Burke's Idiom of Impeachment." *English Literary History* 68 (2001): 397-418.

Shyllon, Folarin. *Black People in Britain 1555-1833*. London: Oxford University Press, 1977.

Singh, Jyotsna. *Colonial Narratives, Cultural Dialogues: "Discoveries" of India in the Language of Colonialism*. London: Routledge, 1996.

Spear, Percival. *The Nabobs: A Study of the Social Life of the English in Eighteenth-Century India*. London: Oxford University Press, 1963.

1. Late Eighteenth-Century Women Dramatists

Starke, Mariana. *The Sword of Peace, or, A Voyage of Love; A Comedy, in Five Acts*. Dublin: H. Chamberlaine *et al.*, 1789.

___. *The Widow of Malabar: A Tragedy in Three Acts. As it is Performed at the Theatre-Royal Covent Garden*, Dublin: Printed for P. Wogan *et al.*, 1791.

Suleri, Sara. *The Rhetoric of English India*. Chicago: University of Chicago Press, 1992.

Sutherland, Lucy S. *The East India Company in Eighteenth-Century Politics*. Oxford: Clarendon Press, 1952.

Thrale, Hester Lynch. *Thraliana. The Diary of Mrs Hester Lynch Thrale (Later Mrs. Piozzi) 1776-1809*. 2 vols. Ed. Katherine Balderston. Oxford: Clarendon Press, 1942.

Travel Literature and India. Proceedings of the First International Conference on Travel Literature and India, 20-21 Feb. 2007, University of Delhi (forthcoming).

Zonana, Joyce. "The Sultan and the Slave: Feminist Orientalism and the Structure of *Jane Eyre*." *Signs* 18.3 (Spring 1993): 592-617.

2. India as Gothic Horror: Maturin's *Melmoth the Wanderer* and Images of Juggernaut in Early Nineteenth-Century Missionary Writing

Andrew Rudd
Trinity College, Cambridge

Charles Maturin's gothic novel *Melmoth the Wanderer* (1820) is not traditionally considered part of the "literature of British India." This masterpiece of Protestant paranoia, written by a debt-stricken clergyman living in colonial Dublin, explores the theme of religious and specifically Catholic oppression of individual freedoms. The Faust-like Melmoth, ancestor of the novel's main narrator, entered into a satanic pact centuries earlier, which granted him a term of immortality during which he must find a victim in a situation so bleak that they are willing to exchange fates with him. If he fails to find such a person, devils will reclaim him at the expiry of the term. Melmoth roams the world looking for scenarios of suffering. The vast majority of these are shown to be the products of the social structures and rituals of Catholic southern Europe; Maturin's family were Protestant French Huguenot emigrants who had no love lost for their former persecutors. A typical situation, and one that introduces the section covered by this essay, involves a young Spanish nobleman, Alonzo di Monçada, who refuses to enter the priesthood at his family's behest. Enraged, they consign him to a monastery, where the cruelty and sadism of his fellow monks drive him to the brink of insanity. On one occasion, they sprinkle the steps of the altar with tiny fragments of glass, causing him to appear to have a fit when he walks barefoot over them during an inspection of the church by the abbot. He is ripe, clearly, for the Wanderer's approach. Yet a considerable portion of the novel is set not in Spain, Italy, Portugal or France – the heartlands of Catholic Europe – but in India. The 250-page-long "Tale of the Indians" at the heart of Maturin's notoriously concentric fiction forms the subject of this enquiry, and marks the culmination of an extraordinary process of textual transmission and transmutation that links colonial reportage to the gothic novel.

First, however, I wish to consider ways in which writing about colonial India can be regarded as "gothic." Patrick Brantlinger found a gathering gloom in nineteenth-century writing on Empire in his *Rule of Darkness: British Literature and Imperialism, 1830-1914* (1988). Writing of Indian Mutiny novels, Brantlinger observed "an absolute polarisation of good and evil, innocence and guilt, justice and injustice, moral restraint and sexual depravity, civilisation and barbarism" that was directly comparable to the dynamics of the gothic mode (200). Alexandra Warwick, in her entry in *The Handbook to Gothic Literature* (1998), identified two broad strands of "colonial gothic" in British literature: the first characterised by a domestic setting that represents "the fear of the incursion of the foreign 'other' into Britain" (the appearance of Mrs Rochester in Charlotte Brontë's *Jane Eyre* is the paradigmatic example); the second set in the colonial contact zone itself, with an experience of otherness "manifested in attempts to control or domesticate the native peoples" (261-62). A third sub-category, which Massimiliano Demata has coined in relation to William Beckford's *Vathek* (1782), is "Oriental gothic": a mingling of fact and fiction, typified by the use of footnotes to provide an illusion of reality, which opens up "a narrative space which discloses to the reader the dangerous proximity and closeness of the alien presence of the other" (21). All these literary phenomena involve ways of looking at otherness in a colonial context that, consciously or unconsciously, occupy the psychological realms of the gothic. Such texts need not be novels in themselves but all share a preoccupation with fear of the unknown, the uncanny, darkness, depravity and vice.

The texts under scrutiny here are British responses to Indian religious practices, particularly those associated with Hinduism. While it is well known that commentators in the nineteenth century took a dim view of customs such *sati* and *thagi*, European engagement with Hinduism was not always marked by moralising disapproval. On the contrary, the eighteenth century and Romantic period saw a flourishing of scholarly and artistic interest in Indian religion. The movement known then as Orientalism (not to be confused with Edward Said's description of a particular European attitude towards the East – although the point is debatable) sought to investigate and present to Europeans the culture of Asia. For the main part, it did so sympathetically. British men of colonial letters, among them Nathaniel Brassey Halhed, Charles Wilkins and, above all, Sir William Jones, disseminated knowledge of Hinduism and its ancient language of expression, Sanskrit, with characteristic Enlightenment zeal. By 1800, Britain could boast that of all European nations it had delved deepest into the history of world religions and discovered several new ones (Sikhism was added to the list in 1788 with the publication of Wilkins's "Observations on the Seeks and their College" in the first volume of *Asiatic Researches*). But, in certain quarters, familiarity bred contempt. Britain's military and economic dominance of the Subcontinent by the turn of the century, together with the progress in Britain of the Evangelical Revival, meant that Indian faiths increasingly came to be viewed as a poor relation of Christianity. Moreover, a mounting sense of providence, manifest in Britain's pre-eminence in South Asia, led to calls for the conversion of the Indians to Christianity.

If the creed that had served Britons so well were extended to Britain's Indian subjects, this argument ran, then not only would the British Empire in the East become an unassailable, unified entity, but millions of heathen souls would be saved. Members of the influential evangelical group known as the Clapham Sect, which included William Wilberforce, Zachary Macaulay and (ironically) Sir William Jones's successor as President of the Asiatic Society of Bengal, John Shore, Lord Teignmouth, lobbied Parliament for the imposition of Christianity throughout British India. They sought to insert the so-called "pious clause" into the East India Company charter, which was due for renewal in 1813. This read: "it is the Duty of the Country to promote the Interests and the Happiness of the Native Inhabitants of the British Dominions in India and such Measures ought to be adopted as may tend to the introduction among them of useful knowledge the religious and moral improvement" (qtd. in Porter 74). The Company forbade missionary activity in their territory on security grounds, following the Vellore Mutiny of 1806, in which native sepoys, alarmed by rumours that they would be forcibly converted to Christianity, rose up and attacked their European officers. It even sponsored various local festivals, notably the ceremony at the temple of Juggernaut in Puri, Orissa. The years leading up to 1813 therefore saw a polarisation of views on Hinduism, with evangelical attacks matched in vigour by Orientalist ripostes.

My first contention is that evangelical polemic played a significant part in steering depictions of Indian religion towards gothic tropes. Consider, for example, the following passage from Teignmouth's *Considerations on the Practicability, Policy, and Obligation of Communicating to the Natives of India the Knowledge of Christianity* (1808):

> Were the same superstitions, or the same barbarous and licentious rites, which are now exhibited on the banks of the Ganges, to be practised on the banks of the Thames, or even the remotest part of the British islands, they would excite the strongest possible feelings of horror, and stimulate our efforts to substitute a purer and more benign system in the place of this compound of cruelty and crime. (57)

When Joshua Marshman, a Baptist missionary based in the Danish enclave of Serampore, recorded his reaction to a *sati*, he similarly (and understandably) reached for the language of the macabre to describe his feelings:

> To have seen savage wolves thus tearing a human body limb from limb, would have seemed shocking, but to see rela-

2. India as Gothic Horror

> tions and neighbours do this to one with whom they had familiarly conversed not an hour before, and to do it with an air of levity, was almost too much for me to bear. (Qtd. in Wilberforce 49)

Others saw Hinduism as simply the most barbarous religion with which Europeans were then acquainted. William Ward, another Serampore Baptist, issued an expansive and influential work, *A View of the History, Literature and Religion of the Hindoos* (1811), in which he denounced that faith as "the most PUERILE, IMPURE, AND BLOODY OF ANY SYSTEM OF IDOLATRY THAT WAS EVER ESTABLISHED ON EARTH" (1: 100). The discourse applied to Hinduism of violence, horror and transgression, in which all manner of natural laws were cast asunder, meant that following the publicity campaign mounted during the charter debate, India found itself cast as a land of religious nightmare. European imaginations ran amok there in multiple collisions of neurosis, fiction and reality.

Reactions to Hinduism found a ready-made analogue in the established anti-Catholic rhetoric of the period.[1] The British popular imagination came to associate both religions with superstition, priestcraft and image-worship, and observers were not behindhand in connecting the two as common obstacles to the propagation of the Gospel as they interpreted it. Edward Moor, author of *The Hindu Pantheon* (1810), which celebrated the "pure" Vedanta strain of Hinduism, contemplated a volume entitled *Pagan and Papal Rome: connecting those ancient and modern pagan rites, ceremonies and legends, with the fables of Hindu mythology: and showing the unchangeableness of popery, and monkery and priestcraft – applicable to the present times*; portions of this were published in his *Oriental Fragments* (1834). Claudius Buchanan, Vice-Provost of Fort William College, Calcutta, cautioned in his *Christian Researches in Asia* (1811) that "while we

---

[1] See Haydon and Wheeler. On perceived links between Hinduism and Catholicism, see Young 91-111.

remain silent and unmoved spectators of the flames of the Widow's Pile, there is no hope that we shall be justly affected by the reported horrors of the Inquisition" (155). Buchanan was referring to the rumoured state of affairs in the Portuguese territories in Goa, which the British viewed with considerable suspicion. Teignmouth, Marshman and Buchanan introduce a moral and aesthetic dimension into their texts that invites the reader to share their feelings and be moved to intervene in scenes of suffering. This reflex that they take for granted derived from eighteenth-century formulations of imaginative sympathy, notably that offered by Edmund Burke in his *Philosophical Enquiry into the Origin of our Ideas concerning the Sublime and the Beautiful* (1757). Early nineteenth-century Evangelicals inherited this imaginative formula, but significantly sharpened its Protestant Christian focus.

A revealing case study is that of Henry Martyn, an East India Company chaplain and the first translator of the New Testament into Urdu. Martyn was a student of the prominent Evangelical Charles Simeon, incumbent of Holy Trinity Church, Cambridge, and "converted" to Christianity in 1799. Martyn's posthumously published *Journals and Letters* (1837) are the chief primary source for his life and opinions, and constitute a fine example of the evangelical imaginary at work. Martyn was inspired by the example of William Carey, founder of the Baptist mission at Serampore, who, unencumbered by the East India Company regulations concerning Christian proselytising, sought converts among the local population. Like many Evangelicals, Martyn considered it scandalous that the Church of England held no jurisdiction in British India. He was bound by regulations, however, and embarked for India in 1805 to minister to Company employees exclusively. During the voyage, Martyn antagonised the ship's passengers and crew with recurrent sermons on the ninth psalm, "the wicked shall be turned into hell, and all the nations that forget God." Nine months later in 1806, as the vessel arrived off the coast, he saw the temple of Juggernaut in silhouette against the setting sun. The apparition dis-

2. India as Gothic Horror

turbed him profoundly. "Here is heathenism staring the stranger in the face on his arrival off the land," he wrote in his diary, "the scene presented another specimen of that tremendous gloom, with which the devil has overspread the land; no house near it, we conceived no noise to be heard along the bare coast, but the hollow roar of the surf" (1: 441-42). Martyn's first impressions are strongly conditioned by his biblical reading and faith, which lead him to conjure an atmosphere of evil around a seemingly innocuous scene. Worse was to come once the chaplain disembarked. Guided through woods one night by the sound of drums and cymbals, Martyn recalled that "never did sounds go through my heart with such horror in my life." Anticipation gave way to what appears (to modern readers) to be something of an anticlimax, when he emerged at a Hindu temple in the midst of a nighttime ceremony:

> The people to the number of about fifty were standing on the outside, and playing the instruments. In the centre of the building was the idol, a little black ugly image, about two feet high, with a few lights burning round him. At intervals they prostrated themselves, with their foreheads to the earth [. . .] I shivered at being in the neighbourhood of hell; my heart was ready to burst at the dreadful state to which the Devil had brought my poor fellow-creatures. (1: 449-50)

What is striking about Martyn's account compared to the Oriental scholars of the preceding generation is its complete absence of curiosity, let alone tolerance. He is also prey to what are entirely imagined horrors, in the manner of an Anne Radcliffe heroine or Catherine Morland in Jane Austen's *Northanger Abbey* (1817). Unlike Catherine, who is finally able to transcend her gothic preconceptions, Martyn finds what he sees genuinely shocking. We should not underestimate the force of his conviction, and, in fairness to Martyn, ultimately he did not distinguish between European and Indian sinners; one day he recorded that he "lay in tears interceding for the natives of this country; thinking with myself that the most despicable Soodar of India was of as much value in the sight of God as the King of Great Britain" (1: 457).

Buchanan manifested fewer outward signs of heightened sensibility than Martyn, but, like him, supported the idea of extending the Anglican hierarchy to India. His book *Colonial Ecclesiastical Establishment* (1813) outlined a plan for creating parishes and dioceses throughout Company territory, and refuted criticism that this would lead to civil unrest. Even more so than Martyn, he viewed this as the fulfilment of divine providence. Buchanan's centrality to this essay lies not in his role as architect of Anglicanism in the Subcontinent but as an observer of the annual ceremony at the temple of Juggernaut, to which, as mentioned earlier, the Company acted as patron. He brought to perfection the tendency established among earlier European eyewitnesses of viewing the scene through a biblical and, later, a Miltonic prism. Said insightfully termed this way of looking a "textual attitude"; that is, a "fallacy" of employing works of literature to order the "swarming, unpredictable, and problematic mess in which human beings live" (93). Earlier accounts of Juggernaut included those of William Bruton and François Bernier, available to British readers in the widely-read *Collection of Voyages and Travels [. . .] from the curious and valuable LIBRARY of the late EARL OF OXFORD*, often known as "Churchill's Collection" or "Churchill's Travels." Bruton and Bernier observed the phenomenon of devotees throwing themselves beneath the wheels of an enormous chariot. Bernier, who visited India in 1658 and again in 1668, wrote "when this hellish triumphant chariot marcheth, there are found (which is no fable) persons so foolishly credulous and superstitious as to throw themselves with their bellies under those large and heavy wheels, which bruise them to death" (*Collection* 2: 198). Bruton, harking back to his travels of 1638, declared the spectacle to be "the mirror of all wickedness and idolatry." He was reminded of the Moabites worshipping Baal mentioned in the Book of Kings and elsewhere. When the statue of Juggernaut ap-

2. *India as Gothic Horror*

peared and worshippers rushed to immolate themselves beneath it, his thoughts turned to "the *Revelat.* and 1st verse, and likewise the 16th and 17th verses of the said chapter, in which places there is a beast, and such idolatrous worship mentioned." He even interpreted the sandal paste on the Brahmins' foreheads as the mark of the Beast described in Revelation 16.3: "And he causeth all, both small and great, rich and poor, free and bond, to receive a mark in their right hand, or in their foreheads" (*Collection* 2: 277).

As might be expected, these seventeenth-century observers were steeped in biblical imagery. Yet a ready recourse to scripture was also characteristic of early nineteenth-century Evangelicals such as Buchanan. He visited the temple on 18 June 1806, having earlier outlined the essentials of the ceremony in his *Colonial Ecclesiastical Establishment*, cited as a source text in Robert Southey's poem *The Curse of Kehama*. On the latter occasion, recorded in his published journal, he counted over 100 human skulls littering the precincts, and recalled seeing dogs, jackals and vultures scavenging. He approached the temple on horseback in the midst of a crowd of devotees. At one point, the crush was so intense that the clergyman was nearly knocked from the saddle. At length, the chariot of Juggernaut appeared, and Buchanan recorded the event in his diary as follows:

> I have returned home from witnessing a scene which I shall never forget. At twelve o'clock of this day, being the great day of the feast, the Moloch of Hindoostan was brought out of his temple amidst the acclamations of hundreds of thousands of his followers. [...]
>
> The throne of the idol was placed on a stupendous car or tower about sixty feet in height, resting on wheels which indented the ground deeply, as they turned slowly under the ponderous machine. Attached to it were six cables, of the size and length of a ship's cable, by which the people drew it along. Upon the tower were the priests and satellites of the

idol, surrounding his throne. The idol is a block of wood, having a frightful visage painted black, with a distended mouth of a bloody colour. His arms are of gold, and he is dressed in gorgeous apparel. [. . .]

I went on in the procession, close by the tower of Moloch; which, as it was drawn with difficulty, grated on its wheels harsh thunder. After a few minutes it stopped; and now the worship of the God began. – A high priest mounted the car in front of the idol, and pronounced his obscene stanzas in the ears of the people; who responded at intervals in the same strain. "These songs", said he, "are the delight of the God. His car can only move when he is pleased with the song". [. . .] A boy of about twelve years was then brought forth to attempt something yet more lascivious, if peradventure the God would move. The "child perfected the praise" of his idol with such ardent expression and gesture, that the God was pleased, and the multitude emitting a sensual yell of delight, urged the car along. [. . .] An aged minister of the idol then stood up, and with a long rod in his hand, which he moved with indecent action, completed the variety of this disgusting exhibition. – I felt a consciousness of doing wrong in witnessing it. I was also somewhat appalled at the magnitude and horror of the spectacle; I felt like a guilty person, on whom all eyes were fixed, and I was about to withdraw. But a scene of a different kind was about to be presented. The characteristics of Moloch's worship are obscenity and blood. We have seen the former. Now comes the blood.

After the tower had proceeded some way, a pilgrim announced that he was ready to offer himself a sacrifice to the idol. He laid himself down in the road before the tower as it was moving along, lying on his face, with his arms stretched forwards. The multitude passed round him, leaving the space

2. *India as Gothic Horror*

clear, and he was crushed to death by the wheels of the chariot. (*Christian Researches* 24-27)

"*Hissing* applause" heard on the approach to the temple refers to the Pandemonium scenes from book 10 of Milton's *Paradise Lost*, where Satan and his fellow fallen angels metamorphose into serpents. Their only sound thereafter is "from innumerable / A dismal universal hiss" (10.507-08). Buchanan's mention of Moloch next transports his readers to the earlier Pandemonium scene, where is found the description of that god as a "horrid King besmear'd with blood / Of human sacrifice, and parents tears" (2.392-96). "Homicide" and "lust hard by hate" mark the "wanton rites" of his worship, and in the scene before him, the minister witnesses acts that appear to confirm his prejudices. The Hindus were popularly believed to descend from the children of Ham, the Ammonites, and these are among the tribes condemned for idolatry throughout the Old Testament.[2] The phrase "the child perfected the praise," presumably in this case by submitting to buggery, is intended to contrast with the behaviour of the children in the Temple in Jerusalem when they worshipped Jesus in defiance of the chief priests: "And Jesus saith to them, Yea, have ye never read, Out of the mouth of babes and sucklings thou hast perfected praise?" (Matthew 21.16) Taken together, Buchanan's ironic quotations from Scripture and cross-references to *Paradise Lost* convey a powerful sense of hell on earth; one, importantly, that it was in Britain's power to redeem. The diary entry closes with Buchanan surveying what he considers a "Golgotha" from a distant hilltop, and dreaming of a Christian establishment in India (27).

Buchanan's accounts of Juggernaut gained currency in Britain as a secondary source in literature and elsewhere. Southey, whose interest in the East Indies was galvanised by the missionary debate, repro-

---

[2] The antiquarian Jacob Bryant repeated this idea in his *Analysis of Ancient Mythology; or, An Analysis of Ancient Mythology* (1774), as did Jones in his discourse "On the Origin and Families of Nations" (1792).

duced extracts from Buchanan's *Colonial Ecclesiastical Establishment* in the footnotes to *The Curse of Kehama*.[3] In the years surrounding the publication of his epic poem, Southey denounced Hinduism in a series of articles for the *Quarterly* and *Annual Review*. For instance, his 1815 review of James Forbes's *Oriental Memoirs* (1813) labelled the Hindu system of government a "diabolocracy" and noted that in Urdu the words for 'lie' and 'jest' are the same, while in Tamil there is no word for 'hope' ("Oriental" 196). Southey's position on the conversion of India to Christianity is worth clarifying, for while he saw Portuguese Catholicism as a threat to British interests, he nevertheless admired the zeal with which the founder of Portugal's East Indian Empire, Albuquerque, propagated his faith. By contrast, "if England were dispossessed of its dominion in India, the natives would retain nothing of all which we could have taught," Southey lamented, "not a trace of our language would remain; and for our religion – the Hindoo would argue that we had none" ("Periodical" 210).

Hinduism was for him, as for Buchanan, Martyn and others, an obstacle to be removed; yet this did not stop the future poet laureate from exploiting its imaginative potential in *The Curse of Kehama*. The poem involved an elaborate recreation of the Hindu cosmos that forms the backdrop to a tale of individual heroism and moral virtue. Buchanan's account, in addition to those of Bruton, Bernier, John Stavorinus, and Johann Niekamp, fed into Southey's dramatic Juggernaut scene. His treatment of them is significant, for it shows the direction that representations of India were increasingly taking: that of gothic horror. At this stage in the poem, the Indian heroine, Kailyal, has been kidnapped and appears on the chariot in readiness for her ritual "marriage" to Juggernaut:

> Up rear'd on twenty wheels elate,
> Huge as a Ship, the Bridal Car appear'd;
> Loud creak its ponderous wheels, as through the gate

---

[3] On Southey's preoccupation with India at this time, see Lynda Pratt.

2. *India as Gothic Horror*

> A thousand Bramins drag the enormous load.
> There throned aloft in state,
> The Image of the seven-headed God
> Came forth from his abode; and at his side
> Sate [sic] Kailyal like a bride. [. . .]
>
> A thousand pilgrims strain
> Arm, shoulder, breast and thigh, with might and main,
> To drag that sacred wain,
> And scarce can draw along the enormous load.
> Prone fall the frantic votaries in the road,
> And calling on the God,
> Their self-devoted bodies there they lay
> To pave his chariot-way.
> On Jaga-Naut they call,
> The ponderous Car rolls on, and crushes all.
> Through flesh and bones it ploughs its dreadful path.
> Groans rise unheard: the dying cry,
> And death and agony
> Are trodden under foot by yon mad throng,
> Who follow close, and thrust the deadly wheels along.
>
> (147)

Southey intended to offset personal liberty and abuses perpetrated in the name of corrupt religion. Accordingly, we confront the worst aspects of religious despotism. Groans rising "unheard" and death and agony "trodden under foot" signify the absence of a normative, Christian sensibility such as Buchanan's. Compassion and sympathy are not to be found among religious fanatics, the poet implies. Kailyal's predicament – the innocent soul fallen among zealots – is familiar from many a gothic novel, although ordinarily in British literature the villains are Catholic. As for many other commentators, Catholicism and Hinduism were linked in Southey's mind. In his later *Book of the*

Church (1824), he wrote of "practices not less extravagant than those of the Indian Yoguees, and more loathsome" being officially sanctioned by the Church in Italy and Spain (1: 305).

This trend is confirmed in Sydney Owenson, Lady Morgan's novel *The Missionary: An Indian Tale* (1811), where the virtues of individual sensibility as opposed to the "cold hand of religion" are extolled even more vigorously (2: 7-8). The title and publication date are significant. By 1811, the debate on missionary activity in British India was already well advanced. Just as her earlier novel, *The Wild Irish Girl: A National Tale* (1806) had examined Irish national identity in the wake of the 1800 Act of Union, Morgan again intervened in contemporary politics under the cloak of fiction. Set in the seventeenth century, the book tells of the illicit love affair between a Portuguese Franciscan friar, Hilarion, and Luxima, a Hindu "Brachmichira" (virgin widow), both of whom act as itinerant preachers. Towards the end of the novel comes what is clearly a contribution to the missionary debate. Spoken by Hilarion, it offers a sentimental programme for the conversion of India to Christianity, and one that is based on voluntary accession not dogma:

> It is by a precious cultivation of their moral powers, we may hope to influence their religious belief; it is by teaching them to love us, that we can lead them to listen to us; it is by inspiring them with respect for our virtues, that we can give them a confidence in our doctrine: but this has not always been the system adopted by European reformers, and the religion we proffer them is seldom illustrated by its influence on our own lives. (3: 95)

Morgan takes particular aim here at the Jesuits, who were active in India during the seventeenth century. Protestants widely regarded their methods, which reportedly included disguising themselves as Brahmins, as underhand. Hilarion at this point is sitting before Jesuit inquisitors who accuse him of heresy, having discovered his relationship

2. *India as Gothic Horror*

with Luxima. The author invites readers to endorse their love, which she sees as conducive to the true spirit of religion; yet orthodox Catholicism and Hinduism pursue their errant votaries in the second half of novel with a malice that again invokes the gothic mode. Two parallel rites of excommunication take place: the first, when Luxima is expelled from her faith by her own father, the Guru of Kashmir, in a ceremony in a subterranean temple; the second, when Hilarion is imprisoned in the fortress of the Inquisition in Goa, which Morgan refers to as "the mansion of horror and superstition" (3: 148-49). In the ensuing *auto-da-fé*, Luxima throws herself onto the flames with a cry of "*Brahma* receive and eternally unite our spirits!" (3: 179): a somewhat predictable comparison of the rite with *sati*. Strictly speaking, *The Missionary* is neither a gothic novel nor an anti-Catholic one – that is to say, it depicts the inhumane Jesuits as the exception and not the rule of Catholic practice – yet it exhibits a vital theme commonly associated with gothic fiction: tension between the sanctity of the individual and religious orthodoxy.

By the time of the *Melmoth the Wanderer*'s publication in 1820, the East India Charter debate was seven years in the past; there is no reason to suppose that Maturin wished to reignite the arguments for and against the conversion of India to Christianity. Rather, his use of Hinduism, and the ceremony of Juggernaut in particular, as an archetype of misdirected religion points to the inadvertent result of the earlier controversy. India had become associated with horror and functioned in a similar way to Catholicism in the gothic novels of the late eighteenth century. Evidence of this lies in the fact that Maturin modulates freely from Catholicism to Hinduism and back again in his novel. The majority of the work, as mentioned in the opening paragraph, depicts scenarios supposedly common throughout Catholic southern Europe: forced consignments of individuals to monasteries and nunneries, priestly corruption, psychological and sexual abuse and so forth. Monçada introduces the "Tale of the Indians" whilst telling his life story to young John Melmoth, who gradually learns the truth about his dastardly forbear. Having been enclosed in the monastery against his will, Monçada is at length transferred to the Fortress of the Inquisition, where he is tried for heresy. By a stroke of providence, the building catches fire, and in the confusion the Spaniard escapes. He seeks refuge in an underground passageway, which leads to the cell of an elderly cabbalistic Jew. The Jew possesses an antique manuscript written in Spanish, which he asks Monçada to translate.

This document contains the story of Immalee, a maiden and child of nature, who, we are told, lived on an island near the mouth of the Hooghly River (familiar to British readers as the approach to Calcutta). The island is initially visited by devotees of the "black goddess Seeva." Here is the first indication of Maturin's displaced anti-Catholic agenda, for this group mortify their flesh and tell rosary beads. The author claims to derive this information from Thomas Maurice's *Indian Antiquities* (1800), and his intention was presumably to lend a veneer of authenticity to the fiction. The discovery of Immalee on the island dispels the malefic routine. Young people, taking her for a *"white* goddess," row out from the mainland in canoes to scatter flowers and light candles in an obvious riposte to the old, corrupt form of worship (279). Immalee is an *ingénue*, blissfully ignorant of the world beyond her island home. At this point the Wanderer approaches. He appears on the beach one day, and offers to instruct Immalee in the folly of the outside world, about which she is curious to learn. Melmoth turns the conversation to religion. "There is only one point on which they all agree," he argues in an effective piece of satire, "that of making their religion a torment; – the religion of some prompting them to torture themselves, and the religion of some prompting them to torture others" (290). To illustrate his point, he trains a telescope on the coast of India. First, Immalee sees "the black pagoda of Juggernaut," then a "Turkish" mosque (erected as part of Tipu Sultan's efforts to enforce Islam throughout his dominions), and beyond that a temple of "Maha-Devi," "one of the ancient goddesses of the country" (291). This composite of Eastern religions, viewed

2. India as Gothic Horror

through what is evidently a very powerful telescope, suits the Wanderer's purposes exactly for it displays the worst imaginable consequences of blind faith. A "vast sandy plain" lies before the temple of Juggernaut, littered with "the bones of a thousand skeletons, bleaching in the burning and unmoistening air." A thousand pilgrims, "hardly more alive, and scarce less emaciated," drag "their charred and blackening bodies over the sands, to perish under the shadow of the temple, hopeless of ever reaching its walls." Vultures flap overhead, while others, driven frantic in their fervour, wear their hands and knees literally through to the bone. "Immalee withheld her breath, as if she inhaled the abominable effluvia of this mass of putrefaction, which is said to desolate the shores near the temple of Juggernaut, like a pestilence" (292).

The footnote to Maurice, together with the phrase "which is said," draw attention to the passage's supposed basis in reality. Demata's observations on "Oriental gothic" are useful here as a means of understanding the *frisson* gothic literature derived from its proximity to non-fictional texts. Maturin reminds his readers that the material is not the stuff of fantasy but actual religious practice, albeit mercifully distant. As the description of Juggernaut unfolds, it becomes clear that the principal source is Buchanan's diary, freely adapted but with several elements reproduced verbatim. The chariot itself echoes Buchanan and Southey, although here it is transformed with didactic explicitness into an emblem of heathen depravity:

> An enormous fabric, more resembling a moving palace than a triumphal car, supported the inshrined image of Juggernaut, and was dragged forward by the united strength of a thousand human bodies, priests, victims, brahmins, faqueers and all. In spite of this huge force, the impulse was so unequal, that the whole edifice rocked and tottered from time to time, and this singular union of instability and splendour, of trembling decadence and terrific glory, gave a faithful image

of the meretricious exterior, and internal hollowness, of idolatrous religion. (292)

As in a game of Chinese Whispers, the description of Juggernaut becomes progressively more lurid as it is transmitted from text to text. Whereas Buchanan saw one person crushed beneath the chariot wheels, Immalee sees "multitudes" perish. Like his source, Maturin highlights biblical quotations that his original readers would have recognised. The 12-year-old boy reappears, who we are told "perfected the praise" of the loathsome idol, "with all the outrageous lubricities of the phallic worship" (Immalee fails to comprehend the nature of the act: we are told that "from the slightest consciousness of the meaning of this phenomenon, her unimaginable purity protected her as with a shield"). Worshippers nearby who "cut themselves with knives and lancets in their manner," evoking the heathen prophets of Baal in the First Book of Kings (1 Kings 18.28).

These particulars confirm the debt of *Melmoth the Wanderer* to Buchanan. However, the novelist's polemical energies are not confined to Hinduism. Taking India as a free-floating signifier of spiritual corruption, Maturin picks off each sect in turn as the Wanderer endeavours to turn Immalee against religion altogether. Thus at the temple of Maha-Devi mothers dance and sing while they hang their babies up in baskets as food for the birds, while outside the mosque "Turks" lash out at harmless beggars as they swagger past on their way to prayers. Only "a small obscure building overshadowed by palm-trees, and surmounted by a cross" fills Immalee with a momentary optimism (297). This glimmer of (Protestant) truth recalls us to Maturin's purpose in attacking Indian religion. He groups it along with Catholicism as systems that are inherently corrupting, and that tend to cut their worshippers off not only from God but also from each other. The relationship is made explicit when the authorial voice reminds readers that the worshippers of Juggernaut place as much faith in their exertions "as the Catholic votarist does in the penance of St Bruno, or the ex-

2. *India as Gothic Horror*

oculation of St Lucia, or the martyrdom of St Ursula and her eleven thousand virgins" (292-93); a scorn for the worship of false gods on Maturin's part that extends to all idolatrous creeds.

The reception of Maturin's earlier tragedy *Bertram; or, The Castle of St Aldobrand* (1816) illuminates the logic of his recourse to Hinduism as an object of gothic horror. Samuel Taylor Coleridge, writing in the *Courier*, denounced the work as "jacobinical" for overturning what he regarded as reasonable moral expectations (342). The preface to *Melmoth the Wanderer* voiced the author's concerns that the gothic novel was increasingly seen as an outmoded and (as Coleridge's comment shows) a politically suspect form of literature. Maturin writes that "a friend" had censured the section of "The Spaniard's Tale"(i.e. the section of novel narrated by Monçada) "as containing too much attempt at the revivification of the horrors of Radcliffe-Romance, of the persecutions of convents, and the terrors of the Inquisition" (5). The Wanderer's speeches against religion also prompt a defensive footnote: "the sentiments ascribed to the stranger are diametrically opposite to mine, and [. . .] I have purposely put them into the mouth of an agent of the enemy of mankind" (303n). Given these anxieties, it can be argued that Hinduism in this case rejuvenated the gothic form when its original wellsprings were drying up. Although the novels of Horace Walpole, Radcliffe and Matthew "Monk" Lewis preserved popular anti-Catholic discourse throughout eighteenth-century Britain, by the time of *Melmoth the Wanderer* first Jacobinism then Bonapartism replaced the Roman church as spectres of continental European otherness. By 1820, Napoleon was secured on the island of St Helena, whilst Joseph Bonaparte had abolished the Spanish Inquisition in 1808.

If Hinduism partially occupied the space left by Roman Catholicism in the gothic imagination, what were the consequences for Hinduism and its practitioners in real life? Throughout the essay, I have sought to trace the proximity of fiction and reality in gothic fiction, and the novelist's somewhat cavalier treatment of documentary sources in crafting the tale. In conclusion, I would say that through this combination of factors, gothic *chiaroscuro* replaced the more temperate, "enlightened" outlook exemplified by Jones's cultural syncretism as the primary mode of portraying Indian religion. The debate over the East India Company charter polarised views on Hinduism, and introduced vivid imagery, ripe for incorporation into fiction, into the public domain. Teignmouth, Wilberforce and evangelical commentators such as Buchanan spoke of feeling compelled to intervene when confronting the "horrors" of ceremony and custom in British India. Authors such as Southey, Morgan and, most strikingly, Maturin exploited these extraordinary scenes and inaugurated a lasting fascination with widow-burning and the notion of Juggernaut (alive today as a word to describe oversized vehicles that crush everything in their path). This is not to hold the gothic mode with its inherent prejudices responsible for providing a vocabulary for nineteenth-century imperialist rhetoric, but there was more than a ghostly resemblance between the imaginative imperatives of gothic writing and the ideology of nascent imperialism. In *Melmoth the Wanderer*, India is presented as a socio-religious worst-case scenario, unworthy even of the Wanderer's attention, for its inhabitants have long since sunk beyond the possibilities of despair and temptation, let alone redemption. Yet in the same way that gothic novels decried the supposed abuses of Catholicism whilst pitying its victims, so British sympathies transferred away from the culture and religion of India onto its people, who were increasingly portrayed as lost souls in need of Christian salvation.

Works Cited

Bernier, François. "The History of the Revolution of the Dominions of the Great Mogol." *A Collection of Voyages and Travels, Consisting of Authentic Writers in our own Tongue, which have not before been collected in English, or have been abridged in other Collections* [. . .]. *From the curious and valuable LIBRARY of the late EARL OF OXFORD*. 2 vols. Vol. 2. London: Thomas Osbourne, 1745. 105-236.

Brantlinger, Patrick. *Rule of Darkness: British Literature and Imperialism, 1830-1914*. London: Cornell University Press, 1988.

Bruton, William. "News from the East Indies; or, A Voyage to Bengalla." *A Collection of Voyages and Travels, Consisting of Authentic Writers in our own Tongue, which have not before been collected in English, or have been abridged in other Collections [. . .] From the curious and valuable LIBRARY of the late EARL OF OXFORD*. 2 vols. Vol. 2. London: Thomas Osbourne, 1745. 267-79.

Bryant, Jacob. *A New System; or, An Analysis of Ancient Mythology: wherein an attempt is made to divest Tradition of Fable; and to Reduce the Truth to its Original Purity*. 2 vols. London: T. Payne, 1774.

Buchanan, Claudius. *Christian Researches in Asia: with Notices of the Translation of the Scriptures into the Oriental Languages*. London: T. Cadell & W. Davies, 1811.

___. *Colonial Ecclesiastical Establishment: being a Brief View of the State of the Colonies of Great Britain, and of her Asiatic Empire, in respect to Religious Instruction*. London: T. Cadell & W. Davies, 1813.

Burke, Edmund. *A Philosophical Enquiry into the Origin of our Ideas of the Sublime and the Beautiful*. 1757. Ed. Adam Philips. Oxford: Oxford University Press, 1990.

Coleridge, Samuel Taylor. *Biographia Literaria*. Ed. Nigel Leask. London: Everyman, 1997.

A Collection of Voyages and Travels [. . .] *from the curious and valuable LIBRARY of the late EARL OF OXFORD*. 2 vols. London: Thomas Osbourne, 1745.

Demata, Massimiliano. "Discovering Eastern Horrors: Beckford, Maturin and the Discourse of Travel Literature." *Empire and the Gothic: The Politics of Genre*. Ed. William Hughes and Andrew Smith. Basingstoke: Palgrave Macmillan, 2003.

Haydon, Colin. *Anti-Catholicism in Eighteenth-Century England, c.1714-80*. Manchester: Manchester University Press, 1993.

Jones, William, Sir. "On the Origin and Families of Nations." *Asiatick Researches* 3 (1799): 479-92.

Martyn, Henry. *Journals and Letters*. 2 vols. Ed. S. Wilberforce. London: R. B. Seeley & W. Burnside, 1837.

Maturin, Charles. *Bertram; or, The Castle of St Aldobrand: A Tragedy, in Five Acts*. London: n.p., 1816.

___. *Melmoth the Wanderer*. Ed. Douglas Grant. Oxford: Oxford University Press, 1998.

Maurice, Thomas. *Indian Antiquities; or, Dissertations, relative to the Ancient Geographical Divisions, the Pure System of Primeval Theology, the Grand Code of Civil Laws, the Original Form of Government, the Widely-Extended Commerce, and the Various and Profound Literature, of Hindostan: compared, throughout, with the Religion, Laws, Government, and Literature, of Persia, Egypt, and Greece*. 7 vols. London: H. L. Galabin, 1800.

Moor, Edward. *Oriental Fragments*. London: Smith & Elder, 1834.

Morgan, Sydney Owenson, Lady. *The Missionary: An Indian Tale*. 3 vols. London: J. J. Stockdale, 1811.

___. *The Wild Irish Girl: A National Tale*. Ed. Kathryn Kirkpatrick. Oxford: Oxford University Press, 1999.

Niekamp, Johann Lucas. *Historia Missionis Evangelicæ in India Orientali*. Halae, 1745.

Porter, Andrew. *Religion versus Empire? British Protestant Missionaries and Overseas Expansion, 1700-1914.* Manchester: Manchester University Press, 2004.

Pratt, Lynda. "Southey the Literary East Indiaman." *Romantic Representations of British India.* Ed. Michael J. Franklin. London: Routledge, 2006. 131-53.

Said, Edward W. *Orientalism.* London: Penguin, 1995.

Southey, Robert. "Periodical Accounts Relative to the Baptist Missionary Society." *Quarterly Review* 1 (May-June 1809): 193-226.

___. *The Curse of Kehama.* London: Longman *et al.*, 1810.

___. "Oriental Memoirs." *Quarterly Review* 12 (Oct. 1814-May 1815): 180-227.

___. *The Book of the Church.* 2 vols. London: John Murray, 1824.

Stavorinus, Jan Splinter. *Voyages to the East Indies.* Trans. Samuel Hull Wilcocke. 3 vols. London: G. G. & J. Robinson, 1798.

Teignmouth, Lord, John Shore. *Considerations on the Practicability, Policy and Obligation of Communicating to the Natives of India the Knowledge of Christianity.* London: John Hatchard *et al.*, 1813.

Ward, William. *A View of the History, Literature and Religion of the Hindoos: including a Minute Description of their Manners and Customs, and Translations from their Principal Works.* 4 vols. London: Baptist Missionary Society, 1811.

Warwick, Alexandra. "Colonial Gothic." *The Handbook to Gothic Literature.* Ed. Marie Mulvey-Roberts. Basingstoke: Palgrave Macmillan, 1998.

Wheeler, Michael. *The Old Enemies: Catholic and Protestant and Catholic in Nineteenth-Century English Culture.* Cambridge: Cambridge University Press, 2006.

Wilberforce, William. *Substance of the Speeches of William Wilberforce, Esq., on the Clause in the East-India Bill for Promoting the Religious Instruction and Moral Improvement of the Natives of* the British Dominion in India, on the 22nd of June, and the 1st and 12th of July, 1813. London: John Hatchard et al., 1813.

Wilkins, Charles. "Observations on the Seeks and their College." *Asiatick Researches* 1 (1788): 288-94.

Young, Brian. "'The Lust of Empire and Religious Hate': Christianity, History and India, 1790-1820." *History, Religion and Culture: British Intellectual History 1750-1850*. Ed. Stefan Collini, Richard Whatmore, and Brian Young. Cambridge: Cambridge University Press, 2000. 91-111.

3. Intrepid Traveller, "She-Merchant," or Colonialist Historiographer: Reading Eliza Fay's *Original Letters*

Nira Gupta-Casale
Kean University

Accompanying her husband, Anthony Fay, to Calcutta in the dawning years of British colonial rule in India, where he hoped to secure a comfortable legal practice, Eliza Fay was truly "an intrepid" traveller. She travelled by land over France, across the Alps, to Italy, and then on to Alexandria, Cairo and Suez, and finally, to India. Even by the arduous standards of eighteenth-century travel, Eliza Fay underwent adventures and disappointments that would have shaken the fortitude and health of a self-styled "poor, invalid female." Fay travelled incognito in Arabian dress through a desert beset by marauders, rode the waters of the Nile pursued by thieves, and, upon finally reaching the shores of India, was held captive for fifteen weeks by a despot who threatened to forcibly enlist her husband in the Nawab's army. She eventually arrived in Calcutta, via Calicut and Madras, over a year after leaving England, but her stay in the city was fated to be short lived. Within two years the Fays' fortunes failed, their marriage dissolved in ignominy; Eliza returned alone to England. Despite this, she repeatedly returned to India, making four more visits, these times not as a wife, but as a rare "she-merchant" in pursuit of an elusive fortune; she tried teaching and running a milliner's shop, owned a ship, and traded in muslin. At the time of her death in Calcutta in 1816 (aged 60), she was engaged in one final business venture – the preparing of her private letters for publication.

Published posthumously in 1817 as *Original Letters From India; Containing a Narrative of a Journey Through Egypt and the Author's*

Imprisonment at Calicut by Hyder Ali, (1779-1815),[1] Fay's letters are now part of the colonial archive, and are a significant chronicle of Calcutta's Anglo-Indian social life during the tumultuous years leading up to the Hastings/Impey impeachment scandal.[2] The collection of letters, part journal, part social commentary, is divided into two parts. The first part consists of twenty three letters addressed to her family from April 1779 to February 1783, the period of Fay's first travels to India and residence in Calcutta. The second part consists of eight letters written in 1815 to "Mrs. L." She is assumed to be a fictive persona, created to sustain the epistolary design of the collection – the letters in this part were meant to provide an autobiographical account of the twenty years in between Eliza Fay's first arrival in Calcutta and her fifth visit.

The narrative structure of Fay's *Original Letters* highlights four dramatic movements: (1) her overland journey through France and Italy and her escape across the Arabian desert, (letters 1-11); (2) her captivity, attempted escape, and release in Calicut, (letters 12-13); (3) her life in Calcutta, before and after her husband's return to England, (letters 15-23); and (4) her three subsequent visits to India between 1784 and 1796. In the first three sections, Eliza Fay appears as the long-suffering wife, distraught captive adventurer, and "astute" purveyor of social customs. Fay's nationalist sentiments and vivid accounts of her travels and encounters with "others" – French, Egyptian, Indian – as well as her observations upon her own countrymen and women, have provided social historians with useful information about travel in the eighteenth century and the early days of Empire. It is in the fourth section, however, in which Eliza Fay portrays herself in an unconventional light. In these later letters she is no longer the passive victim of circumstances, but the agent of her destiny.

---

[1] All subsequent citations are to the 1986 edition.
[2] She is cited in H. E. Busteed's *Echoes From Old Calcutta* (1882), P. Long's articles in the *Calcutta Review*, and P. Thankappan Nair's *Calcutta in the Eighteenth Century: Impressions of Travellers*. See also Basham; Sengupta.

3. Reading *Eliza Fay's* Original Letters

Her volume is prefaced with the promise that her letters will exhibit "a faithful account of certain remarkable occurrences in the history of an individual, whose lot has been to make frequent visits to several distant regions of the globe, to mingle in the society of people of different kindreds [sic] and tongues, and to experience many vicissitudes of fortune" (27), and this promise the text largely fulfils. *Original Letters* abruptly terminates in 1797, with the author's arrival in New York aboard her ill-fated cargo ship of muslins, and there is no account of the last twenty years of her life.[3] *Original Letters From India*, Eliza Fay's only book, received an early reprinting soon after initial publication, even though its sales brought in only Rs. 220. It subsequently appeared in three different editions in the twentieth century, in 1908, 1925, and 1986, the last two with the Hogarth Press and edited by two critically and commercially acclaimed British authors, E. M. Forster and M. M. Kaye.

Such continued interest in *Original Letters from India* begs the question of its reception. Who were Eliza Fay's readers? And why should we read her today? Fay's early readers were drawn to her vivid eyewitness account of social life of Calcutta during the late eighteenth century, but she is more than a chronicler of history; her *Letters* are a multivalent discourse, part travelogue, part autobiography, and their epistolary format constitutes a literary narrative that reads as a commentary on middle-class female subjectivity. Fay is not only an agent of colonialism, but as a merchant and traveller she also represents an emerging cosmopolitanism; the value of her account lies not just in her testimony, where she historicises the relationship of class and gender to issues of colonialism, as recent feminist scholars have argued, but also in her particular subject position as single, middle-class woman negotiating between two worlds and ambitious for improved

---

[3] Her 1908 editor, Reverend Firminger claimed that "The Executors cut the book short where Mrs. Fay had left the printing of it" on the grounds that the rest of the narrative lacked interest.

social and material rank.[4] In this respect Fay resembles the figure of the tropicopolitan subject, defined by Srinivas Aravamudan as "a name for the colonised subject who exists both as fictive construct of colonial tropology *and* actual resident of tropical space, object of representation *and* agent of resistance" (4). Often disenfranchised as a woman, Fay experienced economic hardship; she functions complexly as both a tropicopolitan figure who asserts and resists subjectivity, as well as a "self-actualising metropolitan." We can read Fay as more than a passive mirror reflecting the British-Indian experience, as a subject with agency and a mixed British cosmopolitan and subaltern tropicopolitan identity. The reception of Fay's *Letters* has tended to ignore this aspect of her story; her mercantile adventures and her cosmopolitanism are frequently subsumed by her ability to report, albeit from the margins, on significant historical events. E. M. Forster lauds Fay for her powers of observation; but what exactly did she see, and how does a fuller consideration of her particular perspective, as well as the editorial framing of that perspective, challenge some of the key tenets that inform the British-Indian archive?

Although the recipients of Fay's original letters were her two sisters in England, she begins the first letter by announcing, "I believe before I left England it was agreed that, my Letters should not in general be addressed to anyone particularly, as they will be something in the style of journals" (31). Fay's letters often change their tone and focus, for they move fluidly from personal, intimate addresses to descriptive commentary, revealing as much about the social and political climate of the countries she visited as they do about her personal likes and dislikes, hopes and frustrations. Fay's personal narrative does not always correspond to the hegemonic discourse of nationalism and colonialism in the late eighteenth century, and implicitly challenges British constructions of domesticity and femininity; consequently, her editors have felt the need to contain and explain her.

---

[4] For Fay as a feminist critic, see Grundy (83) and Gupta-Casale.

3. Reading *Eliza Fay's* Original Letters

Posthumous publication compromises the author's discursive authority because the content is mediated through the editor's unauthorised explanatory comments. Revealingly, all three of her editors refer to her class position, marking her style and subject matter, and also our reception of her as a historiographer. Reverend Firminger's edition offers the first full discussion of Eliza Fay and her husband, as well as their historical context, by emphasising their class position. He comments on their petite-bourgeois expediencies, calling "her economies a little too drastic" – he refers to an account of "the inns where beds are procured for 4 sous a night" – and sympathises with her husband: "Poor Anthony [Fay], we feel certain, will sooner or later revolt" (Firminger vi). (Forster was to later cite a contemporary reference in which her husband is described as "a very low man" by Sir Elijah Impey.)[5] Firminger claims that readers of Busteed "are well acquainted with Mrs. Fay's *prattle* about Belvedire, the Harmonic, the beauty of Lady Chambers, the elegance of the second Mrs. Warren Hastings, the troubles of a Calcutta memsahib of the period, etc" (iv). If this commentary was not enough to alert the reader to Fay's class position, Firminger uses the introduction to inscribe his own notions of the ideal British woman when he describes Fay's personality:

> Then again, there is something about Mrs. Fay which fails to charm, something of a too conscious superiority which alienates sympathy in circumstances in which sympathy would not be begrudged. When Mrs. Hastings hinted that our authoress had brought her troubles on herself, 'by imprudently venturing on such an expedition out of mere curiosity,' although we see the injustice of the hint, yet after all we cannot help feeling that if Mrs. Fay would be so audacious, and would do things in a way which no ordinary woman would, or perhaps should, dare to do them, most people would feel inclined to share her critic's view of her sufferings. (v)

---

[5] Cited in Forster's "Terminal Notes" in Fay's *Original Letters* 282.

Firminger contrasts Fay's charmlessness with the "charming" Lady Chambers, her patroness who he eulogises in glowingly approving terms:

> Her treatment of Mrs. Fay is in itself a monument to her kindness and most probably to her forbearance. She was a woman who well knew how to use the world without abusing it and go on her way rejoicing. It cannot, for one moment be denied, that the most helpful thing England can hope to offer to India is the type of noble womanhood so generously represented by Lady Chambers. (x)

Fay's character elides easy categorisation, and Firminger is critical of her style, which he took liberties to "correct" in his 1908 edition: "The reader will note that Mrs. Fay's manner of writing can scarcely be called a 'style,' and that she is none too careful of grammar," he declared, adding, "she frequently arranges her words in such an order that she is bound to get in trouble with her relative pronouns" (xi). While Firminger asserts that Fay deserved to be read in full, and not just for excerpts found in Busteed, Orme, and other historians, he does recognise the circumstances which led to her slap-dash punctuation, "written under the most trying circumstances imaginable," he observes, "her chaotic punctuation remains as a sort of witness to the naturally distracted state of her suffering mind" (xii). Eliza Fay's second editor, E. M. Forster, was no less damning, claiming that she had had a "second-rate career" ("Introductory Notes" 12). Forster acknowledges that "Eliza Fay is a work of art," but qualifies this by saying that "she was also a historical character, who wielded and resumed a pen and from that point of view some brief notes may be acceptable" (7), once again displaying his ambivalence. Does Forster suggest that Fay was a "character" or "a piece of art," and on what does he base this claim? Does Forster suggest that she had constructed a persona for herself that had its own agency, or is he treating her with mock

3. Reading Eliza Fay's Original Letters

humour?[6] The veiled compliment implied in the statement "Fay is a work of art" reveals the gender and class bias of the editor, who, for all his serious appraisal of Eliza Fay, names her style female, even while asserting that the value of the letters rests as much in their historical value as in their humanness: "She wrote as well as she could, she wrote nothing that she herself was not [. . .] Her age produced many greater letters, but so few that so faithfully reflect the character of their author" (16).

Forster links her with the other well-known memoirist of this period, William Hickey, and once again alludes to her class position: "If she is a lady, then Hickey is a gentleman," observing that "their value to us today is that they were never first-rate, never at the top," and that this gives us an "account of Calcutta that would never occur to the well- bred, the highly educated, the sincerely pious, or the satisfactorily introduced" (22). Throughout his "Introductory Notes," Forster sustains this mock humorous tone; he defends her punctuation and grammar against Firminger's critique, and he applauds Fay's acute observational skills: "her ear, like her eye it is always alive! How the cries of the sepoys in Calicut sink into her! And her mouth! How she does relish her food!! She is constantly registering through her senses, and recording the results through a powerful, though untrained mind" (15). While Forster and Firminger provide several instances of editorial framing of Eliza Fay as "not quite Ladylike," I want to focus on how Fay's editors use her references to food to characterise her as "underbred."

An example occurs in a letter describing her domestic situation and comparing it to the English household:

> I will give you our bill of fare, and the general price of things. A soup, a roast of fowl, curry, and rice, a mutton pie, a forequarter of lamb, a rice pudding, tarts, very good cheese, fresh

---

[6] *Pharos and Pharillon*, Forster's vignettes of travelers to Alexandria, included "Eliza in Egypt," which mocked her tourist curiosity.

churned butter, fine bread, excellent Madeira (that is expensive but eatables are very cheap) – a whole sheep costs but two rupees: a lamb one rupee, six good fowls or ducks ditto [. . .] – English claret sells at this time for sixty rupees a dozen. There's a price for you! I need not say that much of it will not be seen at our table; now and then we are forced to produce it, but very seldom. I assure you much caution is requisite to avoid running in debt. (Fay 181-82)

It is not the adumbration of the dinner table, but Fay's frank appraisal of the food that Forster finds so amusing. When Fay confides to her family, "We were frequently told in England you know, that the heat in Bengal destroyed the appetite, I must own that I never yet saw any proof of that; on the contrary I cannot help thinking that I never saw an equal quantity of victuals consumed" (181). Forster's note comments, "our heroine was of the hungry type. People who write long letters often are [. . .] she ate and ate till the end – asparagus, pork, tunny, turtle, preserved peaches, ghi" ("Terminal Notes" 280).

Forster once again refers to her preoccupation with food, even as he praises her style for being "personal." Giving an example, he says, "or consider the following trifle: it begins with all the dreariness and unreality of an ocean log, then curdles into life suddenly. 'Numbers of man-of-war birds and eggs, were taken, which proved to be good eating; they likewise caught the finest turtle I ever saw, but by an act of unpardonable negligence in people so situated, it was suffered to walk overboard in the night'" ("Introductory Notes" 14). Forster's empathy is with the turtle: "Suffered to escape, and she so partial to nourishing food!" His decision to focus on the absconding sea turtle, rather than the author's struggles for independence serves again to illustrate Fay's rejection of the protective mantle of domestic bourgeois ideology which inscribed femininity in the socially sanctioned space of the home and marriage.

3. Reading *Eliza Fay's* Original Letters

Forster does compliment her style; he observes that "her opinions and desires are always sticking out like this, ripping the chaste mantle of literature!" (14). This comment suggests that Forster is celebrating the voice of the commoner, but it is also evident that he implicates Fay as "unladylike." In Forster's opinion, her preoccupation with the stomach, while "real" and "human," is also unladylike, ungenteel, and "underbred." Firminger had also commented on Fay's consumption and domestic economy, and even M. M. Kaye, her most recent editor (and the only one to mention her business career), describes her as "a good trencherwoman with a proper respect for food and drink," a "glutton for punishment" who "thrived on danger", and a woman who "had the heart and stomach of a merchant adventurer and a British merchant-adventurer too!" (n. pag.).

Eliza Fay's talk about food was not the fabulous feasts of Badshahs and Nawabs, but the ordinary fare of ordinary people, and there was nothing glamorous, exotic or even ladylike in that for her editors to admire. Seemingly, she belonged to the wrong class. According to her editors, she was solidly middle-class, pragmatic and plebeian to the extreme, dutifully pious and frankly ambitious – some might say hungry. For such hunger and over-reaching – so overtly expressed – calls into question the ostensible selflessness of Empire-building. All three editors see Fay as an intrepid traveller and colonial historiographer, while they almost completely bypass the mercantile aspects of her later letters; such silence tells us much about the ways that gender and class are imbricated within colonialist discourse.

During the years of Fay's correspondence, Calcutta saw major social and political changes; the city became the commercial centre of a colonial power. Published accounts of the British visiting India, either as merchants, travellers, or administrators, made popular reading for a public increasingly aware of the dealings of the East India Company.[7]

---

[7] Examples include Edward Ives' *A Voyage From England to India in the Year MDCCLIV* (1773); John Henry Grose's *A Voyage to the East Indies with Observations on Various Parts There* (1757); William Francklin's

Fay was one of only two eighteenth-century British women to publish accounts of their travels to India; she offers a rare gendered perspective on the formative years of imperial expansion.[8] During the era of British colonialism, gender differences were often conflated into a master discussion of coloniser versus colonised; Fay's narrative confounds such a conflation.

Colonial ideology in this period asserted a particular British subjectivity that helped justify and entrench their rule; women in the colonies were expected to reflect the domestic ideology of eighteenth-century England and were consciously used to bolster a sense of imperial Englishness that was threatened by the seductive charms of "nativism."[9] However, British women's encounters with colonised cultures, and especially their exposure to other domesticities, led to a gendered response which added a "non-binary, non-monolithic" dimension to hegemonic imperialist discourse (Melman 2). Sara Suleri has noted the "symbolic representation" of the Anglo-Indian woman in colonial discourse: "she was in India as a symbolic representative of the joys of an English home; she was the embodiment of all the Englishman must protect; most significantly she was a safeguard against the dangers posed by the Eastern woman" (76).

Although the epistolary accounts of travelling British women tended to idealise the image of gentle, nurturing, supportive, self-sacrificing British womanhood, the tropicopolitan Fay does not so easily fit this mould. Anglo-Indian domesticity featured in the "letters home," providing readers with insights into the conjugal struggles for harmony and control, ruminations upon cultural differences (especially with regard to female autonomy), and the urgency with which British women

---

Observations Made on a Tour from Bengal to Persia (1790); George Forster's *A Journey From Bengal to England* (1798); and William Hickey's *Diaries*.

[8] Mrs. Jemima Kindersley's *Letters From the Island of Teneriffe, Brazil, the Cape of Good Hope, and the East Indies* (1777) was the first.

[9] See Barr; Macmillan; Spear.

3. Reading Eliza Fay's Original Letters

confronted the issues of identity and alienation.[10] In one of her letters, Fay expresses the muted frustrations of a dutiful wife: "the duty of a wife which is paramount to all other civil obligations compels me silently to witness what is beyond my power to counteract" (199).

Caught in the intersections between two different cultures, the Anglo-Indian woman often needed to show her allegiance; this awareness often expressed itself in a strident assertion of cultural and nationalistic identity, at the very moment that these women were seeking to redefine themselves as individuals. In several instances, Eliza Fay articulates a British nationalism close to jingoism in her disparaging comments about Arabian or Indian "others" – "[H]ave we not a religion more infinitely pure than that of India?" (203) – while at the same time she expresses her identification with the predicament of women, irrespective of cultural or national differences. One significant instance is to be found in the following example.

In the first part of letter 20, where Eliza Fay informs her family of her husband's infidelity, their separation and divorce, and her new state of homelessness and dependency on the "kindness of strangers," she also offers them a description of Indian religion and customs beginning with "that horrible custom of widows burning themselves with the dead bodies of their husbands" (202). Instead of a conventional homily on the evils of *sati*, Fay offers an interesting observation on the hypocrisy of gender relations in all societies, commenting that *sati* was not indicative of the wife's greater love for her husband, "since the same tenderness and ardour would doubtless extend to his offspring and prevent them from exposing the innocent survivors to the miseries attendant on an orphan state, and they would clearly see that to live [. . .] would be the most rational and natural way of shewing their regard" (202). More significantly, she declares that "the practice is entirely a political scheme intended to secure the care and good

---

[10] See Gupta-Casale, "Absenting the Other: The Construction of British Identity in the Eighteenth-Century."

offices of wives to their husbands, who have not failed in most countries to invent a sufficient number of rules to render the weaker sex totally subservient to their authority" (203). Fay makes a cogent cross-cultural comparison about the general condition of women:

> I am well aware that so much are we the slaves of habit *every where* that were it necessary for a woman's reputation to burn herself in England, many a one who has *accepted* a husband merely for the sake of an establishment, who has lived with him without affection; perhaps thwarted his views, dissipated his fortune, and rendered his life uncomfortable to its close, would yet mount the funeral pile with all imaginable decency and die with heroic fortitude. (203)

Here she disrupts the dominant discourse of the day (one that condemned *sati* along with other Hindu practices as barbaric), and also rebukes British observers who assigned a superior character and heroism to Hindu women who were willing to sacrifice their lives upon their husband's death. Fay's assertion that a woman was "ten times more of a heroine than the slave of bigotry and superstition, who effects to scorn the life demanded of her by the laws of country and who endures without complaining the unkindness, infidelity, and extravagance, meanness, or scorn of the man to whom she has given a tender and confining heart" (203) is telling. Her recognition of women's entrapment in social conventions and her own disillusion with domesticity emerged through her own marital dissolution, but this lessens neither this diatribe's discursive impact nor its threat to nationalist ideology. The reality of the experience of imperialism for British women, whether at home or abroad, was that it coincided with what Gayatri Spivak calls "feminist individualism in the age of imperialism," constructed against the backdrop of the complex encounter of the British with the eastern "others" of India and serves to show how "the imperialist project [was] cathected as civil-society-through-social mission" (799).

3. Reading Eliza Fay's Original Letters

To some extent Fay *is* tacitly complicit in "the imperialist project" despite her sometimes frank expressions of frustration against the institution of marriage and the petty politicking and foolishness of her compatriots. In her preface she constructs a narrative persona of a modest, unassuming woman writer who shrinks from thrusting herself into the public eye, despite the requests of her friends to publish. She writes that "she was repeatedly urged by several of her friends to publish some account of the events that had befallen her, which, it was supposed would engage the attention of the public, being connected with important circumstances in the lives of well known and respectable individuals, and illustrative of the character of a Potentate whose movements were the subjects of serious alarm in India" (30). Fay's insight (the interest in anything to do with Hastings) has been borne out by her subsequent reception, but one cannot help but wonder why she did not publish her letters immediately, waiting nearly thirty years to do so. Her own explanation seems a feint; she affects a female reluctance to seem "immodest" and "forward" by pursuing her authorial ambitions, because she "lived in an age which mocked female authors [. . .] a woman who was not conscious of possessing decided genius or superior knowledge could not easily be induced to leave 'the harmless tenor of her ways,' and render herself amenable to the 'pains and penalties' then, generally, inflicted on female authorships" (30). In the light of Fay's many attempts to secure her financial independence between 1783 and 1796, and especially given the indebted financial state at the time of her death, the real motives for publishing her letters may well have been purely commercial – a desire to profit from increasing public interest in Indian travel narratives. However, in keeping with the domestic ideology of inscribed femininity she offers instead, as explanation, the changing attitudes towards women authors: "In this indulgent era [1815] the author presumes to deliver her letters to the world as they have been preserved by the dear sister to whom they were partly addressed, trusting that as this is, in its nature, the most unassuming of all kinds of writing, and one that claims the most extensive allowances, they will be received with peculiar mercy and forbearance" (31). Fay believed epistolary writing to be "unassuming" because throughout the eighteenth century the genre was associated with feminine writing and style. Formal or fictional letters created an aura of autobiographical and historical authenticity, and allowed women to "speak" from their position of powerlessness.[11] That Fay was still consciously trying to affect this feminine style is evident in the tone of the opening statement of the second part, written thirty-five years after her first journey to India; here the feminine style is employed to assert a new kind of agency (that of an independent woman). Eliza Fay announces her reason for again undertaking the perilous voyage to India (and the transition from memsahib to she-merchant), in terms of her desire for independence: "I tried various plans in pursuit of independence; but none seemed to promise success; my friends wished me to remain at home; but Calcutta appeared the most likely theatre of exertion; and you cannot wonder that my heart warmed towards a place, where I had met such friendship and generosity, and where so much general encouragement was given to the efforts of respectable individuals" (229).

There is hardly any description of Anglo-Indian society in these later letters; instead, Fay focuses on the description of her business affairs and her travel experiences on various ships. Social historians have less to cite, since there is less commentary regarding Calcutta society in these later letters. Letter 3 focuses on her attempts at maintaining her social respectability, which a direct association with trade would jeopardise, even though, as Percival Spear points out, "trade and gentility" were not incompatible (37). To that end she engaged a young Englishwoman to travel to Calcutta with her in the hopes of setting her up as the front in the millinery business; "it was agreed that my name should not appear" (238) she declared, but within four

---

[11] See Bakhtin and Goldsmith.

3. Reading *Eliza Fay's* Original Letters

months of her arrival in India Miss Hicks engaged and married a Mr. Lacey, and Eliza Fay was compelled to conduct business in her own name. She succeeded "tolerably well" until 1788, when the millinery business was adversely affected by a general economic slump; Fay's description of how she handled this crisis echoes the tone of Daniel Defoe's fictional she-merchant, Roxana:

> [. . .] I solicited and obtained the indulgence of my creditors for eighteen months under four Trustees [. . .] and such was the confidence reposed in my integrity, that everything remained in my own hands as formerly. Never, I am proud to say, was that confidence abused; pardon the seeming vanity of this assertion; in justice to my own character, I must say this much, and can boldly appeal to those who are best acquainted with the whole transaction for the truth of my statement. [. . .] wherein I was benevolently assisted by many who saw and compassionated my arduous struggles after independence, I succeeded in settling either in money or goods, every claim on me, and again possessed of a little property [. . .]. (240)

In letter 4 she justifies her reasons for leaving her homeland once again: "I rather rejoiced at quitting England, as the whole time of my stay had been imbittered [sic] by a succession of losses and disappointments, arising partly from my individual misfortune respecting the ship, and partly form the general state of commerce at this inauspicious period" (246). Fay identifies herself as part of a larger exodus from England because of hard times; this would not be comfortable to highlight for her posthumous editors. Fay's determination to detach herself from existing emotional ties and seek independence wherever she could find it (even if it meant travelling to distant lands) is remarkable. Finally, she locates her commercial failure not in terms of her individual misfortunes, but as endemic of the national economy.

Letter 5 describes her outward journey from England to India, but it is significant because it registers the experience of a worldlier traveller. Stopping at Madeira and the Isle of Wight, Fay gives her readers a sense of the new world of British experiences. She comments on their hospitality and new forms of entertaining that has become so much the norm for cosmopolitan exchanges – the host treating the guests at a hotel instead of an established household, which results in expenditure for both parties: "A Mr L____to whom I had letters, went with us to a Hotel; for unfortunately his lady being in England, he could not entertain us at his own house. Living in this manner was very expensive and disagreeable, also, we paid 5sh for our wine" (250).

Letter 5 also displays another aspect of British history that Fay experiences directly. Detained on the island of St. Helena because of a court case (she is accused of having sold a young Indian woman into slavery), Fay is made to pay reparations (she borrows the sum from her brother-in-law) and the young woman's passage back to India. Discussing this incident, Forster calls it her "worst action" and feels that Fay probably left the girl in St. Helena instead of continuing with her to England. The casualness with which Fay comments on this incident is evidence of the fact that slave trading was, as Forster confirms, a "normal part of Anglo-Indian life"– something that British official histories were not comfortable in recording. Fay's disruptive writing once again voices something which Anglo-Indian colonialist historiography has marginalised. In the case of the slave girl's accusations against Fay, as much culpability should be directed towards the nation which practiced slavery, as towards the individual.

To confirm just how much class mattered in colonial historiography one need only compare the editorial assertions about Fay with those of Lady Mary Wortley Montagu's *Turkish Embassy Letters*, written earlier in the century. Montagu was a celebrated poet and writer and a member of the London literary elite, and the *Turkish Embassy Letters* were yet another authorial enterprise; Eliza Fay, in contrast, was probably driven to publish her letters out of financial desperation.

3. Reading Eliza Fay's Original Letters

Montagu travelled to the Constantinople in 1717 as the wife of an ambassador and wrote fifty-two letters over a two-year period; her correspondents included Alexander Pope, Abbe Conte, the Princess of Wales, and her daughter (who was the wife of a future Prime Minister). These letters, which are relatively impersonal and formal, were compiled and transcribed in an album for publication by the author, and when published posthumously, achieved instant acclaim. Known variously as *The Turkish Embassy Letters* or *Letters from the Levant*, Lady Montagu's letters are celebrated for their insightful commentary on European and Turkish social customs (in particular her sympathetic approach to gender differences between the two), as well as for their literary style. Her most famous letters describe her visit to the Turkish hamams (baths) – an exclusively female space forbidden to men – and document her significance in being the first European to enter and comment upon such a space. Montagu occupied a completely different class position to Fay; as a member of the aristocracy, her style and subject matter, but also the reception of her correspondence, was markedly different. For example, a review of her *Turkish Embassy Letters* which appeared in London's *Monthly Review*, glossing over the fact that the author had deliberately edited and compiled her letters for publication before death, and instead praising the "naturalness" of the style, declared:

> [T]here is no affectation of female 'delicatesse,' there are no 'prettynesses,' no 'Ladyisms' in these natural, easy familiar Epistles; which [. . .] have not the air of being wrote for the press, as were many of the laboured Letters which are so much admired in the correspondence of Pope and Swift. This may, in some measure be presumed, from the incorrectness of the language in a few instances; for had the Writer originally designed these papers for the public eye, there is no doubt but she who was so very capable of it, would have retouched them, and removed such little flaws, as appear like small

freckles on a fine face; which, notwithstanding, is a fine face still. (Rev. of "Letters" 384-85)

Montagu was classically educated, and her *Letters* describe her privileged access to an exclusive world of female luxury and beauty that charmed and titillated her readers. In contrast, Fay concentrated on the struggles of domesticity; she had an education which Forster described as "vaguely commercial," and scant: "no more should her education detain us than it did her" (9).

Fay performed the travel writer's function of describing foreign places – mountains and terrain in France and Italy, cities in Egypt, people and customs in India – and interlaced observation with commentary reflective of standard prejudices. On Turin Palace, she observed that "I visited the royal gardens, but thought them very uninteresting, as all appear after those that surround the seats of our English nobility and gentry" (57). Displaying her own desperate desire for upward mobility, and as one for whom India meant acceleration up the class system, she also recorded and exposed the mundane aspects of empire building and the petty rivalries of her compatriots. In her observations the Imperial ruling class are displayed as come off as both ordinary and ambitious, consumed with self-interest, prejudice, and a voracious appetite for advancement; her frank appraisal, informed by her wry humour, is unalleviated by moralising or philosophising. Such directness lacks the finish and discretion of the *belles lettres* of a proper lady (such as Montagu); Eliza and her husband, travelling independently of the East India Company, belong to a class of opportunists that, if anything, were more of an embarrassment to the burgeoning Empire than an asset.

Fay's letters elide and confound strict private and public classifications, and as such challenge some of the implicit protocols that shape the British-Indian archive: namely, that the reporting author writing home should erase individual subjectivity in the interest of an objective, almost anthropological gaze. Fay is praised by her editors (espe-

3. Reading Eliza Fay's Original Letters

cially Forster) when accurately and astutely reporting the manners and mores of Indians; she is criticised (or dismissed as unimportant) when she registers more personalised subjective observations about herself. Fay's class position (a financially straitened but ambitious arriviste divorcee) and the perspective it offers complicates our understanding of both the British-Indian encounter, as well as the archive that that encounter has produced.

In "The Problem of Speech Genres," Bakhtin offers us a paradigm for discourse analysis which is particularly useful in understanding the rhetorical significance of private letters and their place in the archives. He identifies different types of speech genres, and explains how even private letters function discursively as agents of nationalist ideologies:

> Various genres can reveal various layers and facets of the individual personality, and individual style can be found in various interrelations with the national language. The very problem of the national and the individual in language is basically the problem of the utterance (after all, only here, in the utterance, is the national language embodied in individual form. (63)

Bakhtin distinguishes between various forms of utterances and states that "letters are primary utterances, novels are secondary (complex) utterances" (62), and it is the secondary which is explicitly ideological. He also claims that "any utterance – oral or written, primary or secondary, and in any sphere of communication – is individual, and therefore can reflect the individuality of the speaker (or writer); that is, possess individual style" (63), which suggests that complex utterances function ideologically, even as they reflect the individual style of the speaker. Fay's letters thus occupy this liminal space; as private correspondence they are primary utterances, but as soon as they are revised for publication, they embody a literary space and function dialogically. The "letters home" written by British travellers, traders and administrators in India enabled the imperialist project through the ex-

83

plicit and implicit articulation of a nationalist and colonialist ideology. In electing to "tell her story in her own way or not at all" (129), Fay upsets the "compositional unities" that Bakhtin describes as existing as an "organic, inseparable link between style and genre" where "each sphere has and applies its own genres that correspond to own specific conditions"; in opting for the familiar (private) style in preference above the formal (public), she upsets protocols, ignoring the idea that "particular styles [. . .] correspond to these genres" (Bakhtin 64).

By revising her twenty-three original letters and composing at least eight more with the explicit intention of publishing them, Fay constructed an epistolary narrative which Bakhtin might recognise as "a complex speech genre." For example, in letter 12, the longest of her epistles, which occurs midway in her correspondence during the first trip to India, Fay describes a particularly harrowing experience. She begins this letter, dated 12 February 1780, by asserting:

> It was my determination never to write to you, during the state of dreadful Captivity in which we have long been held, but having hopes of a release, think I may now venture to give you some account of our sufferings which have been extreme, both in body and mind, for a period of fifteen weeks, which we have spent in wretched confinement, totally in the power of Barbarians. (110)

Before she recounts the circumstances by which she and her fellow passengers at Calicut are held hostage by Sirdar Khan (Calicut governor and brother-in-law of Hyder Ali, who was confronting the British at the time), Fay gives us an emotionally charged insight into her mental state as an explanation for any possible lapses in her narrative style: "such is the harassing confusion of my mind, and the weakness of my nerves, that I can merely offer you a statement of facts, and even that must necessarily be incorrect; for incessant anxiety and constant anticipation of more intolerable evils, have totally unhinged my faculties" (110). She expresses her heartfelt yearning to be reunited

3. Reading Eliza Fay's Original Letters

with her friends for whom her "affection rises now to a pitch of Enthusiasm, of which [I] knew not that [my] heart was capable" (111). What follows is a relatively lucid and detailed captivity narrative; but what is significant is that Fay's "Barbarians" are not only the Sirdar Khan and his henchmen, but her own countrymen as well. Her diatribes against them are scathing. She describes them (including the only other woman in the group, Mrs Tulloh) as petty and foolish, and highlight theirs self-serving cowardice as they scheme to gain passage out of the ship before the Fays are allowed to. The British government which should have afforded its citizens some measure of protection is not portrayed in a positive light; the English Consul had abandoned his post several weeks earlier, and the captives must send their letters of appeal directly to the distant Madras Consul. Fay reserves her strongest indictment for Captain Ayres, a renegade London-born former highwayman captain in Hyder Ali's army: "a volume would not contain half the enormities perpetrated by this disgrace to human nature" (116). The only character who comes out well is the old Jewish merchant, Mr. Isaac, for whom Fay writes a glowing encomium.

During this ordeal, Fay expressed her fear of being raped by Captain Ayre's men, and felt her life several times "hung in the balance over her head by a hair" (111); yet her editors make scant reference to it. Firminger barely alludes to it except to note that she had an "extravagant and dissolute husband" to contend with on top of everything else, and that the couple was probably "not friends" and estranged by this stage. Forster supplies the reader with the historical context for the imprisonment, and also offers supporting documents to corroborate Fay's accounts of the negotiations, as well as her characterisation of the parties concerned:

> She certainly sums up his faults well; and his letter to Sirdar Khan [. . .] fully bears out her charge of pomposity. But he was probably nicer than she says. We must never forget that she herself was a most trying woman, particularly on a boat,

85

and that Mr. Hare would not have found her table manners funny, or appreciated her contempt for the violin. ("Terminal Notes" 276)

Forster uses the self-styled comic touches (even Fay admits that in later days they would see the humour of some of their situations) in her writing to record her plebeian concerns, even while he praises her courage and gallantry:

> She does not conceal her sufferings, but not once does she whine over them, and we get after a few pages a wonderful impression of hardness. Hard as steel? Hardly, for that suggests nobility: but harder than her blockhead of a husband. When the verandah in which they had hidden their savings was twitched off the house by a monsoon, he abandoned himself to lamentations while she calculated the direction of the wind and finally discovered the money in a far away tuft of grass. In her sense, as in her sentiment, she is the child of her century, which despite its palpitations never lost grasp of the main chance. Her floods of tears and fainting fits are always postponed until a convenient moment; they never intrude while she is looking out for her luggage or outwitting her foes. ("Introductory Notes" 14)

While her published letters functioned ideologically in contributing to the colonialist historiography surrounding Warren Hastings's Calcutta, the highly individual style in which this information was conveyed functioned disruptively to produce an alternate, or parallel, narrative of that period. In insisting on drawing attention to her tangential, tropicopolitan, position, Fay's editors alerted readers of her letters to her subject position as "female" and "lower class" and used her style (especially her grammatical inconsistencies) as a marker for this assessment.

3. Reading Eliza Fay's Original Letters

The reception histories of Fay's *Letters* reveal important aspects of the evolution of British-Indian discourse. Each time they have been published they have served as supplement to nostalgia for the glory days of John's Company, but there is also a perceptual shift with each successive publication in terms of how she was read. In 1908, Reverend Firminger was commissioned by the Calcutta Historical Society to edit Fay; in his introductory notes he justified the re-publication of *Original Letters* by contextualising her work specifically in the social history of 1780s Calcutta. Firminger claimed that Fay's letters were most interesting because they "throw light on the social life of the Calcutta of Warren Hastings and Sir Phillip Francis" and explained that the publishers were motivated to re-issue her book in response to the contemporary nostalgic interest in the figure of Warren Hastings, first Governor-General of India (the Hastings trail had been the *cause célèbre* of its age). While acknowledging the intrinsic merit of Fay's letters, Firminger nevertheless conceded that their primary value was archival. The reason that a book "so often laid under contribution, so full of adventures, containing so many clearly cut descriptions of interesting persons and places, has been allowed to fall out of circulation," has to do with the transient nature of the colonial experience, because Calcutta, being a "place of frequent partings is in consequence, a place of short memories [. . .] and perhaps the Calcutta of Warren Hastings days had not for the men of that time the glamour which it has for us today" (Firminger iv).

Fay's *Letters* were published outside India for the first time in 1925 by the Hogarth Press, owned and operated by Virginia and Leonard Woolf; the choice of editor (E. M. Forster) signalled a new reading of the correspondence. This edition came out soon after Forster's novel *A Passage to India* (1924), capitalising on Forster's reputation as a knowledgeable and empathetic observer of Anglo-India. This was also a period of intense nationalistic protests against colonial rule in South Asia, and British readers would have seen it in this light, both reminding them of the founding of the Raj, and gratifying a more recent curiosity for all things Indian. Unlike Firminger, Forster's "Introduction with Terminal Notes" offers the readers the original text of Eliza Fay's letters, as well as an exhaustive commentary on historical figures, places and events mentioned, and evaluates the author as a historic person; Firminger, appalled at Fay's "troubles with her relative pronouns" (xi), had made many unwarranted editorial interventions in the text. Deliberately unscholarly and wittily subjective, Forster's introduction would have had the effect of popularising Fay's appeal to modern readers; like Firminger, Forster recognised her worth as a historical informant, but constantly highlights her on class and gender marginality.

The most recent publication was in 1986, again by the Hogarth Press. The choice of editor, the popular novelist M. M. Kaye, reflects yet another market-driven impetus; Kaye's *The Far Pavilions* had recently enjoyed considerable sales success. The resurgent British interest in India in the 1980s is reflected in the deliberately exoticised choice of book jacket cover for this edition (a buxom painting of an aristocratic Mughal lady sniffing a flower). Unlike Forster or Firminger, Kaye's introduction says more about his own experience of India, and less about Eliza Fay's. The publication history of Fay's *Letters* suggests that their primary value has been in their intimate account of late eighteenth-century Anglo-India society: Warren Hastings, Sir Elijah Impey, Sir Robert Chambers, Sudder Khan and Hyder Ali. But more significant for contemporary readers is the way in which Fay's *Letters* depict a gendered, nuanced, and complex personal world that disrupts and challenges received colonial historiography.

3. Reading *Eliza Fay's* Original Letters

Works Cited

Aravamudan, Srinivas. *Tropicopolitans*. Durham, NC: Duke University Press, 1999.

Bakhtin, M. M. *Speech Genres and Other Late Essays*. Trans. Vern M. McGee. Ed. Caryl Emerson and Michael Holquist. Austin: University of Texas Press, 1986.

Basham, A. L. "Sophia and the 'Brahmin.'" *East India Company Studies*. Ed. K. Ballhatchet and J. Harrison. London & Hong Kong, 1987. 13-30.

Barr, Pat. *Memsahibs: In Praise of the Women of Victorian India*. London: Century Hutchinson, 1989.

Busteed, H. E. *Echoes from Old Calcutta: Being Chiefly Reminiscences of the Days of Warren Hastings, Francis and Impey*. 2nd ed. Calcutta: Thacker, Spink, 1888.

Fay, Eliza. *Original Letters from India (1779-1815) by Mrs. Fay*. Introductory and Terminal Notes by E. M. Forster. 1925. Newly introd. M. M. Kaye. London: Hogarth, 1986.

___. *Original Letters From India; Containing a Narrative of a Journey Through Egypt and the Author's Imprisonment at Calicut by Hyder Ali, (1779-1815)*. Calcutta, 1817.

Firminger, Rev. Walter Kelly. Introduction. *The Original Letters From India of Mrs. Eliza Fay. A New Edition with Introduction and Notes*. Calcutta: Thacker, Spink, 1908. iii-xii. Notes 227-38.

Francklin, William. *Observations Made on a Tour from Bengal to Persia*. London, 1790.

Forster, E. M. "Eliza in Egypt." *Pharos and Pharillon*. 1923. Berkeley: Creative Arts, 1980.

___. "Introductory Notes." Fay 7-24.

___. "Terminal Notes." Fay 273-85.

Forster, George. *A Journey From Bengal to England*. 2 vols. London, 1798.

William Francklin. *Observations Made on a Tour from Bengal to Persia*. 1790.

Goldsmith, Elizabeth, ed. *Writing the Female Voice: Essays on Epistolary Fiction*. Boston: Northeastern University Press, 1989.

Grose, John Henry. *A Voyage to the East Indies with Observations on Various Parts There*. London, 1757.

Grundy, Isobel. "The Barbarous Character We Give Them: White Women Travellers Report on Other Races." *Studies in Eighteenth Century Culture* 22 (1992): 73-86.

Gupta, Nira Mira. "Absenting the Other: The Construction of British Identity in the Eighteenth-Century". Diss. State University of New York at Stony Brook, 1994.

Gupta-Casale, Nira. "The Commerce of Travel: Gender, Genre, and the Eighteenth-Century English Traveller." Conference Paper. Writing the Journey: A Conference on American, British and Anglophone Travel Writers and Writing. 10-13 June 1999. University of Pennsylvania.

Hickey, William. *Memoirs of William Hickey*. Ed. Peter Quennel. London: Hutchinson, 1960.

Ives, Edward. *A Voyage From England to India in the Year MDCCLIV*. London, 1773.

Kaye, M. M. Introduction. Fay n. pag.

Kindersley, Mrs. Jemima. *Letters From the Island of Teneriffe, Brazil, the Cape of Good Hope, and the East Indies*. London: J. Nourse, 1777.

Macmillan, Mary. *Women of the Raj*. London: Thames & Hudson, 1988.

Melman, Billie. *Women's Orients: English Women and the Middle East, 1718-1918: Sexuality, Religion and Work*. Ann Arbor: University of Michigan Press, 1992.

Nair, P. Thankappan. *Calcutta in the Eighteenth Century: Impressions of Travellers*. Calcutta: K. L.Mukhopadhyay, 1984.

Rev. of "Letters of Lady Mary Wortley Montagu." *Monthly Review* 28 (1763). London: Beckett and Dehondt.

Sengupta, Anjali. *Cameos of Twelve European Women in India: 1757-1857*. Calcutta: RDDHI-India, 1984.

Spear, T. G. Percival. *The Nabobs: A Study of the Social Life of the English in Eighteenth Century India*. 1932. Rev. ed. London: Oxford University Press, 1963..

Spivak, Gayatri Chakravorty. "Three Women's Texts and a Critique of Imperialism." *Feminisms: Anthology of Literary Theory and Criticism*. Ed. Robyn R. Warhol and Diana Price Herndl. New Brunswick: Rutgers University Press, 1991. 896-912

Suleri, Sara. *The Rhetoric of English India*. Chicago and London: University of Chicago Press, 1992.

4. The British Woman Traveller in India: Cultural Intimacy and Interracial Kinship in Fanny Parks's *Wanderings of a Pilgrim in Search of the Picturesque*

Nandini Sengupta
Syracuse University

> Roaming about with a good tent and a good Arab, one might be happy forever in India: a man might possibly enjoy this sort of life more than a woman; he has his dog, his gun and his beaters, with an open country to shoot over, [. . .] I have a pencil instead of a gun, and believe it affords me satisfaction equal, if not greater, than the sportsman derives from his Manton. (Parks 2: 191)

This essay offers a reading of the travel journals of Fanny Parks, a British woman who accompanied her husband to India in the nineteenth century. As the wife of a junior civil officer, she spent over two decades of her life in India (1822-1845), travelling extensively through northern India. On her return to England she published the account of her peregrinations under the engaging title *Wanderings of a Pilgrim, In Search of The Picturesque, During Four-and-Twenty Years in the East; With Revelations of Life in the Zenana* (1850). This account of Parks's travels through India forms one of numerous such narratives "penciled" by British women who were placed in the outposts of Empire to enact their roles as "incorporated" wives, sisters or daughters.[1]

---

[1] I borrow this idea of the "incorporated wife" from Hilary Callan for whom the term denotes that "condition of *wifehood* in a range of settings where the social character ascribed to a woman is an intimate function of her husband's occupational identity and culture" (1). Indira Ghose and Sara Mills also refer to Fanny Parks as the "incorporated wife" (3).

It would be limiting, however, to regard Fanny Parks's extremely lively and fascinating journal as the articulations of a colonial wife trying to make sense of a novel environment even while gaining a sense of identity from the performance of duties that her incorporation demanded. Parks repudiates the expectations and limits of that role; instead she constructs through her text the rhetoric of a female vagabond, the *pilgrim* wandering the colonial space: "I awoke [. . .] and my little soul was soon cantering away on the back of an Arab, enjoying the pure, cool, morning breeze. Oh! The pleasure of vagabondizing over India!" (2: 192) Fashioning her persona against that of the male imperialist/adventurer, Fanny Parks presents herself as a free spirit. Astride her Arab, sans male guardian, she explores open, hidden and liminal spaces of the contact zone; bonds with Indians; acquires an understanding of the indigenous religious customs; masters the regional dialects; learns to play the sitar; indeed intimately experiences the eclectic coordinates of Indian life.[2] Yet she is more than just the female imperialist appropriating the colonial space through her textual labour. In re-examining the record of Fanny Parks's fearless "cantering" across the contact zone, I focus on the intensity of her interactions and locate in them manifestations of an interracial, cross-cultural intimacy that reveal the multifarious ways in which the West and East did or could interact with each other; ways that were not simply exploitative or simply acquisitive in nature. The connections that Parks forges on her travels through the colonial space create an alternative intimate field that existed within the parameters of the colonial narrative of subjugation and domination, yet strangely disengaged from it. Her text best animates Mary Louis Pratt's "contact" perspective that seeks to "foreground the interactive, improvisational dimensions of

---

[2] I use Mary Louise Pratt's coinage and definition of the term 'contact zone': "social spaces where disparate cultures meet, clash, and grapple with each other, often in highly asymmetrical relations of domination and subordination – like colonialism, slavery, or their aftermaths as they are lived out across the globe today" (4).

4. *Fanny Parks's* Wanderings

colonial encounters so easily ignored or suppressed by diffusionist accounts of conquest and domination" (7). Within an understanding of relations of power that have placed British women like Fanny Parks in the contact zone, this perspective seeks to unravel the parallel stories generated by the colonial experience and those narratives of interactive encounters that are often obscured by attention to the master narratives of conquest and domination.

In offering this argument I locate myself against established readings of Parks's text that claim that the impulse to possess, map and acquire propels her travels around India. Indeed her avowal of the pencil, in the opening extract, is quite characteristic of British women in India in the early nineteenth century, as Sara Suleri has argued. The use of the pencil allowed the women of Anglo-India to occupy "one of the few socially responsible positions" available to them outside those offered within the domestic domain. As "amateur ethnographers," British women in India collected "peripheral images" of the people and the space they were thrust amidst. Suleri further claims that they produced verbal and visual representations of India that marked their entry into the political domain of their male counterparts but in order to aestheticise rather than to analyse (75). Using the artistic mode of the picturesque these women converted the "subcontinental threats" into watercolors or words in their journals. In Suleri's argument the "picturesque becomes synonymous with a desire to transfix a dynamic cultural confrontation into a still life, converting a pictorial imperative into a gesture of self-protection that allows the colonial gaze a license to convert its ability not to see into studiously visual representations" (76). In my re-reading of Fanny Parks's journal, I counter this argument by claiming that cultural confrontation is not always deferred or transfixed. I emphasise, instead, the centrality of exchange, interaction and reciprocity in Parks's experience of India. This reading of her text moves beyond the imperial picturesque by recognising the intimacies generated between the itinerant Anglo-Indian women and the native "Other" within the cultural matrix of the contact zone.

By calling attention to these intimate spaces of the Empire I broaden our understanding of what constitutes the intimate in colonial relations. Scholarship regarding the intimate spaces of Empire typically revolves around the colonial management of sexual, domestic or private relations. Ann Laura Stoler's work in this field is most influential in framing current understandings of imperial intimacy. Her argument delineating the "connections between the broad-scale dynamics of colonial rule and the intimate sites of implementation" is undoubtedly integral to our understanding of the colonial management of "sexual arrangements and affective attachments" (7-8). Her further claim that "domains of the intimate figured [. . .] prominently in the perceptions and policies of those who ruled" is, however, predicated on an understanding of the intimate as "carnal" or sexual. It *is* essential to acknowledge the importance of sexual intimacy in the construction of colonial categories, yet there are other intimate domains that defy categorisation as they are situated in a position subjacent to these other, more threatening expressions of transgressive sentiments. Alongside the sexual politics that shapes colonial categories and defines licit and illicit desire there also exist a wide range of sentiments facilitated by the proximity, nearness and familiarity in the contact zone – a familiarity that creates an alternative "intimate field" (Berlant 2). I follow Lauren Berlant's thesis in claiming that within the colonial experience intimate attachments also emerged from mobile processes. Formed in unpredictable spaces and following unpredictable trajectories, these connections did impact the people and produced something, but, to quote Berlant again, "perhaps not history in its ordinary, memorable or valorized sense, and always 'something' of positive value" (5).

In Fanny Parks's avid engagement with India she forges such an alternate intimate space. She resolutely places herself not at the periphery of Indian spaces but at their centre and experiences intimately the various coordinates of Indian life: religion, history, culture, architecture and the people. I have broadly labeled this interaction as her *cul-*

4. *Fanny Parks's* Wanderings

tural intimacy with India. I locate this intimacy in the sustained series of moments that situate her at the heart of the Indian landscape and amongst different orders of Indians: her household servants; the oarsmen of her steamer; hybridised Anglo-Indian selves like her; women in the *zenana* of Colonel Gardner; and women in the camp of the Maratha dowager queen, Baiza Bai. The so-called colonising self also permeates an array of social spaces. Parks plants herself within the Indian milieu at "native" fairs, participates in religious celebrations, enjoys the "native" bazaars, voyages along the river Ganga, visits ancient historical structures and enters the coveted space of the *zenana*. The proximity operates on intersecting levels: with the spaces, the people and the cultural matrix that envelope these. In this essay, I examine more closely the dynamics of Parks's robust interest in and her keen engagement with Hindu religious beliefs alongside the creation of alternative bonds of kinship with the interracial family of William Gardner on the one hand, and with the dispossessed Maratha queen Baiza Bai on the other. These resultant attachments with the customs or with the colonial "other" do not de-center the trajectory of imperialism, of coercive and hegemonic policies, or of administrative practices but they do produce an alternative knowledge about the "other" while also fashioning a cross-cultural, interracial subjectivity that is rarely located in this genre of women's travel journals.

The introductory page of Parks's published journal bears testimony to this cross-cultural identity. Her authorship is claimed by a signature in Persian. Dedicating the journal to the memory of her "beloved mother," she begins with an invocation to the elephant god, Ganesh, in the traditional Hindu manner. In a cultural amalgamation of the Hindu and Muslim traditions of the "beginning," she marks her salutes in both Persian and Hindi.[3] She invokes "Māhādeo and Parvutī!" regis-

---

[3] According to the *Oxford Dictionary of National Biography*, the transliteration from the Persian has produced what is actually a misspelling of her name: "Parkes" for "Parks." I use the original spelling, although some scholars prefer "Parkes"; see Raza (*DNB*).

tering her "Salām" to them and aspires to write like Ganesh (1: xix). Her invocation of the Hindu god of prosperous beginnings and the patron of learning coalesced with a typical Muslim greeting not only differentiates her from her contemporaries but it also indicates her complete immersion in Indian culture and its belief systems. Parks reproduces a likeness of her own idol of this deity in the frontispiece of the edition and explains in overbearing details the various articles that constitute her religious altar.

Sara Suleri critiques Parks's "appropriation" of the image reading her use of the deity as a "trope for the cultural hybridity that a feminine picturesque must both record and lull into repose" (84). The god in her analysis is "emptied of any mythological violence"; instead, it represents an "aesthetic object both collectible and transportable" (84).[4] Suleri's argument about Parks's rhetorical move concerns itself with the element of picturesque in the text and this is a familiar focus in most scholarship related to Parks's work. In her reading of Parks's journal, Suleri identifies primarily the acquisitive instinct of the picturesque which "dehistoricizes the subcontinent into an amorphously aesthetic space, it further desacralizes each icon that Parkes represents into an allegory of colonial ownership" (85). Indira Ghose and Sara Mills echo Suleri's premise that as an aesthetic mode of representation, the picturesque serves to fetishise the East whereby the east becomes a curio, much like the idol of Ganesh that Parks describes in her introduction. Yet in turning attention to what Suleri calls "the alternative politics of the picturesque" we also take attention away from the aspect of cultural intimacy which is a neglected dimension of this text. In identifying Parks's impulse as covetous, the cultural journey of this British woman traveler is stripped of its interactive and improvisational dimensions that Pratt has drawn attention to. In opposition to readings by other scholars, I am intrigued by the self-same im-

---

[4] Among the handful of scholars who have examined Fanny Parks's text, Sara Suleri's reading is one of the most established. I have engaged with this reading in detail so as to clarify my own argument.

4. Fanny Parks's Wanderings

pulse that propels Parks to fashion herself as Ganesh and to invoke the blessings of both the Hindu and Islamic traditions before she embarks on her aesthetic and cultural experience of India. This self-fashioning as Ganesh that frames her text is indicative of that sensibility of the avid traveler who willingly initiates an intimacy and is eager to learn, to know, but above all to amalgamate the best of the disparate worlds. Parks's British, Christianised, gendered selfhood desires validation and recognition in purely indigenous ways – she "salaams" and wants to write like Ganesh.

Moving beyond the critique of the picturesque mode, it is possible to view Parks's ramblings as the expressions of sincere curiosity and excitement at discovering a disparate cultural milieu. She is greatly interested in Hindu religious beliefs and practices, yet the strangeness of the religious rituals invoke in her, often simultaneously, the contradictory emotions of repulsion and attraction. On a visit to the local celebrations of "Churruck Pooja" in Calcutta honoring the Hindu goddess Kalee, the penance and the self-inflicted pain of the religious mendicants shock her initially. She writes, "had not the novelty of the scene excited my curiosity, disgust would have made me sick" (1: 27). She describes in detail the manner in which the mendicants are swinging from posts set up for the purpose: "The man swung in a circle [. . .] supported by four iron hooks, two through the flesh of his back, and two in that of his chest." Her repeated admission is pertinent: "I was much disgusted, but greatly interested" (1: 27-28). The evocation of ambivalent emotions illustrates the operations of an engagement with an alien culture that challenges the belief system of the coloniser. At the same time it also demonstrates pockets of "native" beliefs, rituals and customs that resist a framing/containing by the observant I/eye of the traveler. The power dynamics inherent in this episode are fissured since the narrator no longer occupies the stable position of knowledge as curiosity triumphs over disgust. Yet this exposure to the grotesque element in the Hindu religion does not compel her to be immediately dismissive of "native" religions or practices. Familiarity with the grotesque runs parallel with her attachment to the alluring, and both find equal space in her journal. In Parks's rapt engagement with the figure of the *fakir*; in her fascination with the mounds built for the *sati* at the river banks; in her thirst for religious knowledge, to list a few of the many instances from the text, one can locate moments that question our understanding of the British woman's engagement with India. Parks actively seeks out these uniquely Indian spaces that resist colonisation. Her willing placement of herself as an outsider challenges the model that has been employed to examine the imperial gaze. She does not fear cultural proximity, nor does she place herself on the periphery; instead she realises that her gaze is inadequate to faithfully represent or perceive this rigid pocket of alien culture replete with men swinging on hooks and mendicants with withered arms.

In fact, the narrative introduces a politics of curiosity for "native" life that operates on a plane adjacent to the politics of observation, surveillance, and mapping.[5] This politics of curiosity functions as an intellectual engagement that compels her not only to describe a festival or a superstition in its concrete details but also to delve into the myth within which the belief system is enveloped. As a case in point her description of the worship of the *toolsee* (*tulsi*) plant leads her to explore the legend of the devout worshipper transformed by a curse into the plant (1: 42-44). Similarly, she regales her reader with details, sometimes overbearing no doubt, of all the various deities, the different days accorded to each and the festivities followed; the journal was intended to communicate the flavour of her Indian experience to her mother. This partially explains the painstaking efforts undertaken in conveying detailed descriptions. While Parks's sensibility is Oriental-

---

[5] Nigel Leask indicates that the principle of "curiosity" governed most travel writing during the Romantic Period. He outlines two popular meanings of the word: a) wonder aroused by distant lands culminating in a desire to possess a "singular" object; b) inclination to knowledge (4). I follow the second implication of the word in my analysis of Parks's curious impulse, although Leask suggests that Parks's "colonial curiosity" panders to colonial accumulation (242).

4. *Fanny Parks's* Wanderings

ist, her interest in the east is devoid of any larger political aim. Her intellectual and scientific curiosity is intended to satisfy a self-edifying thirst for intimate knowledge of the East.

During her first trip to the holy city of Benares she writes: "The most holy city of Benares is the high place of superstition. I went into a Hindoo temple in which pooja was being performed, and thought the organ of gullibility must be strongly developed in the Hindoos" (1: 66). A year later (1827) this very organ of gullibility is active in her as one finds her "occupied in planting a small avenue of *neem* trees in front of the house; unlike the air around the tamarind, that near a *neem* tree is reckoned wholesome," and indeed this process is deemed essential as is evident from her immersion in the regional proverb that "we had made no advance on our heavenward road until the avenue was planted, which carried us on one-third of the journey" (1: 71-72).[6] This, in itself, is a telling comment on her previous disbelief and scorn at the temple in Benares. She even allows her servants to follow the religious traditions and "marry" the *neem* tree to a *peepul* tree by entwining their branches. She continues to ensure the wellbeing of her own afterlife in Heaven by following the Hindu prescription of sinking a well. Furthermore, almost a decade later she deems it cause enough to beg with the Lieutenant-Governor of Agra, Sir Charles Metcalfe, to desist from destroying the same avenue of *neem* trees she had so lovingly and devotedly planted.

The nature of Parks's request and her internalisation of the social, cultural, and religious belief systems of the colonised culture demonstrate a brand of intimacy that transcends the picturesque impulse. The

---

[6] Parks frequently uses regional terms for trees, for religious festivals, and other points of reference. Each regional use in the case of a tree, like the *toolsee*, *neem*, or *peepul* mentioned here, is annotated with its scientific/Latinised version. I have used the version used by her within the text. The use of regional terms is a further indication of the self-fashioning of her cross-cultural identity.

colonising self not only seeks a definition and perception of the self through the cultural fabric of the colonised, but also locates the scientific rationale embedded in these seemingly superstitious/gullible practices. The West located in and through Fanny Parks opens itself to the east and reveals alternative avenues of receptivity. The incidents that crowd the text may in themselves seem inconsequential; what could be worthwhile in a journal painstakingly cataloguing Indian traditions, trees, plants, vegetables, superstitions, myth, or the devoted belief in the air around a particular species of trees? By paying attention to these details I indicate the lack inherent in our examination of colonial texts. I identify the emotional excesses embedded in the very text through which scholars have formulated arguments about colonial excesses: domination, appropriation and exhibition. Before we can examine Fanny Parks's collusion in the colonial project through her deployment of the picturesque, we need to pay close attention to her sensibility and the impulse that propels her to cast her identity in the guise of the Hindu god Ganesh; urges her to learn the Hindi and Persian scripts; and devote reams in an attempt to capture the minutiae of Hindu religion. This involvement on Parks's part indicates the paralleling possibilities of an intellectual engagement not commonly attributed to the memsahib.

In developing this argument further I claim that Parks's narrative captures intimate spaces and intimate moments that range *beside*, borrowing Eve Sedgwick's premise, that colonial story that has placed her in India in the first place.[7] An interpretation of Sedgwick's concept allows us to imagine parallel narratives for colonialism so that Parks's insertion of her selfhood within the cultural milieu of the "other" exists alongside her identity as a colonial wife whose very presence in the contact zone is predicated on the other narratives of

---

[7] Eve Sedgwick proposes the notion of the *beside* that, she claims, would liberate us from the dualistic mode in literary analysis (1-24).

4. *Fanny Parks's* Wanderings

conquest. Undoubtedly all travel texts written by British women in this period do, to differing extents, participate in colonial politics, yet a single-minded approach to the texts neglects the equally potent manifestations of local, spontaneous and transitory involvements like those displayed by Parks. These attachments reveal the often unpredictable ways in which colonialism functions. In the context of the historical moment, when administrators like William Bentinck sought to abolish *sati* and curb, what they believed to be the evils of Hindu religion; when the Evangelical zeal of administrators and missionaries sought to proselytise in the contact zone, Parks presents herself through that very objectionable rhetoric of Hinduism, as I have indicated above. Her attachment with the religious spirit of India works in tandem with the official male rhetoric that sought to create a distrust of Hinduism.

Looking beyond the dualistic approach, my attempt is to re-focus the attention on the texture of lives and the models of affect that impacted the existence of ordinary lives *within* the wider spectrum of imperial forces. Following this approach, Fanny Parks's insistence on retaining the avenue of *neem* trees is not the caprice of an overly-curious, over-zealous British middle-class woman; neither is it an expression of colonial high-handedness. Parks's detailing of the religious legends, interest in the practice of *sati*, her use and belief in Oriental proverbs are a parallel process of production of knowledge that is not wholly acquisitive in nature, although it might be partly so. What her impulse amply demonstrates is a key element of the colonial process that is often ignored in colonial studies: the element of reciprocity. This gathering of knowledge about native life and culture is an alternative to the mapping, annexing, and containing impulse that shapes the plot of political alliances or even shapes the impulse of the "Great Game" so astutely captured in Rudyard Kipling's *Kim*. This process does not always stereotype Indians and their customs as barbaric, heathen, or uncivilised, contrary to what Sara Mills claims. In Mills's analysis, Parks "produces knowledge about India as a place of strange and barbaric customs, which she observes from a distance or is told about, but which does not contaminate her" (44-45). Fanny Parks's preference for regional languages, her invocation of Hindu gods and goddesses at the beginning of all her endeavours, her devotion to native beliefs, her insertion of her self at sites of native celebrations all indicate the potential insufficiency of Mills's critique. The knowledge that Parks produces emanates from an intensely experienced process of familiarisation that often debunks the myth of India as barbaric.

In the fullest understanding of the term, Fanny Parks *interacts*. This is not only a unilinear process of revealing the secrets of India to her metropolitan audience, but as much a revelation of the impact of that life on her and her avid response to it. When she requests Charles Metcalfe to save a few trees, her request is embedded in a respect for the people who form the fabric of her everyday life: her servants. She astutely understands the impact of those trees on the Indians – these trees are regarded as sacred by the Hindus, thus defilement would be an act of sacrilege – an understanding beyond the limits of colonial politics and governance. I argue that Parks's narrative encapsulates moments that offer a surprising moment of connection that has not been hitherto examined. Fanny Parks's fascination with the "great curiosities" of India, her "interest," her sense of things "remarkable," even her disgust, all indicate embodied moments of bonding with the texture and fabric of Indian life. These affective encounters do not overtly question, challenge, or subvert any hegemonic processes which are at play in the current historic moment, but they do indicate that the official narrative of colonialism circulates images of distrust, violence, and hate to the exclusion of these moments of affinity. I am not claiming that the existence of these affective moments justifies the colonial impulse in any way, instead I am more interested in an understanding of such cross-cultural encounters that created alternative images of the colonising self and its "other" in the colonial moment.

4. Fanny Parks's Wanderings

The attachment to the cultural milieu discussed above is intensified by Parks's intimate association with the people she encounters on her travels. Of particular interest are her interactions with the women of the *zenana*. The titillating invitation enclosed within the original title of her journal, *Revelations of Life in the Zenana*, belies the sincere bonds formed within this space. The *zenana*, or the female quarters, becomes for her a coveted space of India that she wants to penetrate but is frustrated in all her efforts. That she places herself in a tradition of writers who have produced images of the *zenana* is evident when she invokes Lady Montagu: "The perusal of Lady Mary Wortley Montague's work has rendered me very anxious to visit a zenāna, and to become acquainted with the ladies of the East" (1: 59).[8] It is important at this point to comment on the class politics of this encounter. Parks is not intimately allied with a life of privilege, in England or in India. As the wife of a junior officer in the civil service, she does not belong in the hallowed circles comprising the senior diplomatic officers and their wives. Thus invitations to royal households are hardly ever directed to her. Her curiosity and fascination in this regard are evident in her avid involvement in the letters that her more fortunate peers send of their royal visits. Her position in the class hierarchy is thus an element in the production of her fascination with the women of the *zenana*.

It is her encounter with the interesting figure of Colonel William Gardner that eventually triggers for her a long association with ladies of "rank." Through him a different order of life in India is opened up to her. This is the world of the interracial Anglo-Mughal community. Colonel Gardner's *zenana* was a prototype of the elite household to which Fanny wished to belong; Gardner was both a wealthy land-

---

[8] Lady Mary Wortley Montagu (approx. 1689-1762) was a well-known poetess and essayist in the early eighteenth century. She accompanied her husband on his embassy to Constantinople. Her *Letters Written During her Travels* (1764), also known as *The Turkish Embassy Letters*, are one of the earliest records of the Oriental harem by a British woman (see Isobel Grundy [*DNB*]).

holder and the head of an interracial household.[9] Fanny was clearly fascinated by him: "a most charming old gentleman." Such phrases are regularly showered upon him: "that delightful man [. . .] such a high caste gentleman!"; "very handsome [. . .] so dignified and interesting" (1: 181-85). William Dalrymple suggests that she was clearly a little in love with him (xviii). Gardner was a link to a world she was extremely eager to experience, and his status as a wealthy European, the "great favourite at present" of both the British resident and the independent king of Oude, as well as the guardian of a hybrid household peopled with women who claimed a royal lineage, was ideal. It was a world where the class hierarchy of the Anglo-Indian society became insignificant, yet it worked to create an allied sense of social snobbery in her as through Colonel Gardner she found a connection to other royal households ("he will give me letters of introduction to some of the ladies of the palace," she claims [1: 183]). Repudiating the hierarchised world of Anglo-India, she gained a sense of pride from her association with this parallel world of wealth and privilege.

This intimate involvement with the Gardner family forms the most engaging section of Parks's journal, bringing to a culmination all the knowledge that she has already absorbed from her travels. This opportunity to be a part of his household comes to her a decade after her arrival in India, and it gives a more concrete shape to her cross-cultural proclivities. Parks operates, at least initially, under a few standard tropes of the *zenana* that she has imbibed from her readings. For instance, she reiterates the notion that women inside the *zenana* are beautiful. She carries this stereotype with her into the *zenana* of Mulka Begum, whom she first encounters in James Gardner's (the son

---

[9] Colonel William Linnaeus Gardner (1771-1836), born of Anglo-American parents, spent all his adult life in India. Described mostly as a military adventurer who served the Maratha rulers, his romance with an Indian princess was conducted across the *purdah*; Gardner tells Fanny that he fell in love with a pair of "the most beautiful black eyes in the world," peering at him through a gap in the curtain (1: 417) (see H. M. Chicester [*DNB*]).

4. *Fanny Parks's* Wanderings

of Colonel Gardner) household. A romantic aura is already built around this figure; Mulka Begum had eloped with James Gardner while she was still married to another prince of Delhi. Parks's first glance of this famed woman is however disappointing. It comes as a shock to her to find the Begum under the effect of opium: "I had heard so much of Mulka's wonderful beauty, that I felt disappointed" (1: 380). It only adds to her astonishment to witness the Begum feed her children a bit of opium as well.[10] This discordant initiation into the *zenana* sets the stage for her future encounters as she gradually becomes intimate with the inhabitants. Mulka Begum is transformed when Fanny Parks meets her in the evening, "looking like a dazzling apparition" (1: 383). Fanny's fascination results in overwhelmingly detailed descriptions of every move, every limb and every detail of the dress of this lady. She directs an eroticised glance as she seems to place herself in the guise of the male coloniser who is suddenly given a glance of the forbidden. She exults:

> How beautiful she looked! how very beautiful! Her animated countenance was constantly varying, and her dark eyes struck fire when a joyous thought crossed her mind [. . .] by lamplight she was a different creature; and I felt no surprise when I remembered the wondrous tales told by the men of the beauty of Eastern women [. . .] Her figure is tall and commanding; her hair jet black [. . .] her hands and arms are lovely! (1: 383-84)

While validating the male tradition of fascination with Eastern women, Fanny Parks also sub-consciously intensifies the homoerotic nature of this encounter that displaces, for the time being, the class

---

[10] The use of opium was a well-known weakness in the Mughal Court. Thus Mulka Begum's languid state in the morning, even though it disgusts Parks, is in actuality a sign of her nobility and lineage.

politics which, in part, shapes this fascination for her.[11] The detailing pays close attention to the body of the colonised woman, revealing yet another layer of this intimate view into the *zenana*: the body politics of this encounter. The awe and fascination with royalty and royal love stories that Parks displays throughout her text is translated here into a rapt engagement with the body of the Indian woman. Parks is captivated by the lure of the transparent veil that "hides not; it merely veils the form, adding beauty to the beautiful, by its soft and cloud-like folds" (1: 384). The interest is entirely focused on the erotic charge that this Muslim lady exudes; the jewels adorning the throat and waist, the "delicate and uncovered feet," and the nose-ring, which is a symbol of the love-token from groom to bride. These visions of the Begum follow Parks even to her dreams: "my dreams were haunted by visions of [. . .] the beautiful Begam" (1: 385-88).

Scholars have devoted ample attention to the dynamics of these Western women's East-West encounter through the *zenana*. Yet most of these readings, while revealing an essential aspect of western women's experience of India, do not convey any real sense of interaction across cultural borders. They trace the location and placement of the western woman's body in the alien space without assessing the embodied interaction between the bodies in that secluded space. Fanny Parks's observation and fascination with Mulka Begum is part of a larger process of exchange and genuine intimacy with the women of the Gardner family, whereby fascination and familiarity, perhaps even some amount of contempt at their languid, opium-addicted state, are intricately bound together. The homoerotic overtones of the first description soon replace a more humdrum interaction where both exchange knowledge about women's education in each other's cultures. The exchange also extends to material manifestations: Parks is

---

[11] Both Ghose (52-70) and Nair (224-45) provide useful insights into the various ways women in the *zenana* have been represented in the journals of British women.

4. *Fanny Parks's* Wanderings

adorned in Indian bangles, the objects she had earlier coveted. This experience of the *zenana* also reveals the gradual Indianisation of the western woman's body as it becomes the object of reverse scrutiny. Parks is given a room inside the *zenana* and becomes an object of curiosity herself when the slave girls gaze at her, startled, in turn, at the number of garments worn by a European woman. The gaze she directs at the Begum returns to her as she willingly offers herself up to the reverse gaze. The vulnerability of the European female body is now exposed under the curious eyes of the attendants. The colonising body and eye is no longer the stable locus of power. This proximity exposes both the British subject and the secluded Indian woman. Parks too is the cynosure of eyes in the *zenana* and her conduct is as surprising to the inhabitants there as their habits (smoking the hookah, consuming opium, blackening teeth with antimony) are to her. She writes of the picture she presents to them:

> The conduct that shocked them was our dining with men not our relations, and that too with uncovered faces. A lady going out on horseback is monstrous [. . .] My not being afraid to sleep in the dark without having half a dozen slave girls snoring around me surprised them [. . .] in fact, they looked upon me as a very odd creature. (1: 151)

This exchange indicates the dynamics of an intimate engagement that is ignored in other readings; Parks acknowledges that there are cultural barriers that make her and all other Englishwomen "curious creatures" to women like Mulka Begam and Colonel Gardner's wife, Nissa Begam (1: 451). Parks's engagement with the women in the *zenana* thus reveals the multi-directional workings of the politics of curiosity. It further amplifies the need for an alternative understanding of privilege and power that would take into account the complicated nature of this cultural intimacy.

This intimacy also has emotional connotations as Parks becomes for the Gardner household the "adopted daughter" and is often referred to by Colonel Gardner as "my child." His wife, Nissa Begam, receives Parks as her own child and showers affection befitting a mother. The Gardner household becomes for Parks a surrogate family. Her experience of this quasi-Indian, quasi-European family progresses gradually from a fascination into a familiarity that overcomes her initial consuming desire to *see* a *zenana*. It develops into an intuitive connection encompassing a range of emotions from the paternal and maternal feelings of Colonel Gardner and his wife, to the filial feelings Parks experiences towards them.

This familiarity is also crucial to an understanding of interracial relations in 1830s, when the joint fervour of the Evangelicals, Utilitarians and Radicals in Britain sought to reverse the trajectory of Orientalism. Interracial relationships came under scrutiny and were increasingly discouraged. Parks's abiding encounter with this interracial family with its mixture of fair and dark faces, Muslim and English names, native and European cuisines constitutes a fast vanishing world – a subliminal culture that exists on the shadows of both mainstream native and Anglo-Indian cultures. Her work, as Dalrymple suggests, is important for its record of "this very attractive (and largely forgotten) moment of cultural and sexual interaction," and for its description of a world "far more hybrid" with "far less clearly defined ethnic, national and religious borders, than we have been conditioned to expect" (xxiii).

Fanny Parks's intimate association with the dispossessed Maratha queen, Baiza Bai, reveals another dynamic of interracial interaction in the contact zone. Baiza Bai presents a completely different image than the women in the Gardner family; she is an ambitious matriarch. She presides over a world of women warriors and her story is a precursor to the later, more glamorised, history of Rani Laxmi Bai of Jhansi, who is known to have fought bravely and independently against the

4. Fanny Parks's Wanderings

British forces in the events following the Sepoy Mutiny in 1857.[12] Thus the feminised, eroticised world of the Gardner *zenana* is offset by this world of fierce, spear-toting, armed Maratha women, who protect their own *zenana*, manage their own horses and even ride as a group in public, albeit veiled.

The fascination with eroticised visions in the *zenana* is replaced here with a more somber respect for the dowager queen: "The Baiza Bai is rather an old woman, with grey hair [. . .] there is a freedom and independence in her air that I greatly admire – so unlike that of the sleeping, languid, opium-eating Musulmans" (2: 3). The friendship begins with a mock display of Parks's skills in horsemanship aimed to satisfy the curiosity of the Maratha women to see an English woman "ride crooked." This becomes the source of entertainment among the women and Parks submits herself good-naturedly to being the butt of laughter. Yet she proves her mettle among the Maratha women when she accepts their challenge to ride their horse in the "Mahratta style" clothed in their costume. This event endears Parks to the queen and their pluck becomes the basis of a sound interracial friendship, a sisterhood of sorts, as Parks gets the privileged title of "The Great-aunt of my Grand-daughter": "This was very complimentary, since it entitled me to a rank as the adopted sister of her Highness" (2: 7). The filial bonds with the Gardner family (even that *zenana* privileges her as a beloved aunt) are replaced here by more sisterly bonds between the

---

[12] The Baiza Bai was the widow of Daulat Rao Scindia (1794-1827), the adopted son of Mahadajee Scindia, who was one of the more powerful opponents of the British in the late eighteenth century. After the death of her husband, Baiza Bai was crowned Queen of Gwalior, the seat of their kingdom. She herself was without a male heir but adopted a relative, Jankee Rao, to groom him as her successor. Her subjects revolted against her placing her adopted son against her. Fearing murder, she fled Gwalior and surrendered herself to the protection of the East India Company. It is at his historical moment that Parks meets Baiza Bai (Ghose and Mills; Sleeman).

two women, indicating possibilities of connection across national, cultural and race borders.[13]

Yet the designation as aunt, sister, child, privileging as it is for Parks, also reveals a significant dimension of this intimacy. It introduces the idea of kinship commonly predicated on blood relations. The filial or sororal bonds forged indicate the multiple possibilities inherent in colonial relations. Her acceptance into both the households, especially in the Maratha camp where there is no common European link, is at once transgressive. The naming as sister/aunt subtly indicates the symbolic mingling of blood and, more importantly, the utter ease of acceptance of such cross-racial mixing. Parks's intimacy with the Maratha women indicates that there are possibilities of bonding between Indian and British women that are not founded upon unequal (memsahib and *ayah*) or self-empowering sympathetic instincts (British woman as educator) on the part of the British women. This encounter can neither be classified as an instance of class-envy for Parks since Baiza Bai is a dispossessed queen at this moment in history. This intimacy opens up a space for more egalitarian bonds outside the dynamic of power or privilege. This is evident in their exchange regarding the status of women in their respective societies:

> Speaking of the privations endured by Hindoo widows, her highness mentioned that all luxurious food was denied them as well as a bed; and their situation was rendered as painful as possible. She asked me how an English widow fared?
>
> I told her, "An English lady enjoyed all the luxury of her husband's house during his life; but on his death she was turned out of the family mansion, to make room for the heir, and pensioned off; whilst the old horse was allowed the run

---

[13] Colonel Gardner's son James Gardner refers to her as "Fani Bhua" or "father's sister" (Parks 1: 443). Baiza Bai designates her "Khala," which is a term for "mother's sister" (2: 7).

4. *Fanny Parks's* Wanderings

of the park, and permitted to finish his days amidst the pastures he loved in his prime." (2: 8)

The conversational pattern of "she asked me" and "I told her" progresses seamlessly into a "we." The narrative here plays upon lines of contiguity and similar degrees of subordination that binds these diverse women to a common interest in the status of women. The homoerotic desire, displayed in Parks's observation of Mulka Begum, is refigured into more empathetic bonds of understanding and solidarity. There are many such exchanges recorded by Fanny Parks in her narrative. Parks learns to ride astride and to wear the Maratha costume; she teaches the Maratha women how to make tea; how to ornately dress a camel. She spends hours in the Maratha camp participating in their festivals, always enjoying the visits thoroughly, "the most agreeable visits" in her mind. And it is an exchange in the fullest understanding of the term. Baiza Bai visits Parks's famous river-boat, the Seagull, and allows Parks to play the host as well, thus flouting the protocol generally followed in such instances: the superior always received the inferior. This is significant since Fanny Parks holds no official clout or designation where such a visit would be justified.

The power dynamics of this sisterhood are nuanced. Through the years of her bonding with the Baiza Bai and her coterie of women, Fanny Parks learns to identify herself as one of them and claims, "Were I an Asiatic, I would be a Mahratta" (2: 38). Yet she always refers to Baiza Bai as "her Highness." In spite of her status as a queen, Baiza Bai welcomes Parks as a friend and sister, knowing fully well that a friendship with Parks was not likely to garner her any additional attention from the British authorities. Parks's acceptance at the Gardner household, on the other hand, was partially mediated through Colonel Gardner, and fully possible on the basis of her racial kinship with him. Parks does find the Muslim *zenana* of Colonel Gardner enthralling; she becomes familiar with the women and their attendants, fascination co-exists at all times with a familiarity, but without the sense of identification she shares with the community of the female Maratha warriors. Yet this identification and this camaraderie are not without their obverse. In spite of the emancipatory and transgressive potential of this intimate bond, it has to bow to political exigency that forms the plot of other colonial narratives. Fanny Parks is painfully made aware of her "otherness" that obstructs her free and unlimited access to the camps of the Bai. She also comprehends that her dear friend is being used as a pawn in the exploitative game of power.[14] Baiza Bai's ambitions were being thwarted by both the Indians and the British; while under British protection, her soldiers rose in mutiny and made her a prisoner within the encampment. Yet Parks's request to visit her friend was turned down by the agent for the government. Even though she was allowed to accompany the agent, she had to disappear among the Maratha women, while official terms were negotiated with the ex-queen. It is clear that Parks became, in some sense, a representative of the adversary, perhaps more for her own people than for the Marathas, and could not be permitted within earshot while state affairs were being conducted. In a similar fashion, when the queen is given an ultimatum by the British to reside with a pension at Benaras, a city not to her liking, Parks can only sympathise when asked for advice: "Thus called upon, I was obliged to give my opinion; it was an awkward thing to tell an exiled Queen she must submit [. . .]" (2: 39). She feels the cruel treatment of the Bai, yet is unable to rectify it in any way. While Parks sits in the comfortable confines of her home, a humble British subject, she feels the contrast with her friend: "She who once reigned in Gwalior has now no roof to shelter her [. . .]she is forced to live in tents, and is kept here against her will [. . .]" (2: 51).

Baiza Bai's plight highlights the current disparity between the two women, and the existence of borders that this sisterhood cannot cross. It also indicates that there are spaces within the colonial world that in

---

[14] William Sleeman's unpublished pamphlet recounts the unfortunate fate of Baiza Bai at the hands of both the British and her own retainers.

4. *Fanny Parks's* Wanderings

spite of the oppressor's infiltration can remain suitably free of malice or vengeance, spaces in which such sisterhoods and friendships can exist. These spaces breed a connection that seems to defy the stereotypical representations of colonial relations. The political story of annexation, exploitation, acquisition, and alliances plays out on an adjacent plane, along with the story of two women's interracial bonding. This bonding is subversive in its own sense, yet not threatening enough to reverse the stem of the Bai's cruel treatment at the hands of the British; she is moved from camp to camp, money rightfully belonging to her is taken away by force, and she becomes, as Parks indicates, a prisoner at the hands of the British.

In the final analysis, what Parks's journal reveals is an understanding of interstitial spaces of interaction. Ketaki Kushari Dyson's assessment of a cluster of travel texts and journals from this period is pertinent in this respect. She writes that these texts reveal "the *interface* of things: between the observer and the observed, between one human being and another, between an individual and a group, between one culture and another" (ix). I augment Dyson's concept of this *interface* by positing that the colonial encounter is multidimensional, there are multiple nooks and crannies concealed within the corpus of colonial discourse that are yet undefined or register only as residues. My reading of Parks's work attempts to penetrate one such crevice and examine the keen interactions of this British woman with the space, culture, and people of India: an interaction, that, I argue, questions the repeated attempts to read journals by British women as only colluding in the work of empire-building. This is not to claim that all British women were equally passionate or open-minded in their relationship with India and Indians. I use Parks's journal as a particular instance of under-reading certain colonial texts. A minute reading reveals that Parks's text opens up for examination a space for the accommodation of a healthy interest, respect and sometimes even awe for the Indian way of life. And more compelling than the respect and awe is the genuine attempt to understand the mainsprings of a completely different cultural impulse. William Dalrymple asserts in his reading of Parks's work that she "did her best to understand and build bridges across the colonial divide" (xxii). Such attempts at understanding, at building bridges, at bonding with the other, irrespective of whether transitory or abiding, deserve our attention because they reveal pockets of interaction and mixing that lie alongside the larger colonial story of power, domination and mistrust of the "Other."

Works Cited

Berlant, Lauren, ed. *Intimacy*. Chicago: University of Chicago Press, 2000.

Callan, Hilary, and Shirley Ardener, eds. *The Incorporated Wife*. London: Croom Helm, 1984.

Chichester, H. M. "Gardner, William Linnaeus (1771-1836)." Rev. James Lunt. *Oxford Dictionary of National Biography*. Oxford University Press, 2004. 13 June 2006 <http://www.oxforddnb.com.libezproxy2.syr.edu/view/article/10377>.

Dalrymple, William. *Begums, Thugs & Englishmen: The Journals of Fanny Parkes*. New Delhi: Penguin, 2002.

Dyson, Ketaki Kushari. *A Various Universe: A Study of the Journals and Memoirs of British Men and Women in the Indian Subcontinent 1765-1856*. 1978. New Delhi: Oxford University Press, 2006.

Ghose, Indira. *Women Travellers in Colonial India: The Power of the Female Gaze*. Delhi: Oxford University Press, 1998.

Ghose, Indira and Sara Mills. Introduction. *Wanderings of a Pilgrim in Search of the Picturesque*. By Fanny Parkes. Manchester and New York: Manchester University Press, 2001.

Grundy, Isobel. "Montagu, Lady Mary Wortley (*bap.* 1689, *d.* 1762)", *Oxford Dictionary of National Biography*, Oxford University Press, 2004. 28 Sept. 2006 <http://www.oxforddnb.com.libezproxy2.syr.edu/view/article/19029>.

Kipling, Rudyard. *Kim*. New Delhi: Penguin, 1994.

Leask, Nigel. *Curiosity and Aesthetics of Travel Writing, 1770-1840: 'From an Antique Land'*. Oxford, New York: Oxford University Press, 2002.

Mills, Sara. "Knowledge, Gender and Empire." *Writing Women and Space: Colonial and Postcolonial Geographies*. Ed. Alison Blunt and Gilliam Rose. London, New York: Guilford, 1994. 29-50.

Nair, Janaki. "Uncovering the *Zenana*: Visions of Indian Womanhood in Englishwomen's Writings, 1813-1940." *Cultures of Empire: Colonizers in Britain and the Empire in the Nineteenth and Twentieth Centuries*. Ed. Catherine Hall. New York: Routledge, 2000. 224-45.

Parks, Fanny. *Wanderings of a Pilgrim In Search of the Picturesque*. 1850. Introd. and annot. Esther Chawner. 2 vols. Karachi: Oxford University Press, 1975.

Pratt, Mary Louis. *Imperial Eyes: Travel Writing and Transculturation*. London and New York: Routledge 1992.

Raza, Rosemary Cargill. "Parks, Frances Susanna (1794-875)." *Oxford Dictionary of National Biography*. Oxford University Press, 2004. 28 Apr. 2006 <http://www.oxforddnb.com.libezproxy2.syr.edu/view/article/40907>.

Sedgwick, Eve Kosofsky. *Touching/Feeling: Affect, Pedagogy, Performativity*. Durham: Duke University Press, 2003.

Sleeman, William Henry. "The Story of Bysa Bae." Unpublished Pamphlet. British Library, London.

Stoler, Ann Laura. *Carnal Knowledge and Imperial Power: Race and the Intimate in Colonial Rule*. Berkeley: University of California Press, 2002.

Suleri, Sara. *The Rhetoric of English India*. Chicago: University of Chicago Press, 1992.

5. Inconsequential Lives: *The Voyage Out* and Anglo-Indian Fictions of Voyaging and Domesticity

Pia Mukherji
Tufts University

Three years before she died of heat exhaustion in 1906, Mary Curzon, political wife and colonial traveler, described the sacrifice of her health in the service of Viceroy Curzon's imperial life thus: "India, I know, slowly murders women. Yet, I suppose, many inconsequential lives must go into the foundations of all great works and all great achievements" (Fowler 281). Her statement represents the gendered service to nation and Empire performed by émigré British women in Anglo India at the close of the nineteenth century. The gradual feminisation of Anglo-India after the initial years of active colonialism has been broadly analysed as a reinstatement of Victorian domestic ideology to help settle an early colonial culture.[1] Between 1899 and 1911, over 200,000 women traveled to the colonies from England, seemingly prepared for the tasks of housekeeping and Empire building, and compliant with a manifest destiny that established them as homemakers in exile. A large company traveled to India as wives, missionaries or educators – to domesticate and civilise the new commonwealth colony. Popular "memsahib" fiction, exemplified in the novels of Maud Diver, Flora Annie Steele, Ethel Savi, and Sarah Duncan, appears colonially situated, repeating the consolations and discontents of a dominant bourgeois culture. However, a closer examination of such representations of the feminised Anglo-Indian passage and colonial domesticity provides evidence of feminist self-fashioning and an assertive politics identified with *fin-de-siècle* "new women" in the metropolis. The complexities of representation in each discourse helps

---

[1] For colonial constructions of the "incorporated wife," "maternal imperialism," "missionary feminism" see Strobel, Chaudhury, Davin, Purvis, and Bailey.

contextualise textual passages connecting public and private, and England and the colony, in a variety of narratives, thus mapping a significant discourse of gender and modern identity that compels us, as Simon Gikandi observes, "to read Englishness as a cultural and a literary phenomenon produced in the ambivalent space that separated, but also conjoined, metropolis and colony" (xii).

The genealogy of images tellingly frames an exemplary moment in the modern British canon. The publication of *The Voyage Out* (1915) initiated a feminist exploration of modern subjectivity, a project Virginia Woolf developed in her later fiction. Rachel's voyaging in the novel may be studied in relation to two coincidental late nineteenth-century projects of feminist self-representation: colonial romances of the Anglo-Indian passage, and the emergent discourse of the "new woman" in England. These narrative displacements emphasise that modernist texts are in conversation with marginal narratives and non-metropolitan histories, thus reframing the territorial politics of modernism. This hypothesis must necessarily bring crucial questions of "emplacement" to bear upon the canon. What is the established terrain of literary modernism? How does it coincide with the political landscape of early twentieth-century imperialism? How is the specific text "situated" in relation to authorial (dis)affiliations and (dis)placements within metropolitan cultural maps of exchange, citizenship and gender?

The literature of the Anglo-Indian passage (a specific nineteenth-century cultural narrative of voyaging) was, in a sense, overdetermined. The construction of the "Western imperial subject of modernity" and his global authority had been legitimised by two coincidental traditions of voyaging and their representations: the tradition of imperial adventure which, as Mary Louise Pratt identifies, used circumnavigation and cartography to chart its course, and the tradition of scientific voyaging, which appropriated unknown spaces within modern systems of instituted knowledge (Pratt 29-30). By the nineteenth century, stories of adventurous voyaging were being published by the

5. *Inconsequential Lives*: The Voyage Out

popular press alongside accounts of expeditions and conference proceedings promoted by the British Association for the Advancement of Science. By mid-century the advent of steam made women's mobility within this culture of travel possible. Apart from travelogues by the occasional tourist, colonial and quasi scientific explorations were now recorded in a growing body of women authored texts within the dominant tradition: Mary Kingsley, Isabella Bird, Harriet Martineau are such exemplary references.

Nineteenth-century accounts of the voyage to India thus drew on a narrative tradition of adventurous seafaring tempered by the practice of scientific geopolitics. This discourse, constituted by the accounts of travelling statesmen, soldiers, and bureaucrats, further consolidated the notion of a modern and imperial masculinity competently engaged in the enterprise of colonization.[2] The rhetoric of modernization is evident in social texts describing the technology of such voyages – in personal memoirs, travel guides, and geographical surveys. *Homeward and Outward*, an early traveller's companion to the new and more efficient route to India, describes reconstitutions of time, space and identity, and the resourceful deployment of the "public careers" of the modern administrator and technocrat as a function of the new technology of travel. "India would be forgotten [. . .] were [it] not for the doings of that great magician – STEAM. By that wondrous power, [. . .] time and space are annihilated and gigantic India and her proud ruler, small sized but mighty hearted England, are brought into close contact and made to afford a noble amplification of the power of science in the nineteenth century" (preface vi).

William Delafield Arnold's *Oakfield, or Fellowship in the East* (1853), effectively a counterpoint to the examination of national culture by Matthew Arnold, describes the transportation of collective national identity to the borders of Empire. Oakfield, a gentleman "cadet of infantry in the Bengal establishment," watches the Hoogly river in

---

[2] See Richard Phillips's account of masculinist colonial narratives.

Bengal as "the steamer from England came into sight. Here was another installment of English power: a fresh supply of that material from which soldiers and statesmen were to be formed. What generals, what council may that ship contain, besides young ladies coming out to their parents, brothers, husbands ---" (1).

Arnold's transported women transform the nineteenth-century colonial passage. Margaret Macmillan's important study of Anglo-Indian emigration describes the rapid feminisation of the passage following the establishment of a new overland route, as well as with the opening of the Suez Canal (16-21). With the increased arrival of colonial wives, sisters, and servicewomen, new stories of female migration and colonial domesticity complemented an existing tradition of masculine travel. Marriage, housekeeping, and motherhood (the ideological foundations of metropolitan female subjectivity) were incorporated within narratives of seafaring to gender a received tradition.

Macmillan records extraordinary journeys undertaken by intrepid Englishwomen during a period of rapid technological modernisation. From the late seventeenth century, the East India Company had shipped young women to India. Made in tiny wooden vessels which had to round the Cape of Good Hope, the voyage lasted about six months. In 1830, the first steamer was put into service, and in 1840 The Peninsular and Oriental Steamship Company signed an agreement with the government of India to provide a regular bimonthly service between Suez and certain Indian Ports.[3] A shorter overland route was established in 1845 when passengers crossed a narrow strip of Egyptian desert to reach the Red Sea, and then sailed across the Indian Ocean. The opening of the Suez Canal in 1869 further reduced the voyage to four weeks, and the pleasanter journey considerably increased the traffic of women travellers, "unkindly termed the fishing fleet," to the cities and outposts of the Indian Empire. The author of *Indian Outfits, A Guide for Women* (1882) was enthusiastic: "for those

---

[3] P&O became almost synonymous with the journey to India (Macmillan 20).

5. *Inconsequential Lives*: The Voyage Out

who like the sea, the voyage is very pleasant. There are generally many nice people on board, a band, and on fine nights, dancing on deck, glee parties and theatricals" (Macmillan 20). Guidebooks recommended that "ladies baggage include a chintz bag for laundry, and a provision bag with a spirit lamp, tea, and biscuits." The *Complete Indian Housekeeper and Cook* (1898) advised jocularly that "the general rule was a tweed costume for Homi-side and light dresses for Suez-side" (Steel and Gardiner 205; qtd. in Macmillan 21). Aided by technology, the feminisation of the colonial voyage had been accomplished.

By the turn of century, the exercise of rewriting the imperial "English" experience of India by service women and imported wives was evident. International routes of information exchange across the borders supported the marketing of such literature. As ships from England carried newspapers and the mail to the colonies, Anglo-Indian romances made their way to a growing readership in England.[4] These narratives of travel and marriage, housekeeping and domesticity in exile, appear transparent, a displacement of metropolitan prescriptions for the conventional and gendered life. However, the radical dislocations which shaped these "colonised" fictions point to a more complex relationship with both situated ideologies and metropolitan feminist politics. This conflict finds expression in the emotions of the voyaging heroine of Sara Duncan's 1893 novel *The Simple Adventures of a Memsahib*. Helen Francis Brown, a new bride aboard the steamer at the Royal Albert docks, feels the complexities of her situation as "[s]he felt often she was a parcel being shipped to young Brown in Calcutta, but sometimes she also felt with satisfaction that she was the first bride Canbury had contributed to India, its first feminine connection with the Empire" (24).

This journey from metropolis to periphery was shadowed by another passage, that from the private to the public sphere. Charles Tay-

---

See Bhupal Singh's *A Survey of Anglo-Indian Fiction*.

lor describes the counterspacing of the domestic and the public as fundamental to the genesis of modern identity. Even as domestic space was seen sentimentally as a "haven" in an industrialised world, middle-class female subjectivity found expression within the institutions of patriarchal marriage, the bourgeois home, and domestic work. However, the new politics of a late nineteenth-century feminist discourse challenged the association of women with the "shadowy interiors of the household" (Hannah Arendt; qtd. in Landes 85), essentially separated from the public realm of economic production and political expression. The public debate concerning women's political rights, conducted extensively in the press,[5] also renegotiated the binaries of public versus private. The emergent new woman claimed a public identity and function by revisiting the discourses of marriage, motherhood, domestic management, and thus reconstructing herself as an emancipated citizen in a reformed public culture.

The evolving politics of self-representation involved self-narration as well as critical dialogue. As the public sphere was being reformed by legislative interventions (instituting for example, rights within marriage), it was flooded by texts produced by women engaged in ideological campaigns.[6] Popular romances and conservative essays by Marie Corelli, Mrs Oliphant, Eliza Lynn Linton and social reviews in newly established journals such as *The Englishwoman's Review*, *The Girl's Own Paper*, and *Woman's World* often attempted to preserve gender relations. In contrast, a radically modern sensibility emerged in the feminist novels of "new women" and modernist writers, such as Grant, Schreiner, Syrett, Woolf, Richardson, Mansfield, as well as in essays in publications like *Votes for Women* and the *Common Cause*.[7] Commenting on Sarah Grand, Heilmann observes that the new woman

---

[5] See the 1888 debate initiated by Mona Caird in the *Daily Telegraph* (Heilmann xxvi).

[6] E.g., the Married Women's Property Act (1882), prosecution for marital rape (1891), provisions for alimony in desertion (1886) (Ledger 11).

[7] See Gardiner 1-5.

5. *Inconsequential Lives*: The Voyage Out

"strategically affirmed her domestic and maternal function to claim her political mandate and to legitimize her public persona" (xiii). The rejection of conventional marriage was framed within a social logic of development and civic regeneration. Discussing the morality of marriage in 1897, Mona Caird declared that "[w]oman purchase holds back the race from its best development." Inequality in the status of marriage partnerships and parenting are "methods which reduce human progress which alone can bring social regeneration." The emancipation of women would be "a sign and safeguard of our national liberties" (qtd. in Heilmann 16-17). Most tellingly, metaphors of the new world inhabit a new feminist imagination: "There is a whole world yet to explore in the direction of social developments and it is possible that the future hold a discovery in the domain of spirit as great as that of Columbus in the domain of matter" (qtd. in Heilmann 111).

The re-imagining of domesticity as part of a feminist self-fashioning underwent strange transformations when transported to the colonial borderlands. Usually read as conventional stories that support conservative imperial ideology, Anglo-Indian romances of travel and housekeeping also help identify the complexities of gendered self-definition.[8] As in the writings of Woolf, Richardson, and Mansfield, these exiled romances also suggest that modernist conceptions of gendered identity are marked by anxiety, dislocation, and alienation within bourgeois culture. The texts become complex sites where the gendered politics of metropolitan identity are rethought or affirmed. Maud Diver's *The Englishwoman in India* deconstructs the notion of an unified gendered identity even as it works to describe a coherent colonial subject, while Sara Duncan's *Simple Adventures of a Memsahib* disrupts the conventional order of domestic management in the Anglo-Indian home, thus unsettling a national discourse instituted as the modern discipline of domestic science in English schools; Con-

---

[8] E.g., Benita Parry's reading of "lady romancers" (*Delusions and Discoveries* 6).

stance Sitwell's *Flowers and Elephants* proposes a new aesthetic response as it rejects both the colonial voyage and the marriage plot.

Maud Diver's *The Englishwoman in India* (1909) can be read as a conventional account of the female colonial subject, a structural analysis which uses chapter headings (maid, wife, mother, housekeeper) to construct the analyzed subject. She is defined in opposition to underdeveloped Eastern Womanhood; her proper function is teaching, nursing, home-industries, and needlecraft. Despite the seemingly confident categorisations, Diver emphasises the fragility of such social identification. As the "sister-woman" of English femininity, the Anglo-Indian woman occupies a space of absence in relation to official history, as Diver notes: "These unrecognised women are a nation without a history. Their history rarely supplies effective material for fiction and, in consequence, their existence has come to be doubted this side of the ocean" (21). Disobedient to the requirements of the culture of domesticity, she is described as "a creature primarily social, secondarily domestic" (33). Visiting Englishwomen notice signs of quiet indiscipline, described in reports of the absence of daily worship in the Anglo-Indian home, or of how the ladies "keep late hours and drink too much" (Barr 89). Even as Anglo-Indian domestic life became more elaborate and established, "the sequence of the mofussil" appears monotonous to the Englishwoman confined within her home. Here, she feels acutely the routine of "recurring baths and siestas, recurring notes of the same polka, the flat stare of the white bedroom walls ----. A monotonous life" (Barr 149). She is told to practise organization, economy and supervision in her housekeeping, but subverts the ethic of work by her access to infinite leisure. Diver seems to concede her dissociation: "In her cool dim drawing room with its soft carpets and easy chairs, the Englishwoman in India seems the incarnation of limitless leisure," and preserves a "grace lost to the Englishwoman in these bustling times, in this material age ---" (53).

The fundamental instability in her construction lies in the impossibility of resolution of two radical functions: that of wife and mother.

5. *Inconsequential Lives*: The Voyage Out

The contradictions of "the tragic note of this separation, which is the keynote of Anglo-India" (46), bring her to a "moment of Crisis," and mark her life "with the rival claims of India and England: of Husband and child. Sooner or later the lurking shadow of separation take definite shape; asserts itself as a harsh reality – whispering the inevitable question 'Which shall it be?'" (37). As a counterpoint to such colonial deconstructions, a continuing national discourse of imperial as well as reformist maternalism increasingly supported feminist claims of responsible citizenship.[9]

Narratives of domesticated femininity, crucial to a national feminist discourse, remain similarly unsettled in colonial adaptations. Sara Jeanette Duncan, American journalist and colonial wife, published the *Simple Adventures of a Memsahib* in 1893. The text records the development of Helen Brown, a brand-new memsahib, as she consolidates her identity as Anglo-Indian wife, mother, and housekeeper. Helen's progress is interrupted periodically as experiences in the kitchen and with her Indian domestic disrupt the efficient implementation of rational supervision and accounting. The narrative is positioned in relation to an ideological project in which both metropolitan and Anglo-Indian attempts to systemise and modernise domestic work prescribed that such management was necessary for the efficient functioning of the middle-class kitchen and, by extension, the nation and its colonies.

In this context, a new practical education for the modern Englishwoman increasingly institutionalised domestic arts as civic instruction. Instruction manuals advised that the school curriculum should formalise the methods of rational home management into an academic discipline to ensure public order and civic progress. A 1911 essay observes that "we have come to see that method and system are better than rule of thumb and guesswork. Housekeeping is as a science as an art --- and the Board of Education has done much to help further this aim"

---

[9] See Anna Davin's "Imperialism and Motherhood" and Jane Purvis's *Women's History*.

(*Home Arts*; qtd. in Gardiner 93). Sarah Grand calls on the "womanly" feminist to "set the human household in order, to see that all is sweet and clean and comfortable for the men who are fit to help us make a home in it" (276). A 1910 manual comments that "unless women's work is well done, they [nations] cannot succeed. For unhappy homes cannot a happy nation make" (*Home Management*; qtd. in Gardiner 94).

Colonial narratives of responsible domesticity often express a similar political consciousness. Flora Annie Steel and Grace Gardiner published *The Complete Indian Housekeeper and Cook* in 1898, to advice "English girls tasked to be house mothers in the Eastern empire," and who, upon arrival, "find themselves bereft of all the familiar landmarks of efficient housewifery" (qtd. in Barr 153). The essential homemaker's companion observes that "the Indian household can no more be governed peacefully without dignity, order, and prestige than can the Indian Empire" (Steel and Gardiner 9). Recognizing that "the memsahib's only remedy is to equip herself with sufficient knowledge to assert her authority and bring Western order to Eastern chaos," the text systematically and exhaustively describes the methods necessary to negotiate the details of Anglo-Indian domestic life. At its heart lies the distinct challenge of the colonial kitchen. The Indian kitchen and its native labour is particularised as the necessary object of surveillance, management and sanitised order. The unreformed kitchen is "a black hole, the pantry is a sink, the only help is a sulking savage with a red broom ---" (qtd. in Barr 153). The labouring memsahib transforms the space, making it "airy and wholesome," efficiently managing the accounts and the supplies, and inspecting and routinely "purging all dirty customs so ingrained in native cooks." Steel and Gardiner exactingly demand "bright glass, shining silver, crisp napkins and wholesome broths" on the colonial table and board. Confronting the memsahib's authority is the native cook, untutored, yet potentially threatening in his ability to deceive his innocent mistress and undermine improving regulations (qtd. in Barr 154-55). *The English Bride-*

5. *Inconsequential Lives*: The Voyage Out

1908, a guide for new memsahibs, cautions, "Be patient with your servants and treat them like children. Remember they like praise, and too much cannot be expected of them. They are slow to change their ways and innovation must be cautiously employed" (qtd. in Macmillan 144). The effective supervision of native staff demanded firmness, consistency, kindness, and significantly, linguistic proficiency. The guidebooks are unanimous: "To administer and give intelligible orders to her servants, it is necessary that the mistress should learn to speak in Hindustani ---. One of the main reasons why so many [Englishwomen] remain strangers in a strange land for years on is their inabililty to communicate with the Indian in the vernacular ---. This is a grave omission" (Steel and Gardiner 3-4).[10]

In *The Simple Adventures*, it is significant that Helen's disruptive kitchen prevents authoritative housekeeping. Her domestic authority is mediated through politicised structures of language that she is excluded from and which are re-appropriated by the unmethodical subordinates in their acts of obedience. Helen's domestics, Kali Bagh (cook) and Chui (ayah), challenge Anglo-Indian values of ordered domesticity and contented motherhood. Helen recognises early that Kali Bagh, the head bawarchi, whose disorderly and mysterious domestic methods exceed "understandings accustomed to kitchen ranges of Christianity and civilization," is an "eminently suitable subject for discipline." However, even as "Helen found herself confronted with her little domestic corner of the great problem of India – the 'native's way' – [she realized that] she had no language with which to circumvent it, or remonstrate with it" (86).

The text delineates the coloniser's acquisition of the language of government: "the Government of India has done nothing to stimulate intercourse with the native population among memsahibs. So the memsahib picks up the language in an artless way, gathers her vo-

---

[10] Anglo-Indian wives were encouraged to become linguistically proficient, but the same was not true of their servants (Macmillan 144).

cabulary from every region, makes her own rules, adds her own admixture of English. She subdues the language to her own use, and the natives she knows are governed by them" (227). Helen's dinner dialogue with her cook ends with the instruction, "You can plum pudding do. And dekho, curry hazri na muncta, tiffin muncta." The text qualifies the exchange thus:

> The last statement is to the effect that curry does not want breakfast, it wants lunch, but the heathen mind never translates the memsahib directly. It picks the words it knows out of her discourse and links them together upon a system of probabilities which long application has made remarkably correct. Then it salaams and acts. The usually admirable result is misleading to the memsahib who naturally ascribes it to the grace and force and clarity of her directions. Whereas it is really the discernment of Kali Bagh the cook that is to be recommended. (229)

The exchange in the kitchen is a telling instance of how the conventional narrative obliquely subverts domestic hierarchy and communicative rationality, so valued in the Western liberal public sphere.

Constance Sitwell described her *Flowers and Elephants* (1927) as "the travel impressions of a young lady who went to stay with her brother in India, where she had one or two offers of marriage, --- she attends Brigade sports and peeps at maharajas and bazaars, she idles in clubs" (11). "How well one knows it all!" (11) remarked E. M. Forster in the preface to the novel, cataloguing the familiar episodes structuring Anglo-Indian women's lives. But Forster also notes that Sitwell's account defamiliarises the generic narrative by attempting a deliberate negotiation between the Anglo-Indian marriage plot and a new aesthetic response to this cultural imperative. The voyage out, for instance, is described in a paragraph in which orientalist and modernist discourse intersect.

5. *Inconsequential Lives*: The Voyage Out

> I can hear the swish of the sea now as I write, and the quiet noise of the ship as we go very smoothly through the gulf of Suez. I am alone on deck. There are some Lascars rolling up some awnings in front of me. The lithe figures in fluttering indigo and their bare brown legs are dark against the sparkling sea. I do want, when I travel, to write of those unforgettable little spaces of time that come when imagination is merged into living in a special way, and the thing becomes like a work of art, intense, significant, separate. (23)

The protagonist evades proposals throughout her Indian season, fearing they "would draw her out of her world of the imagination and pattern seeking," and that marriage would make her feel "captive, indefinite" (59). Intensely alienated, she asks herself, "what am I here for?" (84), and returns to England. There she feels the absence of India: "there are moments when England seems pale and mild and grey." There are no "scorching suns, stupendous snows, ash colored staring figures." The "sharpness of feeling is blunted," the "transience of things stabs my mind." But then, a sudden moment of epiphany concludes the narrative. "The disquiet falls away from me. I feel reality, I know permanence. I shall find the vision, the flowers, the jungles --- where the pattern of these things eternally dwells" (151-53). The novel is tentatively attentive to the radical possibilities of aesthetic practice, and as such shares a platform with metropolitan modernist texts.

These thematic correspondences between colonial romance and domestic feminist discourse describe a representational field that, through rewriting new fictions of female subjectivity, collapses the binaries of metropolis and periphery. *The Voyage Out* seems radically informed by just such a reconfigured sense of space and responsive to its political implications. Such multiple locations suggest that literary constructions of colonial voyaging in modern fiction often share space with social texts of modernity which negotiate the geographies of Empire. By examining how the gendered voyage in Woolf's narrative maintains a strategic relationship with a wider imperial discourse, we remain attentive to a "border" discourse that infiltrates the official culture of modernism by de-territorialising it from within.

Woolf's stories describing the migrations of modern identity often revisit the spatial image of the sea; her essays consistently analyse how the imperial sea voyage is used to support a variety of constructions, such as history, subjectivity, and aesthetics. Several essays, including "Richard Hakluyt," "Trafficks and Discoveries," "The Elizabethan Lumbar Room," use emblematic colonial journeys of Elizabethan "voyages, traffics and discoveries to unknown lands" on "the uncharted Elizabethan sea" – that answer a summons to explore, to bring back dyes and roots and oil, and to find a market for wool and iron and cloth ("Elizabethan" 46-47). The process describes how the colonizing nation state is permeated by alien materials. The constitution of a modern national landscape is dependent upon this exchange: "Gradually, owing to the boldness of private travelers, the native stock was improved and embellished." "Beasts and herbs" were imported, and along with them the seeds of "the damask rose and the tulip." As little groups of merchant men settled here and there on the "outskirts of the world," the "precious stream of colored and rare and curious things began slowly and precariously to flow towards London"; English fields were "sown with new flowers ---" ("Reading" 160-161). As such, the essays describe how a history of adventurous, scientific and commercial travel abroad informed domestic English identity. "Strange must have been their thoughts," Woolf imagines, "strange the sense of the unknown, and of themselves," – "the isolated English, --- burning on the very rim of the dark," and "the dark full of unseen splendors" ("Reading" 161). Such transformations of consciousness are reflected in a new poetics – "Thus we find the whole of Elizabethan literature strewn with gold and silver." From narratives of adventure which are marked by the absence of the psychological subject, Woolf notices the development of autobiography, the scripting of a

5. *Inconsequential Lives*: The Voyage Out

"growing consciousness of self, the brooding over the mysteries of the soul --- with talk of Guiana's rarities and references to that America --- which was not merely a land on the map, but symbolized the unknown territories of the soul" ("Elizabethan" 49).

The Voyage Out is Woolf's first attempt at a narrative recasting of the colonial voyage that arrives at a new feminist aesthetics of self-representation while maintaining a critical relationship with an imperial, seafaring tradition. It is also Woolf's first significant revision of received notions of gendered identity. Adapting the conventions of the *Bildungsroman*, the narrative interrupts the protagonist's formation and presents tragic schisms between interior and public identities. The voyage of the vessel "Euphrosyne," sailing to the "forgotten" colony of Santa Marina as "a bride going forth to her husband," introduces the marriage plot in which Rachel's identity is defined, and also connects the narrative with a past colonial history: "Three hundred years ago, five Elizabethan barques had anchored where the Euphrosyne now floated. Half drawn up on the beach lay an equal number of Spanish galleons, unmanned, for the country was still a virgin land behind a veil" (*Voyage* 96). [11]

The image reminds us that literary constructions of colonial voyaging in fiction register specific intertextual and ideological references. Lorna Sage observes that the metaphor of the voyaging ship is repeated within texts which engage with a particular "literary trope," in the words of Henry James, that of "the conception of a young woman confronting her destiny" (qtd. in Sage xix). Rachel's literary antecedents, like the voyaging women of popular colonial romances, seem constructed as repositories of "essential cultural signification and continuity", transporting such metropolitan values across history as they do across the landscape of the Empire. Sage notes that Woolf "turns the image around" in an act of modernist disruption. (xix). In *The*

---

[11] See Karen Lawrence's analysis of the Euphrosyne as a "proliferating" symbol (154-56).

Voyage Out, the voyaging ship and its significant journey rearranges notions of settled gendered identity and imperial spatial relations. The metropolitan text uses the trope of the (colonial) voyage to explore a disruptive identity politics – the feminist negotiation of the distance between the public and private. Sage's observations suggest that it is the transportation of such ideological practices to colonized locations that initiated a radical aesthetic response to the crisis of gendered identity. The narrative traces the trajectory of Rachel's education in the demarcation of spheres, but she ultimately rejects the old dialectic of public/private by recognising the "domestic" as the colonised other of a patriarchal public order. *The Voyage Out* stages the "private" instead; a space of interiority, absence, and proto-feminist self-consciousness offers a modernist rejection of prescribed subjectivity.

While Woolf was working on an early first draft of the novel in South Wales during the summer of 1908, she described the sea there: "It is the sea that does it! Perpetual motion, and a border of mystery, solving the limits of fields and solving their mystery" (letter 1, 438). In the novel, the seascape offers a spatial arrangement of metropolis and colony and the fluid spaces in between. The novel visually dislocates spatial relations of power. At the start of the narrative, the Euphrosyne embarks upon the dark waters of the Thames and the narrative perspective moves along with the ship and away from London. The imperial city recedes, and is rendered immobile, circumscribed, scarred. The metropolitan "situated" imagination, which cannot admit expansions, is replaced in the text by an unfettered voyaging perspective, which escapes the notice of the landlocked gaze:

> They were now moving steadily down the river, passing the dark shapes of ships at anchor, and London was a swarm of lights ---. It seemed dreadful that the town should blaze forever in the same spot; dreadful at least to people going away to adventure upon the sea, and beholding it as a circumscribed mound, eternally burnt, eternally scarred. From the

5. *Inconsequential Lives*: The Voyage Out

> deck of the ship, the great city appeared a crouched and cowardly figure, a sedentary miser (*Voyage* 13).[12]
>
> But while all this went on by land, very few people thought about the sea ---. For all they imagined, the ships when they vanished in the skyline dissolved, like snow in water ---. The people in ships, however, took an equally singular view of England. Not only did it appear to them to be an island, and a very small island, but it was a shrinking island on which people were imprisoned. (29)

The voyage carries the narrative to Santa Marina, and the vast and minute spaces of an alien landscape. The early expedition of the hotel guests to Monte Rosa lays out extensive and intimate vistas of South American land to visiting English eyes. The ascent brings them to vistas of "immense space, gray sands running into forests, --- the infinite distances of South America ---. The effect of so much space was at first rather chilling. Then Evelyn exclaimed "Splendid!" --- 'North – South – East – West' said Miss Allen" (146). The narrative presents the experience of a de-historicised South American landscape, often in terms of a "humanistic geography," where characters inhabit a subjective world in which relations of power find symbolic expression as fantasies of colonisation.[13] The political categorisation of colonial references is significant, however. The dreams of adventure engendered by the landscape divide into fantasies of colonial empowerment and those of anti-colonial identification. These categories ally themselves with moments in the text which focus on the possibilities of female participation within, or its exclusion from the public sphere of modernity. A displaced perception surveys and appropriates new territories and occasionally scrutinises fixed spatial relations of power.

---

[12] The text quoted in this chapter is from Lorna Sage's edition of *The Voyage Out*.

[13] Forster commented that it was "a South America not found on any map, and reached by a boat which would not float on any sea" (qtd. in Lawrence 53).

During the expedition "the great size of the view seemed to enlarge [Rachel's] eyes beyond their natural limit, she looked at the ground; it pleased her to scrutinize this inch of the soil of South America so minutely that she noticed every grain of earth and made it into a world where she was endowed with supreme power" (157). Thornbury and Eliot become "anxious to name the places beneath them [and add to them] information about armies and navies, political parties, navies, and mineral products – all of which combined, they said, to prove that South America was the country of the future" (151). Evelyn imagines "fighting, revolution," the conquest of territory, and "longs to be a man." "If, instead of a picnic party, this was a party of patriots, and she, red shirted like the rest had lain among grim men, flat on the turf, aiming her gun [---]" (144), she would "raise a troop and conquer some territory, and make it splendid" (151).

Evelyn's desire to enter official history is contrasted with Rachel's sense of epistemic exclusion from patriarchal learning. "Oh how I detest modern life!" Evelyn regrets. "It must have been so much easier for the Elizabethans! --- how I'd have liked to be one of those colonists, to cut down trees and make laws and all that, instead of fooling about with all these people who think one is just a pretty young lady" (*Voyage* 216). When Rachel's lack of schooling in the classics is analysed by Hirst as either "lack of training or native incapacity," her alienation from the "indifferent, sneering" eyes of the company at the ball transports her into a gendered Oriental fantasy which confirms her distance from domestic patriarchal culture: "She would be a Persian princess far from civilization, riding her horse upon the mountains alone, and making her women sing to her in the evening, far from all this, from the strife of men and women ---" (172-73). Hirst sends Rachel Gibbon's *Rise and Fall of the Roman Empire* as an introduction to the classics, but it is an anti-colonial poetics in the book which catches her attention:

5. *Inconsequential Lives*: The Voyage Out

> The invading generals, in the early part of his reign, attempted the reduction of Aethiopia and Arabia Felix; --- but the heat of the climate soon repelled the invaders, and protected the unwarlike natives of those sequestered regions --- the northern countries of Europe --- were filled with a hardy race of barbarians, who despised life when it was separated from freedom. Never had any words been so vivid and so beautiful – Arabia Felix – Aethiopia. But those were not more noble than the others, hardy barbarians, forests, and morasses. --- Such was her excitement at the possibilities of knowledge now opening before her that she ceased to read, ---. (196)

The textual representation of a non-metropolitan territory, aestheticised as an object of colonial desire and politicised as the site of patriarchal domination, becomes the stage of Rachel's de-socialisation. The marriage plot which charts Rachel's cultural destiny is projected into this space, and the narrative trajectory is poised between the possibility of social individuation and the threat of dissolution. Ultimately, the refusal to negotiate an identity politics based on the separation of the spheres impels the narrative toward a radical crisis and Rachel's death. Identifying the breakdown of the marriage plot (which "preserves and is predicated upon the notion of separate spheres") as crucial to the tragic movement of the narrative, Christine Froula notices how "Rachel is slow to grasp the idea of separate spheres so crucial to the marriage plot" (145). Rachel's destiny is poised between dual alternatives: a happy conclusion which includes love and marriage, *or* the impossibility of its achievement; the fulfilment of a socialised destiny, *or* the retreat into a space of privacy separated from the imperatives of gendered location.

In a speech delivered in London to the National Society for Women's Service, Woolf described a contemporary "political" murder: that of the "angel in the house," and wondered whether "having rid herself of falsehood, so we may put it, [the modern woman] now only had to be herself ---. But what is herself? I mean, what is a woman?" ("Professions" 60). Woolf points to the political dimensions of the reconstitution of modern subjectivity; Hewett in *The Voyage Out* reflects upon persisting gender exclusions in the public sphere, in essence, a dichotomous world: "what a miracle the masculine conception of life is – judges, civil servants, army, navy, Houses of Parliament, lord mayors – what a world we've made of it! --- It'll take at least six generations before [women] are sufficiently thick skinned to go into law courts and business offices" (240).

Exploring the "private and public negotiations" in Woolf's life and work, Anna Snaith notes her ambivalence toward the possibilities of the new politics of public identities and functions for women. "The suffrage movement, the most public issue confronting women at that time, evoked varying responses from Woolf," Snaith observes; "when the suffragettes first used violent tactics, Woolf questioned her commitment ---, [and] she could not support a campaign that single mindedly believed that political power would bring an end to all other types of oppression of women" (30). In *The Voyage Out,* the implicit rejection of the "public political" is communicated by a consistent identification of the unified imperial subject, (the anti-thesis of the decentered modernist subject), as the agent of the "public political" sphere (exemplified by Clarissa and Richard Dalloway's boarding of the Euphrosyne). Rachel's first political conversation is with Richard Dalloway, whose description of the conditions of modern society's gender and economic relations is predicated upon conservative, patriarchal, and imperial ideas. The expansion of an imperial culture characterised by its rational efficiency depends upon gendered divisions for its material and political well-being. Before Richard's adulterous kiss (which initiates Rachel into the dangers of male seduction and betrayal), Dalloway states his Utilitarian ideal: to be "the citizen of the Empire," to promote "Unity. Unity of aim, of dominion, of progress. The dispersion of the best ideas over the greatest area", as a function

5. *Inconsequential Lives*: The Voyage Out

of being "English, [who are] whiter than most men, their records cleaner" (67). The conception of the unified subject is central to a modern public order of organic action and organised functioning. "The human being is not a set of compartments, but an organism," Dalloway declares; "we citizens are parts of [a modern machine-state] ---, yet if the meanest screw fails in its task, the proper working of the whole is imperiled" (69).

At the close of this description of citizen-identity, the ships of Empire sail past the Euphrosyne:

> [Clarissa] had sighted two sinister gray vessels, low in the water, and as bald as bone, one closely following the other with the look of eyeless beasts. Consciousness returned to Richard immediately. "By George" he exclaimed----. "Ours Dick?" said Clarissa. "The Mediterranean Fleet", he answered. The Euphrosyne was slowly dipping her flag. Richard raised his hat. Convulsively Clarissa squeezed Rachel's hand. "Aren't you glad to be English?" she asked. (72)

This narrative critique of political assimilation within a compromised public sphere forces the consideration of an alternate space: the domestic. Rachel is "twenty four years of age, daughter of a ship owner, has never been properly educated" (159), with "face that was weak rather than decided, [marked by] a lack of colour and definite outline" (15). Her formation into "a woman like her mother" (i.e., a Tory hostess for her father's home and a suitable wife for Terence) are possibilities available at the start of the voyage. The movement toward the possibility of a happy narrative conclusion using the convention of marriage is crucially undermined by consistent interrogations of settled categories. Woolf declared in *The Three Guineas* that "the private and the public worlds are inseparably connected, the tyrannies and servilities of one are the tyrannies and servilities of the other" (258).

Several voices in the novel describe the "tyrannies and servilities" of domesticity. Contemplating marriage to Rachel, Terence presents his "case against marriage," characterising it as a bourgeois compromise inimical to authentic individuation: "He tried all sorts of [mental] pictures, taking them from the lives of friends of his, for he knew many different married couples; but he saw them always, walled up in a warm fire-lit room. When, on the other hand, he began to think of unmarried people, he saw them active in an unlimited world; above all, standing on the same ground as the rest, without shelter or advantage" (281). Terence and Rachel both recall the conditions of female domesticity, which are marked by silence, isolation, invisibility, and routine service performed for fathers, brothers and husbands.

Terence observes: "I've often walked along streets where people live all in a row, and one house is exactly like another house, and wondered what on earth the women were doing inside ---. There it was going on in the background, for all those thousands of years, this curious, silent, unrepresented life" (245).

Evelyn M, who is most nearly the "new woman" of Santa Marina society, notices the political consequences of the spatial confinements of marriage: "love was all very well, and those snug domestic houses, with the kitchen below and the nursery above, which were so secluded and self-contained, like little islands in the torrents of the world; but the real things were surely the things that happened, the causes, the wars, the ideals, which happened in the great world outside, and went on independently of these women" (373).[14] Her rejection of the domestic implies an active, public commitment to feminist politics and socialism. "Of course they were happy and content, but there must be better things than that," Evelyn observes; "surely one could get nearer to life, one could get more out of life" (374).

Though Rachel and Evelyn both escape domestication, the novel emphasises the location of Evelyn's self-definition within the "public-

---

[14] For an overview of the politics and literature of the "new women" activists, see Snaith; Ledger 45-46.

5. *Inconsequential Lives*: The Voyage Out

ity" of social modernity and its difference from the "privacy" of Rachel's self-construction. Evelyn's socialisation contrasts with Rachel's recourse to radical privacy, her aesthete's apprehensions of an "intolerable" intercourse with the world which impedes her. Rachel suffers divisions between the self and the world: "She disliked the look of it immensely – churches, politicians, misfits, and huge impostures – men like Mr. Dalloway, men like Mr. Bax, Evelyn and her chatter --- her own body was the source of all the life in the world, which tried to burst forth here --- and was repressed now by --- the weight of the entire world" (301).

Rachel's crisis, Tony Jackson suggests, reflects the "epistemological shift in sensibility [displayed in] modernist art. "Superficially individualist, it frees the individual from the social frameworks of country, church, and family," Jackson notes, "but the individuality thus achieved, quite unlike nineteenth century affirmative liberal selfhood, is deeply collective, apprehended through the body, the unconscious, and the mediating functions of language and myth in relation to the conscious" (55). Often, Rachel's reveries of "self-forgetting" are represented in an "aesthetics of dissolution," which seem appropriate to Woolf's political suspicions of the "threat of egotism." The narrative consistently betrays Rachel's virginity and sexual inexperience: "There are terrors and agonies. Women one sees on the streets --- Things one guesses at," she observes. "You were never told?" Terence asks. "She shook her head. Here came in the great spaces of life no one had penetrated" (247). She had a body "with the angles and hollows of a young woman's body not yet developed," and "her twenty four years of life had given her a look of reserve" (238). Rachel's conversations are often failed attempts at connection, and she seeks in music the notations missing in words. In a sense, the textual reluctance to compromise such a reserve, the attempts to (fatally) arrest her maturity constantly undermine the conventional structure of the female *Bildungsroman* and suggest a larger representational project:

Woolf's rejection of the epistemic and philosophical basis of the unified subject of realism.

On occasion, Rachel celebrates her exclusion and neglect. "A girl is more lonely than a boy. No one cares in the least what she does," she reflects, "and that is what I like ---. I like the freedom of it ---. It's like being the wind or the sea" (248). Hewett, depressed, thinks "she would never care for one person more than another; she was evidently quite indifferent to him." He remains apprehensive and aware of the impossibility of connection, desire, and consummation. He wonders, "What did she feel? Did she love him, or did she feel nothing at all for him, or for any other man, being, as she had said that afternoon, free, like the wind or the sea?" (283).

The radical indifference of Rachel and her desire for freedom, isolation, withdrawal and eventually death, registers an implicit rejection of domesticity and the marriage plot, as an alternative to the ideologically compromised "public political." Rachel's last expedition on the Amazon is an emblematic episode, crystallising the symbolic movements and ideological crossings of the longer narrative journey undertaken by Woolf's voyaging imagination. The river passage brings to her an acceptance of a proposal of marriage, but also brings her close to fevers, dreams, deliriums, dissolution, an apprehension of "the body, the unconscious, the unsettling mediations of language and myth" (Jackson 55). Vulnerable to tropical airs and infections which thwart a conventional closure to the marriage plot, the voyage into the heart of the jungle brings the narrative to an appropriate space where a new aesthetic response is presented.[15] Here, a conventional resolution

---

[15] Woolf's letters indicate a distaste for foreign landscapes and people, and an intense fear of dirt, infection and contamination that made her describe travel as "a disease from which the brain recovers in a day or two" (letter 1, 187). After a trip to Greece in 1906, her brother Thoby, her sister Vanessa, and her friend Viola Dickenson all contracted typhoid; Thoby died from the attack within a month. Woolf asserts, "The only thing in this world is music – music and books, and one or two pictures. I am going to found a colony where there

5. *Inconsequential Lives*: The Voyage Out

to the marriage plot is rejected, and the formation of gendered identity within patriarchal and imperial spaces is definitively and finally interrupted. As the infection invades her body and mind, the closing scenes of Rachel's sick room bring the reader close to the acuteness and extravagance of Rachel's senses: the dreams of submergence, the hallucinations and deliriums most intensely expressing her withdrawals into a singular privacy, the breakdown of the coherent self, the death of the body which may have been traditionally socialised and consolidated.

After a three-week-long bridal voyage aboard the SS Aurora in 1898, Mary Curzon arrived at a "pageant of dangerous heat and tropical illness" staged in the grand Government House in Calcutta, her home where "squalid bats and fever laden mosquitoes appeared among the brocade and the ormolu" (Fowler 256). As Rachel lies dying of tropical fever, she imagines a certain deliverance:

> The sights were all concerned in some adventure, some escape. --- Now they were among trees and savages, now they were on the sea ----. But just as the crisis was about to happen, something invariably slipped in her brain, so that the whole effort had had to begin over again. The heat was suffocating. At least the faces went further away; she fell into a deep pool of sticky water, which eventually closed over her head. She saw nothing and heard nothing but a faint booming sound, which was the sound of the sea rolling over her head. (397).

Rachel's last delirium stages the crisis, repeats the vocabulary of a familiar imaginative landscape of an "adventure and an escape," of

---

will be no marrying --- no human element at all, except what comes through Art" (letter 1, 43).

trees, savages and an engulfing sea, and significantly transforms a defining cultural narrative.

Works Cited

Arnold, W. D. *Oakfield, or Fellowship in the East*. London: Longman, Brown and Green, 1854.

Bailey, Susan F. *Women and the British Empire: An Annotated Guide to Sources*. New York: Garland, 1983.

Barr, Pat. *The Memsahibs: Women of Victorian India*. London: Secker and Warburg, 1976.

Caird, Mona. *The Morality of Marriage*. London: George Redway, 1897.

Corelli, Marie, Flora Annie Steel, and Susan, Countess of Malmesbury. *The Modern Marriage Market*. London, Hutchinson, 1898.

Davin, Anna. "Imperialism and Motherhood." *Tensions of Empire: Colonial Culture in a Bourgeois World*. Ed. Frederick Cooper and Ann Laura Stoler. Berkeley: University of California Press, 1997. 87-151.

Diver, Maud. *The Englishwoman in India*. London: W. Blackwood and Son, 1909.

Duncan, Sara. *The Simple Adventures of a Memsahib*. New York: D. Appleton and Company, 1893.

Fowler, Marian. *Below the Peacock Fan: First Ladies of the Raj*. Ontario: Penguin, 1979.

Forster, E. M. "Forword." *Flowers and Elephants*. By Constance Sitwell. New York: Harcourt Brace, 1911. 7-14.

Froula, Christine. "Out of the Chrysalis: Female Initiation and Female Authority in Virginia Woolf's *The Voyage Out*." *Virginia Woolf: A Collection of Critical Essays*. Ed. Margaret Homans. Englewood Cliffs, NJ: Prentice Hall, 1993.

Gardiner, Juliet, ed. *The New Woman: Women's Voices 1880-1918*. London: Collins and Brown, 1993.

5. *Inconsequential Lives*: The Voyage Out

Gikandi, Simon. *Maps of Englishness: Writing Identity in the Culture of Colonialism.* New York: Columbia University Press, 1996.

Grand, Sarah. "The New Aspect of the Woman Question." *North American Review* 158 (1894): 270-76.

Heilmann, Ann, ed. *Marriage and Motherhood. The Late Victorian Marriage Question.* London: Routledge,1998.

Jackson, Tony E. *The Subject of Modernism: Narrative Alterations in the Fiction of Conrad, Woolf and Joyce.* Ann Arbor: University of Michigan Press, 1994.

Landes, Joan B. "The Public and the Private Sphere: A Feminist Reconsideration." *Feminism: The Public and the Private.* Oxford and New York: Oxford University Press, 1998. 135-63.

Ledger, Sally. *The New Woman: Fiction and Feminism at the Fin de Siècle.* Manchester: Manchester University Press, 1997.

Lawrence, Karen. *Penelope Voyages: Women and Tradition in the British Literary Tradition.* Ithaca: Cornell University Press, 1994.

Macmillan, Margaret Olwen. *Women of the Raj.* London: Thames and Hudson, 1988.

Parry, Benita. *Delusions and Discoveries: Studies on India in the British Imagination.* Berkeley: University of California Press, 1979.

Phillips, Richard. *Mapping Men and Empire: A Geography of Empire.* New York: Routledge, 1997.

Pratt, Mary Louise. *Imperial Eyes: Travel Writing and Transculturation.* London and New York, Routledge, 1992.

Purvis, June, ed. "An Introduction: White Women, Race and Empire." *Women's History: Britain 1850-1945.* London: UCL, 1998. 261-68.

Sage, Lorna. Introduction. *The Voyage Out.* By Virginia Woolf. Oxford: Oxford University Press, 1992. xii – xxix.

Singh, Bhupal. *A Survey of Anglo-Indian Fiction.* Oxford: Oxford University Press, 1934.

Sitwell, Constance. *Flowers and Elephants.* New York: Harcourt, Brace, 1911.

Snaith, Anna. *Virginia Woolf: Public and Private Negotiations*. New York: Palgrave, 2000.

Steel, Flora Annie, and Grace Gardiner. The *Complete Indian Housekeeper and Cook*. London: W. Heinemann, 1898.

Strobel, Margaret, and Nupur Chaudhuri, eds. *Western Women and Imperialism: Complicity and Resistance*. Bloomington: Indiana University Press, 1991.

Taylor, Charles. *Sources of the Self: The Making of Modern Identity*. Cambridge, Mass.: Harvard University Press, 1989.

Woolf, Virginia. *The Voyage Out*. London: Hogarth, 1915.

___. *The Voyage Out*. Ed. Lorna Sage. Oxford: Oxford University Press, 1992.

___. "The Elizabethan Lumbar Room." *Collected Essays*. Ed. Leonard Woolf. Vol. 1. London: Hogarth, 1966. 46-54.

___. "Professions for Women." *Virginia Woolf: Women and Writing*. Ed. Michele Barrett. London: Harcourt, Brace, 1979. 57-64.

___. "Trafficks and Discoveries." *The Essays of Virginia Woolf*. Ed. Andrew McNeillie. Vol. 2. London: Hogarth, 1986. 326.

___. "Richard Hakluyt." *The Essays of Virginia Woolf*. Ed. Andrew McNeillie. Vol. 3. London: Hogarth, 1986. 450.

___. "Reading." *The Captain's Deathbed and Other Essays*. Ed. Leonard Woolf. New York: Harcourt Brace, 1952. 151-80.

___. *Three Guineas*. 1938. London: Hogarth, 1952.

___. *The Letters of Virginia Woolf*. Vol. 1. Ed. Nigel Nicholson and Joanne Trautman. New York: Harvest, 1978.

6. Remade Womanhoods, Refashioned Modernities: The Construction of "Good Womanhood" in *Annisa*, an Early Twentieth-Century Women's Magazine in Urdu

Rekha Pande, K. C. Bindu, Viqar Atiya
Maulana Azad National Urdu University, Hyderabad

> [T]he underbelly of every attempt towards identity has been a redescription of women of different classes. (Vaid and Sangari 9)

In recent times, the figure of the Muslim woman is seen as a cause of concern as well as a site of "reform" in the public discourses in India. Her alternating figure swings between the image of the oppressed victim and that of the perpetrator of a threatening minority culture. The national (read 'majority community') perception in India, due to many accidents in history, coincides with the figure she has become in the international scene also after the tragic events of 11 September 2001. But the construction of the Muslim woman's image within the community has not been discussed enough. This is the context which takes us back into the colonial past.

"Re-forming" the Muslim woman

The late nineteenth and the early twentieth centuries were periods of the extension of control and influence of colonial ideology in India. The understanding of these times as formative periods in modern Indian history is unquestioned. During that period, almost all the communities in the country underwent profound changes in negotiating with modernity. Identities were changing or being formed.

Along with other changes in the public sphere changes in the family structure occurred. For the nascent middle classes, the private sphere was being moulded into a particular shape during this period. Many communities moved towards notions of the modern individual. This imagined individual was ideally placed within a nuclear family. Gender, it has been well documented, served as an important site for such a transformation and "reform." Recent works on this period even suggest that the process of gendering was central to the programme of "reform" itself (Vaid and Sangari 9; Devika 6). Social reform in India did not come about through the sudden emergence of the "individual" in the public field. In the context of sharp caste and religious divisions, the reform agenda could only be taken up on a community basis. The Nationalist movement later appropriated (and many say, silenced) reform movements within communities (Chatterjee 233-53). While Bengali forward-caste Hindu modernity has been well documented from this perspective,[1] very little effort has been made to hear the voices of other communities. The aspiration for modernity among the minority communities in India has rarely been taken up for study. The formation of gender identities within the community would reveal the particular contours of this modernity. This paper tries to do precisely that.

As a theorist has put it, the practice of *purdah* "literally as well as figuratively" veils the Muslim woman (Minault 2). Assuming that the group most likely to be articulate about their historical situation will be the elite Muslim women at the turn of the century, our effort in this paper is to unravel the making of these women during the turn of the twentieth century by looking at one particular Urdu journal.

The Deccan region, with Hyderabad as its capital, had a different history from other places of comparative Muslim dominance. Ruled by the Nizam, the area was officially not a British province and therefore not subject to direct rule. Yet, the advent of colonial modernity was experienced in this area just as in many other places in British India. For the Muslim community though, the state of

---

[1] Most of the well-known work on colonial modernity, for various reasons, takes Bengal and along with it the forward-caste identity as its study object. Two studies picked at random would be Lata Mani and Mrinalini Sinha.

6. The Construction of "Good Womanhood" in Annisa

Hyderabad, as the largest princely state in India still represented one of the last bastions of Islamic glory and power.

Literature, as we understand it, was a very important vehicle for the propagation of reformist ideas. But the inclusion of the regions, minority identities, and questions related to women belonging to minority communities requires that one does not confine oneself to the English language. Conversely, Urdu print literature serves as a very good source to see the advent and spread of modernity in the nineteenth and the twentieth centuries among a specific community in the Deccan.

Journal publishing for women during the turn of the twentieth century was crucial for social reform groups throughout India. The Muslim community, like others, took up their social reform through this method, and Urdu journals proliferated during this time.[2] The Muslim social reform movement produced a number of husband-wife teams who were both equally involved in raising questions related to the community and who served as models of social reform. There are a number of examples of journals for women started by these reformist couples. For example, Sayyid Mumtaz Ali and his wife Muhammadi Begum (who served as the editor till her untimely death) started *Tahzib un-Niswan* (*The Civilized Woman*) in 1898 from Lahore. In a similar vein, Gail Minault notes that Shaikh Abdullah and his wife Wahid Jahan Begum of Aligarh starting a magazine for women, *Khatun* (*The Lady*), in 1904 (110). The main purpose of the magazine was to advocate women's education and to convince men of the need for it.

From Deccan, Begum Sughra Humayun Mirza (1884-1958) was one of the important figures who worked for issues related to Muslim women's education, situating this issue within the general matrix of

---

[2] Anwaruddin gives a detailed list of all journals from Hyderabad, dividing it into different fields like Medicine, Culture, Law, Literature, Agriculture, Education, Poetry, Children, and journals of various educational institutions (351-56).

the reform of the community. She was the daughter of Captain Haji Safdar Hussain and Mariyam Begum. During her childhood in Hyderabad (now in Andhra Pradesh state) she learnt Urdu and Persian from her parents. After her marriage, she travelled widely and was quite well-read and knowledgeable.

Begum Mirza served as the editor of many journals related to women. They include *Annisa* (*The Woman*) and *Zebunnisa* (*The Beautiful Woman*). She was quite prolific as far as literary output was concerned and had come out with works like *Musheer-e-Niswan* (*Women's Advisor,* 1920), *Mohini* (*Mohini*, 1931) *Safarnamah-e-Iraq* (*Travelogue of Iraq*, 1915), *Majmuah-yi-Nuhahjat* (*A Collection of Elegies,*, 1989 edition), *Mukhtasar Halat Hazrat Bibi Fatima* (*A Short Life History of Hazrat Bibi Fatima*, 1940) and *Nasihat ke Moti: Majmuah-yi-Nasaeh* (*Pearls of Instructions: A Collection of Advice*, 1955) Most of them were written using her pen name "Haya."

This paper analyses one of the magazines edited by Begum Mirza to examine the constructions of elite Muslim femininities at the turn of the twentieth century in India. The difficult balance between modernity and tradition which the women's journals were advocating during those times would serve to show the present-day gender constructions as well. For our detailed study, we will be looking into one particular journal for Muslim women published during the 1920s in Urdu from Hyderabad, the magazine *Annisa*.[3] Edited by Sughra Humayun Mirza, *Annisa*, along with other such journals, served to fashion the "good Muslim lady" at the turn of the century.

The journals were not the only mechanism for propagating the idea of the "good woman." This was being continuously enforced through various institutions like family, women's associations, religion, etc. The good woman was supposed to be educated in affairs to do with the home, her children, Islam, and sometimes, on her special

---

[3] Referred to differently as *Al-Nisa* in Tharu and Lalitha (378) and *An-Nissa* in Minault (151).

6. The Construction of "Good Womanhood" in Annisa

community identity, as a Deccani. We can see the refashioning of Muslim patriarchy through the eyes of this journal.

Perhaps the story of *Annisa* cannot be told without a preceding story – the story of *Mu'allim-e-Niswan (Women's Teacher)*. Edited by Muhibb-e-Hussain, *Mu'allim-e-Niswan* was a pioneering journal in Urdu for women. It was published from the 1880s onwards from Nizam's capital, Hyderabad, and lasted for fourteen years. In the 1880s the discussion on women's education was only just beginning, but this did not prevent Muhibb-e-Hussain and his magazine from taking up controversial topics for discussion, including *purdah*.[4] Gail Minault notes that as a result of the editor's outspoken opposition to *purdah* the magazine had to be closed down in 1901 (109).

After the demise of *Mu'allim-e-Niswan*, there was a gap of some years before women's journals started appearing again. This time, the difference was that many of these journals were edited by women themselves. According to Minault, *Annisa* appeared between 1919 and 1927 (151). But Mohammad Anwaruddin, who has worked on the early journals from Hyderabad and Deccan, claims that it appeared from 1918 onwards continually for three years only (194). Our own search took us to an issue in 1919, and we could manage to get issues up to 1925, but not continuously. Anwaruddin also says that due to Sughra's ill health and her European travels the publication stopped for a while and restarted after a break (194).

The story of the magazine is connected to the other reform activities at the all-India level. There were many women's organisations, including Muslim women's organisations which were started during this period by various elite women, often under the influence of their husbands, who encouraged literacy among women. Sughra Humayun Mirza must have been influenced by the Tayyiba Begum Khediev Jung (1873-1921), a social reformer who was her contemporary. She

---

[4] In 1880, Hyderabad had only eleven girls' schools (Minault 205).

also frequently acknowledged her husband's influence in her life choices.

The magazine's audience was not limited to the Deccan region. It spread throughout the mainland of British India, which included Lahore, Delhi, Lucknow and Aligarh, as can be inferred from the introduction of writers or references to earlier writings in the magazine itself. Though announced as a women's magazine, the intended readers (and sometimes writers) were also progressive men, who had to be converted to support issues related to women. The following couplet, printed on the title page of most issues shows how the magazine saw itself:

> Dakin mein is tarah taleem-e-niswan ki taraqqi ho
> Ki pardeh mein bhi har khatoon aflatoon-e-dauran.

> If there is such development of women's education in Deccan
> Every woman, even in veil, will become a Plato of her times.

It shows the main agenda of the magazine – women's education. The profusion of women's journals edited by women themselves was already under way by the time *Annisa* appeared. For example, *Humjoli* (*A Woman Friend*), a magazine from Hyderabad, was edited by Sayyida Begum Khwishgi.

It is important to note that *Annisa*, rather than the feminist journal that one expects, was educational and didactic. Also, we cannot compare it to contemporary popular women's magazines of India like *Women's Era* or *Femina* which are overtly consumerist. This is not just because of the small circulation of the magazines but also because they started functioning with a clear reform agenda. Print had not yet proved its capitalistic potential. Published by local printing presses, the magazine contained very little illustrations and no photographs. *Annisa* was printed at different presses including Matba-e-Nizam-e-Dakin, Taj, Gangasagar, Shamsul Islam, Moin-e-Dakin, Matba-e-

6. The Construction of "Good Womanhood" in Annisa

Mufeel-e-Dakin, Imad, Matba-e-Rahbar-e-Dakin, etc. According to information in the magazine issues most of these presses were in Chatta Bazar, where even today printing is done.[5] *Annisa* had the subtitle *Women's and Girl's Monthly Urdu Journal* and had around forty pages in a standard issue. The usual fare included childcare, health and hygiene, cooking, home management, religious thoughts, recipes, discipline, travelogues, novels, poetry, biographies along with reformist and educational information. Writing contests for women writers were organised and prizes distributed.

Various organisations for Muslim women were also spreading throughout the country during the same time, and the magazine should be seen in this context. Very often, these journals served as mouthpieces for the organisations. An example of such an organisation was the Anjuman-e-khavatin-e-Islam (Association of Muslim Women). Gail Minault observes that it was started in 1914 by the Begum of Bhopal who presided over the function. According to Minault, it was formed "as part of the colourful ceremony inaugurating the new residence hall at Aligarh Girls' School" by Shaikh Abdulla and Wahid Jahan Begum who worked behind the scenes (285). Perhaps as a sister organisation, Anjuman-e-khavatin-e-dakin (Association of Deccan Women) began functioning in 1919 with Tayyiba Begum Khediv Jung as its President. But due to Tayyiba's ill health, Sughra served as the "chief motivator" (Minault 210). The organisation stood for Muslim women's education and social reform. The proceedings of the Anjuman meetings were published in the magazine every month, thus confirming the mouthpiece status of the magazine.

---

[5] We do not know who owned these presses. *Annisa* had an Asfiya registration number (24) for the registration in the Nizam's domain, as well as a British Government registration number (1294).

Muslim modernity at the turn of the twentieth century

While the above-mentioned would be the immediate and local context in which one can see the inception of the magazine, the larger context would place it within Muslim modernity at the turn of the century itself. The magazine and the articles in it should be read in the context of the Khilafat movement. After World War I, the Ottoman Empire with which the muslim subjects of British India had felt a strong identification, faced imminent dismemberment. Under the leadership of the Ali brothers, Maulana Muhammad Ali and Maulana Shaukat Ali, the Muslims of South Asia launched the Khilafat Movement to try and save the Empire. This unified the Indian Muslim community with an international Islamic brotherhood against the Western powers, especially the British. In India, this was also the time of the non-cooperation movement launched by Gandhi. This led to an alliance with the majority community which was organised around nationalist sentiments. Sughra Humayun Mirza, belonging to an elite family, must have strongly identified with the urge for national integration and Hindu-Muslim unity. Her adopted son Yousuf Ali Mirza in an interview said that she was a supporter of the Congress Party, with Sarojini Naidu being a close friend.[6] He also added that her brother Baquar Ali Mirza was the first Member of Parliament who won from a Congress ticket in Hyderabad after independence.

Yet, as a minority community, the Muslims in colonial India and Deccan could not ignore the specific identity of their community. We see this being forged through efforts like *Annisa*. However, it was not an assertion or revival of older traditions that was happening at that time. The most important function that the magazine and perhaps Muslim social reformers of those times took upon themselves was to mould a special identity, that of the modern Muslim community. *Annisa* was in the forefront of this enterprise. Let us examine the

---

[6] Interview by K. C. Bindu and Viqar Atiya on 4 May 2007.

6. The Construction of "Good Womanhood" in Annisa

specific contours of this modernity in general before proceeding to the question of gender.

There are a lot of discussions around the general theme of modernity in the journal. The attempts of a community to reorganise itself for a different and modern kind of life is seen in many of these articles. This happens through a variety of processes and is sometimes not quite open. One can for instance read this aspiration in prescriptive and didactic poems which deal with time and its value, such as *"Wakht"* ("Time").[7] It can perhaps be connected to a world that was defining itself more and more in terms of the emerging capitalism in the country. Yet another instance would be the Urdu translations of quotations from English classics, strewn in *Annisa*; sometimes these were even out of context. One example among many would be a philosophical poem on death, "Shaher-e-Khamooshan" ("The Cemetery") that has a quote from the famous cemetery scene of *Hamlet*. We can see which class of readers or at least intended models of class the magazine wished to reproduce through these examples.

Also evident is the imagining of a "modern" individual through the pages of the magazine. This modern individual is built by discarding what is useless and "backward" in tradition. An example would be the article "Tark-e-Rasumat-e-Fuzool" ("Get Rid of Bad Customs"), which warns the women of the community to get rid of useless customs and move forward with times. While the first surprise comes with the fact that women alone are identified as the culprits responsible for the backwardness of the community, the next one comes with the listing of avoidable customs. Most of these are quite

---

[7] A note on the referencing of *Annisa* articles: We have used the full name of the authors as given in the articles. This makes following the Western standard of having the surname followed by the first name difficult. For this reason, we have used the Urdu titles of the articles for in-text citation and alphabetical listing in the list following the Works Cited below. If the cited articles form a series, we have also used the author's name in the in-text citations.

local in character and had become a way of life before modernity. Moreover, they are also customs related to women's lives. Thus, *viladat,* or customs related to birth, *rozah kushai,* the function when the child opens her/his first fast during *Ramadan, mangni* or engagement ceremony, *mehndi* or ritually putting *henna* on the hands of the bride, *chawthi* or the bride and the groom putting colours on each other, etc. are all seen to be an unnecessary waste of money and un-Islamic. The understanding of "wasteful" expenditure for feudal customs shows a shift towards capitalism and modernity with puritan values. We can also see that the move to get rid of useless customs was taking the community towards a more "modern," i.e. scriptural, tradition of Islam that was refashioning local Islams.

The construction of Islam as more text-bound and scriptural, rather than based upon customs and local rituals, has to be seen as a sign of the shift towards modernity itself. Middle Eastern feminists have noted this trend in Islamic countries and have also commented on the loss of women's power over some of the ritual spaces with this kind of a reinterpretation of the religion. For instance, Leila Ahmad in an interview has commented on the "difference between living, oral traditions and written texts," which in the context of Islam means a divorce between the "living Islam of Muslim women and the official Islam" (Ahmed 8-9). While one need not romanticise the pre-modern as a heavenly women's space, one can yet read the changing notions of patriarchy that modernity seemed to advance. This analysis of Islam does not mean that the other communities were taking totally different turns. A similar move had already occurred in Hindu communities with attempts seen as "reducing orality to textuality" along with colonialism (Pande 22).

Another point to be noted is the curious intermixture of Islam, India, and the West that the magazine and perhaps Islamic reform movements themselves were advocating. It was not at all a complete and unproblematic acceptance of Western ideas. On the contrary, there are clearly anti-colonial sentiments expressed in the magazine,

6. The Construction of "Good Womanhood" in Annisa

very often as an assertion of Islamic identity. These also appear in perhaps unexpected areas. For instance, in a travelogue, *"London ka Ajaebkhanah"* ("The London Museum"), an author, while describing the London Museum (perhaps the British Museum?) and the wonders he encounters there, notes that the museum showcases almost all the glories of the Islamic world. While taking note of Tipu's sword, kept in display, he feels it is Islam's very sword which is taken from its roots and displayed in the museum. In fact, the advocacy of modernity in these pages, rather than blindly following of the West is the imagination of an Islamic modernity. As mentioned earlier, the magazine originates at a time when Hindu-Muslim unity is talked about and is tried out in the national scene, and yet the special identity of a minority community is visible even at that time.

The importance of social concerns, expressed in terms of community, is very often pointed out in the magazine's discussions. The word *qaum*, which means nation, also has shades of the meaning of community in Urdu. For instance, the simultaneous use of the terms *vatan* 'own land' and *qaum* in the following poem is not a rare occurrence at that time:

> Abna-e-vatan keliye hain uzoo-e-muattal
> Late hain yahi qaum pe adbar nikhattu. ("Taranah-e-amal")

> Useless to the mother land are they who sit idle
> As body parts are which have stopped working.
> A burden to the community are those lazy ones. ("Poem on Work")

The word, which is used more often than not to refer to the social, seems to be 'community,' rather than 'mother land.'

In these journals, history becomes a rallying point for Muslim identity formation; the point to be noted is that it is not only a national but an international Islamic identity that is being created. The connection that is made with the wider Islamic world, in the Middle East and elsewhere, is clearly visible in the magazine's pages. Thus Muhammad Ibn-e-Rashid, introduced as an important Muslim thinker in one of the series titled "Famous Muslims and their Achievements" by Syed Humayun Mirza ("Musalman Namvaron Ke Karname"), is from Spain.

There are rarely instructional articles which deal with the specific local identity of being a Deccani Muslim. Perhaps, when the call seems to be to build a national and even international Islamic modernity, the local was too uncomfortable to be foregrounded. An example would be the article "Khandhar-e-Deccan" which is about the historical importance of the place Khandahar in Deccan. But even here, the recounting of local history is meant to contribute to a global Muslim identity and alliance by equating Deccan's Khandahar with Afghanistan's city of the same name, a very important place for South Asian Muslims. One of the reasons for this absence of the local might be that Sughra herself, though born in the Deccan, but belonging to an elite family, might have identified more with the high culture of Lucknow or other North Indian cities rather than with the Deccan.

Islamic contributions to science are very important for the building of a global Muslim identity at this stage when the national/global identity of the Muslim is being forged in early twentieth-century India. An example of an important Muslim who figures in the above-mentioned series is Allama Mohammadbin Moosa, known for his contributions to Algebra; his achievements are highlighted by the editors in "Musalman Namvaron ke Karname" ("Famous Muslims and their Achievements"). In this editorial, a comparison with other cultures, especially those of the West, is evident. It is yet another effort to build alternative roads to modernity other than those imposed by British colonialism. The point seems to be that when the rest of the world, including the Western world, was in darkness, the Islamic world was blooming in the Middle Ages.

The identity of the community is built through constant comparisons, especially with Western colonisers. There are direct

6. The Construction of "Good Womanhood" in Annisa

comparisons with the British in many articles, and one can read the sub-text of this comparison in almost all the general articles as well. An example of a direct comparison occurs in an article on women's education where the writer brings in a direct reference to European women, who are perceived to be able to do everything as well as their men. In "Talim-e-Niswan" ("Women's Education") the author, Noorani Begum Saheba, wonders how the children who are brought up by these women will turn out to be compared to "our children." There are also other comparisons at work, mostly with the rest of the elite communities in India with whom middle-class Muslims may have been competing. In a piece of fiction titled "Ladki Tumhari Ghar Mehman Hai" ("A Girl is a Guest in Your House"), again on the methods of education, a "modern" Muslim father admonishes his wife for the brutal methods she uses in imparting religious education to their daughter. He compares his house, where the mother is shouting at the daughter for being such a fool, to the more "sophisticated" Bengali Hindu friend's house in Calcutta. In this ideal household, children do their work and play when they should. The girls learn piano and sewing, both Victorian occupations of an elite woman. There is an *ayah* who comes home to instruct the children. Thus, the desire for a different life in the house in which women's education plays a major role is expressed by the male character through comparison with the more "advanced" upper caste Hindus.

Yet another community to which Muslims are compared is the Parsi community, where women are perceived to be better dressed and more presentable: "Look at women from other communities. For example, we feel happiness in seeing the cleanliness of Parsi women, the simplicity of their clothes, and the way their houses are kept. ("Saleeqah" ["Good Ways"]). This method of comparison was not singular to the Muslim community. All over India, community reforms were going on and comparisons, either with Europe or with other communities in India competing for modernity, were constantly made.

The effort to build a modern identity is visible in the pages of the magazine. This effort does not constitute a total acceptance of the Western way of life; neither does it totally replicate the Hindu upper-caste campaign for reform. The Islamic identity expressed is quite specific in the sense that it attempts to build a global Muslim identity which is constructed in comparison, contrast, and sometimes in alliance with many other communities. Thus, while the global Muslim is an ally, the West sometimes appears as a category worthy of emulation, and sometimes as a competitor. Other elite communities also serve the function of fashioning elite Muslim identity.

Gender in Urdu journals

While the community was building its own special brand of modernity, we should also remember that gender played a central role in this. As Yoginder Sikand observes

> Muslim women needed to be educated in order to enable the community to resist the challenge of western culture, protect and promote Islamic "authenticity" and prove to be ideal wives and mothers in order to groom ideal Muslim families. The Muslim woman came to be seen as the first school of her children, and hence as key to the development and future of the Muslim community as a whole. The "backward", "superstitious" and "illiterate" Muslim woman was depicted as a major hurdle in the progress of the community, being seen as the repository of a range of "un-Islamic" beliefs and customs. Only by "reforming" her through proper education, it was stressed, could the community as a whole prosper.
> (3774)

Thus, one of the ways in which women played an important part in this scheme was by being a site of culture, tradition, or Islam itself. We must remember that the upper strata of Hindu communities were

6. The Construction of "Good Womanhood" in Annisa

going through a similar confrontation, in their case, with the missionary construction of India as barbaric. Nationalism emerged from a creative use of the ideas coming from Orientalists scholars (such as Max Müller) who, as Chatterjee observes, built an "untouched" inner sphere for the colonised located in the home, family, and spirituality. Women had become an important point of contention in both missionary as well as social reform narratives.

Annisa also tries to build an untouched "inner sphere." This happens through a mode of presentation adopted by many women's journals at that time, namely by offering explicit instruction about what is good and bad. While this appears to be non-gendered in nature, a closer examination will reveal that the good and bad qualities are often covertly gendered. Thus, in a general article praising "Self-Respect," ("Khuddari") there is a call to distinguish between pride and self-respect, which becomes a specific address to women. Another example is the article "Sabr-vo-Himmat" ("Patience and Courage") which defines the qualities given in the title as desirable. These are of course qualities which are important in any human being. Yet, while one reads on, one understands that the space given to *sabr* 'patience' is not equal to that given to *himmat* 'courage.' Also, the author's concluding remarks make one understand that patience itself is courage in a woman. The supposedly neutral analysis is thereby explicitly gendered.

Upper-caste Hindu reformers of the late nineteenth and early twentieth centuries, as Chakravarty suggests, had installed the figures of Gargi and Maitreyi onto the popular consciousness of the nation as exemplifying the glory of Indian women during Vedic times (Chakravarty 27-28). In a comparable move, we find many female figures from Islamic history being glorified in the pages of *Annisa*. Many of these women were heroines and warriors who fought Islamic wars; but this does not mean that they escaped the usual familial roles prescribed for women. These women warriors were usually shown to be fulfilling their familial responsibility itself by going to war. Thus, in "Musalman Auraton ki Bahaduri Aur Behan ki Mohabbat" ("The Courage of Muslim Women and a Sister's Love"), Khaula, an Islamic heroine who fights the Byzantines for the life of her brother, is remembered as a brave warrior.

Women become very important in the perceived resurgence of both the community and the nation; *Annisa*, like other magazines, makes this connection between womanhood and nation or community. A clear example of this is in the serialised novel *Mulk ka Mustaqbil Auraton ke Hath Mein* (*The Future of the Country is in the Women's Hands*), appearing in the 1920s, whose title itself makes the connection very clear. Of course this womanhood is an efficiently domesticated womanhood, mirroring the Victorian ideals of the colonisers. *Annisa*, like Victorian conduct books, also offers the female reader training, not only in intellectual matters, but also titbits on how to keep a house clean or how to keep eggs fresh.[8]

Almost nowhere in the pages of *Annisa* is there an argument urging equality with men. Instead, there are discussions on the different and complementary nature of women and men. In "Aurat Kya Cheez Hai" ("What is Woman?"), Janab Maulavi Rafiuddin Saheb Rifat dispels any doubts about whether a woman is an incomplete man or not. However, he does not argue that she is a complete human being either, but suggests that she is a *different* person altogether. Maulavi Rafiuddin also claims that if men and women became like each other, women would stop being women. His fears are explicitly voiced; equality will mean the end of love between men and women.

In the few instances where equality is considered, the argument comes from Western women. In one issue, Khaja Ahmed Mutalim translates Mary Connely, an English author. In "Sinf-e-Nazuk" ("The Fair Sex"), she speaks about how uncomfortable men become when women speak about equality. This article, very rare by *Annisa* standards, considers women as having – like men – independent roles

---

[8] For instance, see *Annisa* 1.5 (Aug. 1920): 9.

6. The Construction of "Good Womanhood" in Annisa

in life. She speaks about the contributions that women have made and demands equality. Another rare example that can be quoted is a report, "Auraton ki Azadi ki Tehreek" ("Women's Movement for Independence"), again from the West, of an International women's meeting in Rome where Indian women participated. This article reports that the meeting strongly demanded equality with men.

What are given as instructional materials from within the country would be articles which define the wife's duties. The wife's main purpose in life seems to be to keep her husband happy, which the author of one article, "Insan ka Koi Kaam Gharaz se Khali Nahin" ("No Human Action is Devoid of Purpose"), claims will also keep God happy. Maulana Rafiuddin in the already quoted "Aurat Kya Cheez Hai?" ("What is Woman?") stresses companionship between men and women as well as woman's role as mother. These roles, needless to say, define women purely in relation to men. This construction of the reform woman – an ideal companion, yet not equal to a man, and finding ultimate meaning and fulfilment in motherhood – can be found everywhere in *Annisa*.

Constructing the educated Muslim woman

The issue of women's education assumed such importance perhaps because it stood for all reformist debates in a concentrated form. The building of the educated and "reformed" Muslim woman was seen as the most important step towards modernity. Sughra Humayun Mirza, along with other women, had established schools for girls to apply her theories on women's education.[9] At least one piece in each issue of *Annisa*, catering to the Muslim community, emphasised the importance of education for Muslim women. The question of women's education that the magazine took up with missionary zeal is

---

[9] The Safdariya school, the Urdu medium girls' school started by Sughra Humayun Mirza in 1934, still exists in Humayun Nagar (the area named after Sughra's father) in Hyderabad.

therefore worthy of examination. The importance of education and national progress is explicit in some of the articles, e.g. in "Ahl-e-Mulk ki Taraqqi ka Ek Tariqah" ("A Method to Develop the People of the Nation").

A closer examination of the articles in support of women's education reveals the contradictory nature of modernity built around "reforming" women. One example is the article, "Mardon ki Taleem Muqaddam Hai ya Auraton Ki?" ("Is Men's Education or Women's Education More Important?"), which apparently supports the latter even at the expense of the former. This gendered argument, however does not support women's education for its own sake; in fact, the argument is quite patriarchal. The greater importance of women's education is derived from the view of women as the first educators of men. Such arguments underline the importance of the female roles of wife and, above all, mother.

Sometimes men take more responsible stances regarding women and their education. An article written by Janab Maulavi Muhibb-e-Hussain Sahib, "Kya Purdah Nashinan-e-Hind ki Taleem Angrezi Zaban ke Zarieh Zaroori Hai?" ("Should the Education of India's Veiled Women Necessarily be through the English Language?") takes the position that women need not be given an English education.[10] What prompts the author is not the usual expectation that women should not surpass men; he is clear that women have a right to English education. Instead, his driving force is practicality: he argues that women have very little time for education from the age of eight till the age of fifteen, when they would be removed from school due to marriage. He takes the stand that it is not wise to expect them to become proficient in another language *and* also acquire a decent education. Moreover, the author thinks that not just women, but men as well should be educated in their mother tongues.

---

[10] The author was the editor of another important journal mentioned above, *Mu'allim-e-Niswan*.

6. The Construction of "Good Womanhood" in Annisa

Sometimes the debate provided aesthetic entertainment along with intellectual pleasure. Thus, the comic poem by Mirza Mohammad Bahadur Saheb, "Shikayat-e-Niswan" ("Complaints of Women"), describes the debate in well-turned-out Urdu rhymes. In this poem, the illiterate husband blames the wife, saying her life is easy, unlike a man's. Men have the responsibility of supporting the family, he argues; women, on the other hand, can while away their time. The clever wife answers by saying she bears as much responsibility as the man, because she looks after the family, and therefore she requires and deserves an education.

The debate on women's education, while sometimes veering towards demanding women's human rights, actually stops short of doing so; instead what it urges is a redefining of existing patriarchy. Women's education was a special field fraught with contradictions; ironically, the anxieties of social conservatives regarding women's education were often shared by reformists themselves. As a result, many of the articles (including those by women) supporting education seem to be more apologetic than militant. When they write supporting the cause, they seem to constantly be on guard to distinguish themselves from loose women or non-religious people. For instance, in "*Hum aur Hamari Taleem*" ("We and Our Education"), the woman author has to constantly qualify her words, saying that "my intention, when I speak about women's education is not that she should be educated and become fashionable" (19). Women, when given education, should ideally become "truly" religious (instead of what is conceived as blindly superstitious, uneducated, traditional women) as well as be ready for secular life. They should think about the community's welfare. In line with this thinking, the Hobart school in Madras is explicitly criticised for not giving enough attention to religious education and for failing to observe *purdah* (young girls were found wandering freely within the school, the author observes). The fear of Westernisation is also evident in her criticism that a "higher strata of girls use English words instead of Urdu" (20). This anti-English sentiment is religious as well as nationalistic; she quotes Lala Lajpat Rai's statement that the use of a foreign tongue instead of one's own mother-tongue is the first sign of the colonised people. Yet in the article it is difficult to see whether the author is angrier at the women using English or the English themselves.

One of the strategies women used to build popular consensus for women's education was to bring in the sanction of religion. For instance, Qaisari Begum, in *"Zakat"* ("Charity as Prescribed by Islam"), says that the Prophet himself was supportive of women's education and that opposing this is opposing the Prophet. She asserts that women's education is important for the development of the nation, urging women to speak within the community to justify any move towards modernity. Otherwise, they would lose all legitimacy within the group they are addressing.

This complex position of woman, where education is required, but should remain within the limits prescribed by religion, is fraught with contradictions. They manifest themselves in the welcoming of modernity (brought by the colonisers) and the simultaneous demand for a traditional space within the home. While the aspiration to building the modern individual is there, it is also inscribed within the (reinterpreted) textual sanctions and scriptural traditions of Islam. The debates on women's education thus most poignantly encapsulate the contradictions of the social reform movement itself. Of course, similar attempts to construct "authentic" communities, religions, and nations which were conducive to modernity occurred among all groups and were not specific to Muslims. The Muslim elite women, in that sense, should be seen as part of a broader group of upper-caste or aspiring middle-class women emerging in colonial India.

The class basis of *Annisa*

While there is an effort discernible in *Annisa* to build a universal Muslim identity (with the special inflections of gender written into it),

6. The Construction of "Good Womanhood" in Annisa

one need to be clear that it is a particular class that is articulating this need. The magazine clearly stands for the elite sections of Muslims in the country; there are many instances where the class basis of *Annisa* is revealed. Most of the writers are from aristocratic backgrounds; only they could have taken up the cause of the community at that time. Often their right to speak is supported by a proud display of families and social backgrounds, and sometimes this class basis is revealed in the very names of the authors themselves. Women gain this legitimacy by announcing that they are the wives, sisters, or daughters of aristocratic and "honourable" gentlemen. For example, Mehmooda Begum Sahiba, in "Insan ka Koi Kaam Gharaz se Khali Nahin" ("No Human Action is Devoid of Purpose"), announces herself as Mehmooda Begum Sahiba Mahal Nawab Qadir Nawaz Jang Bahaddur, i.e. the wife of Quadir Nawaz whose military title (in the Nizam's army) is Jang Bahaddur and whose aristocratic lineage is signified by the title Nawab. As Vir Talwar points out, this practice was not confined to the Muslim community at that time (Talwar 209).

Sometimes this class bias is revealed quite openly in the magazine. For example, in the appeal for charity towards the poor (central to the Islamic religion itself). One volume announces in an advertisement that *Annisa* copies will be given to poor women who request it.[11] The charitable activities of many of the patrons are listed along with the monthly meeting proceedings of the Anjuman-e-khavatin-e-dakin (All India Deccan Ladies' Conference). The contradictions of charity are clearly visible in the "Shazrat" ("Editor's Comment") of one issue of the magazine. The author mentions the increase in the number of beggars and recounts how forty beggars, most of them women and children, died due to starvation in Bombay. She is also concerned about how many more will die from diseases. While she says it is important to wipe out begging, she also describes a group of beggars who are out to exploit the hard-working and generous people from good families.

---

[11] *Annisa* 1.4 (July 1920): 22.

The phrase she uses to describe these beggars in Urdu is *hatte, katte mustande* 'hale and hearty.' The contradiction between this and her own observation that so many beggars are dying from diseases is not noticed by the author. She goes on to criticise the custom of *khairat* or giving alms to beggars propagated by Islam.

Though claims about a universal Muslim identity seem to be made constantly, the magazine is exclusive in its scope. The class identification of its contributors and readers clearly defines its ideology. It is within this context that gender should be analysed in the magazine.

Conclusion

Annisa should be seen in the context of "reform" literature that populated the Indian scene from the nineteenth century onwards. Representing Muslim identity by trying to fashion the good Muslim woman (a reformist agenda based on community) seems to be a mission taken up by the magazine. However, the qualities of the subjects elaborated in the magazine show the contradictory position that gender seemed to occupy in the social reform discourse; the debate surrounding women's education encapsulates this contradiction of vouching for women's education, yet trying to limit it at the same time.

The fact that women were taking up the pen for the first time, using print media as editors, publishers, and writers would make them inscribe themselves as subjects into a hitherto male sphere. But that they primarily spoke of matters related to the private realm, or were mainly concerned with the creation of a private realm of a particular shape, made the use of print media a contradictory step for women. Gender should not be read based solely on the identity of a community. The class assumptions of a venture like *Annisa*, and by extension, the social reform movement itself, need to be considered in any analysis of modernity and gender.

6. The Construction of "Good Womanhood" in Annisa

Works Cited

Ahmed, Leila. "An Interview with the Author." *A Border Passage: From Cairo to America, A Woman's Journey*. By Leila Ahmed. New York: Penguin, 2000. 5-9.

Amena, Zafer. "Urdu Research Centre Mein Maqzoona Resala Zebunnisa ka Isharaiy" ("The Catalogue of the Monthly Zebunnisa Preserved in the Urdu Research Centre"). M.Phil. thesis University of Hyderabad, 2006.

Anwaruddin, Mohammad. *Hyderabad Deccan ke Ilmi-va Adabi Rasael* ("Educational and Literary Journals of Hyderabad Deccan"). Hyderabad: Maktabah-yi-Shadaab, 1997.

Chakravarty, Uma. "Whatever Happened to the Vedic Dasi? Orientalism, Nationalism and a Script for the Past." *Recasting Women: Essays in Colonial History*. Ed. Sudesh Vaid and Kumkum Sangari. New Delhi: Zubaan, 2006. 27-87.

Chatterjee, Partha. "The Nationalist Resolution of the Women's Question." *Recasting Women: Essays in Colonial History*. Ed. Sudesh Vaid and Kumkum Sangari. New Delhi: Zubaan, 2006. 233-53.

Devika, J. *En-gendering Individuals: The Language of Re-forming in Early Twentieth Century Keralam*. Hyderabad: Orient Longman, 2007.

Mani, Lata. *Contentious Traditions: The Debate on Sati in Colonial India*. Berkeley: University of California Press, 1998.

Minault, Gail. *Secluded Scholars: Women's Education and Muslim Social Reform in Colonial India*. New Delhi: Oxford University Press, 1998.

Pande, Rekha. *Religious Movements in Medieval India*. New Delhi: Gyan, 2005.

Sikand, Yoginder. "Islamic Education for Girls." *Economic and Political Weekly* XLI 35 (2006): 3774-76.

Sinha, Mrinalini. *Colonial Masculinity: The "Manly Englishman" and the "Effeminate Bengali" in the Late Nineteenth Century*. Manchester: Manchester University Press, 1995.

Talwar, Vir Bharat. "Women's Journals in Hindi, 1910-20." *Recasting Women: Essays in Colonial History*. Ed. Sudesh Vaid and Kumkum Sangari. New Delhi: Zubaan, 2006. 204-32.

Tharu, Susie, and K. Lalita, eds. *Women Writing in India Volume 1: 600 BC to the Early Twentieth Century*. New Delhi: Oxford University Press, 1991.

Vaid, Sudesh, and Kumkum Sangari. Introduction. *Recasting Women: Essays in Colonial History*. Ed. Sudesh Vaid and Kumkum Sangari. New Delhi: Zubaan, 2006. 1-26.

Annisa Articles

"Ahl-e-Mulk ki Taraqqi ka Ek Tariqah" ("A Method to Develop the People of the Nation"). By the editor. 1.5 (1920): 9-16.

"Aurat Kya Cheez Hai?" ("What is Woman?"). By Janab Maulavi Rafiuddin Saheb Rifat. 2.1 (1920): 5-13.

"Auraton ki Azadi ki Tehreek" ("Women's Movement for Independence"). By Begum Abdul Munam Saheb. 5.4 (1923): 22-23.

"Hum aur Hamari Taleem" ("We and Our Education"). By Janab Hamsheerah Saheba Ghulam Dastagir Saheb, Madras. 3.8 (1922): 18-21.

"Insan ka Koi Kaam Gharaz se Khali Nahin" ("No Human Action is Devoid of Purpose"). By Mehmooda Begum Sahiba Mahal Nawab Qadir Nawaz Jang Bahaddur. 1.4 (1920): 8-9.

"Khandhar-e-Deccan" ("Deccan's Khandahar"). By the editors. 1.4 (1920): 1-2.

"Khuddari" ("Self-Respect"). By Meharunnisa Begum. 6.8 (1925): 12-14.

"Kya Purdah Nashinan-e-Hind ki Taleem Angrezi Zaban ke Zarieh Zaroori Hai?" ("Should the Education of India's Veiled Women

6. The Construction of "Good Womanhood" in Annisa

Necessarily be through the English Language?"). By Janab Maulavi Muhibb-e-Hussain Sahib. 3.8 (1922): 4-9.

"Ladki Tumhari Ghar Mehman Hai" ("A Girl is a Guest in Your House"). By the editors. 6.11-12 (1925): 1-8.

"London ka Ajaebkhanah" ("The London Museum"). By Hussain Ali Mirza Khalf Mej and Muhammad Ali Mirza Saheb. 1.4 (1920): 29-30.

"Mardon ki Taleem Muqaddam Hai ya Auraton Ki?" ("Is Men's Education or Women's Education More Important?"). By Ruqayya Sultan Begum Saheba Hamsheerzadi His Highness Nawab Saheb Laharo. 1.4 (1920): 16-22.

"Mulk ka Mustaqbil Auraton ke Hath Men" ("The Future of the Country is in the Women's Hands"). By Muhammad Marghoobuddin. 1.4 (1920): 13-15.

"Musalman Auraton ki Bahaduri Aur Behan ki Mohabbat" ("The Courage of Muslim Women and a Sister's Love"). By Bint-e-Sultan Mahmood Muhiuddin Saheb Qadri. 6.8 (1925): 7-9.

"Musalman Namvaron ke Karname" ("Famous Muslims and their Achievements"). By the editors. 1.4 (1920): 4-5.

"Musalman Namvaron ke Karname" ("Famous Muslims and their Achievements"). By Syed Humayun Mirza. 1.5 (1920): 21-25.

"Sabr-Vo-Himmat" ("Patience and Courage"). By Manik Bai Sahiba Mrs. Shahpurji Okarji. 1.4 (1920): 6-7.

"Saleeqah" ("Method"). By Hamsheerah Saheba Mansoor Jung Bahadur, Rafia Sultan. 5.4 (1923): 18.

"Shaher-e-Khamooshan" ("The Cemetery"). By Lateefa Muzaffaruddin Saheba. 1.4 (1920): 22-25.

"Shazrat" ("Editor's Comments"). 1.4 (1920): 31-32.

"Shikayat-e-Niswan" ("Complaints of Women"). By Mirza Mohammad Bahadur Saheb. 1.5 (1920): 1-9.

"Sinf-e-Nazuk" ("The Fair Sex"). By Khaja Ahmed Mutalim. 2.3 (1920): 13-18.

"Talim-e-Niswan" (Women's Education"). By Janab Noorani Begum Saheba Binte Munshi Fazil Mohammad Shamsuddin Saheb Bodhan. 6.11-12 (1925): 8-10.

"Taranah-e-amal" ("Poem on Work"). By Janab Naushabah Khatton Sahebah. 3.8 (1922): 8.

"Tark-e-Rasumat-e-Fuzool" ("Get Rid of Bad Customs"). By Naushaba Khatoon Saheba. 1.2 (1920): 4-11.

"Wakht" ("Time"). By Sajed Valiullah Husain Saheb Vakeel. 1.4 (1920): 9-12.

"Zakaat" ("Charity as Prescribed by Islam"). By Qaisari Begum. 1.5 (1920): 18-20.

Selected Work by Sughra Humayun Mirza

Majmuah-yi-Nuhahjaat (*A Collection of Elegies*). Hyderabad: Media Press, 1989 edition.

Mohini (*Mohini*). N.p., 1931.

Mukhtasar Halat Hazrat Bibi Fatima (*A Short Life History of Hazrat Bibi Fatima*). Humayun Nagar: Sughra Manzil, 1940.

Musheer-e-Niswan (*Women's Advisor*). Hyderabad: Humayun Manzil, 1920.

Nasihat ke Moti: Majmuah-yi-Nasaeh (*Pearls of Instructions: A Collection of Advice*). Humayun Nagar: Sughra Manzil, 1955.

Safarnaamah-e-Iraq (*Travelogue of Iraq*). N.p., 1915.

7. Abu'l-A'la Mawdudi: British India and the Politics of Popular Islamic Texts

Masood Ashraf Raja
Kent State University

Most studies of the literature of South Asia focus primarily on traditional forms, privileging vernacular poetry, prose, the novel, and other forms of narrative fiction and non-fiction as the only important genres worthy of critical attention. However, the production of Urdu religious texts was also one major form of cultural production in the British India. Barbara Metcalf captures this reality in the following words:

> The use of Urdu continued to be a notable feature of the writing of the period. It served [. . .] for notes and translations of religious classics. But it was also the language of an original religious literature in Urdu. [. . .] This literature both exemplified and furthered the new use of Urdu prose. The Urdu newspapers of the day, themselves providing examples of the entrenched range and simpler styles that were gaining currency, frequently commented on the novelty of religious writing in Urdu. (206)

Metcalf is suggesting that nineteenth-century religious textual production in Urdu, along with traditional literary genres, transformed it into the language of popular Muslim identity. Later Islamic reformers of the early and mid-twentieth century further simplified the language, and used their writings to politicise and mobilise Muslim popular opinion about the Raj and Western civilisation. This paper aims at a close reading of one particular collection of essays by Abu'l-A'la Mawdudi, one of the leading Indian (and later Pakistani) Muslim religious reformers of his time. As a reformer, Mawdudi was famous for his conversational style and simple Urdu prose, a prose more easily understood by an average reader, or more importantly, listener. His works are influential even now, as they still provide the basic guiding principles of modern political Islam in India and Pakistan, especially through the Pakistani political party, the Jama'at-i-Islami.

This paper discusses works from a collection of Mawdudi essays entitled *Tanqihat: Islam aur Maghrabi Tehzeeb ka Tasadum aur us se Paida Shuda Masail per Mukhtasar Tebsare* (*Investigations: Brief Commentaries on the Problems Caused by the Clash of Islam and the Western Civilisation*).[1] Most of these essays were published in the late 1930s and focus primarily on the dilemmas of Muslim life within the colonised space. This chapter will focus on these essays within their immediate historical context, trace their impact on the Muslim politics of that time, and then highlight their significance for the current understanding of political Islam and its interface with metropolitan, postmodern cultures.

As one of the most prominent Muslim reformers of his time, Mawlana Sayyid Abu'l-A'la Mawdudi's intellectual legacy affects not just South Asia, but further afield; his writings have appealed to Muslim readers from across the Islamic world. Seyyed Vali Reza Nasr touches upon this significance of Mawdudi's life and works in the following words:

> He was one of the first Islamic thinkers to develop a systematic political reading of Islam and a plan for social action to realize his vision. His creation of a coherent Islamic ideology, articulated in terms of the elaborate organization of an Islamic state,[2] constitutes the essential breakthrough that led to the rise of contemporary revivalism. His writings were prolific, and the indefatigable efforts of his party, the Jama'at-i-

---

[1] All direct quotations from the Urdu are provided in my translation.
[2] This is a reference to Mawdudi's magnum opus *Islami Riasat* (*The Islamic State*), which explains the most important aspects of a modern Islamic state in the light of *Shariah*.

7. *The Politics of Popular Islamic Texts*

Islami (Islamic Party), first in India and later in Pakistan, disseminated them far and wide. (3)

Published in 1939, *Tanqihat* contains twenty-one brief essays that were written, as Mawdudi informs his readers in the introduction, "at various times about the problems caused by the clash of Islam and Western civilisation" (4). A brief explanation is necessary to first explain my choice of translating the *Tasadum* of the title as a "clash." In Persian and Urdu *Tasadum* implies a head-on collision between two objects. Mawdudi's specific usage of the term does not imply a violent clash or a war-like condition, but rather a clash of Muslim sensitivities and beliefs with the influences of the West (in India's case Britain), both within India and in the rest of the Islamic world. According to Mawdudi, the clash occurs not because Muslims must clash with the West, but because Western powers are present as colonising forces within the Muslim public sphere. Even though these essays are occasional pieces pertinent to a specific Muslim colonised space (i.e. British India), they do have a transhistorical and transnational appeal. This brief chapter will attempt to read two major essays from *Tanqihat* to discuss how Mawdudi articulates and elaborates this conflict and assesses what could be the possible ramifications of his work in today's world.

The two essays discussed in this chapter, "Hamari Zehni Ghulami aur us ke Asbab" and "Millat ki Ta'meer-e-nau ka Sahi Tariqa," can be given the following English titles respectively: "Our Intellectual Slavery and its Causes," and "The Right Method of Reconstructing the *Millat*." Thematically, these essays have been chosen for their concern with the fall and recovery of a specifically Muslim way of life. While the first essay traces the itinerary of what Mawdudi sees as the main problems of colonised Muslims, the second essay attempts to highlight a conceptual framework to free the *Millat* (the global Muslim community), from the perceived "pernicious" influences of Western civilisation.

"Our Intellectual Slavery and its Causes" analyses the nature of Muslim experience in a colonised space dominated by the West, specifically the British in India. The commentary therefore aims to critique the hegemonic impulse of Western constructions of an ascending sociopolitical order. Mawdudi theorises two forms of political power: the intellectual and the political (5). According to this division of power, the state of Muslim societies can be summed up in the following words:

> Power[3] has two forms: the intellectual and psychological, and the political and material. The first kind of dominance happens when a nation is so advanced in its thought that other nations take its concepts as truth and then absorb them as the only true form of knowledge, hence adopting the dominant nation's thought and knowledge as a criterion for right and wrong, true and false. The material form of dominance occurs when one nation becomes so strong politically and materially that the other nations fail to maintain their freedom against its power and dominance. (Mawdudi 5)

Based on this analysis of a two-pronged power, Mawdudi also provides his readers with its resulting concomitant conditions – two forms of subjugation: "the intellectual and political" (5). He is careful to point out that these two forms of dominance and subjugation need not coalesce in a given political scenario: "it is not imperative that a place under the intellectual dominance of a power should also come under the sway of the direct political control of the same power" (5). But this division of power into two aspects – material and psychological – does lead to one important conclusion: "The nations that develop their

---

[3] Mawdudi uses the Urdu/Persian terms *Isteila*, and *Ghalba*, which literally mean 'dominance'; I am translating both these terms as 'power' because he goes on to articulate the two forms of power that correspond to the Gramscian concepts of dominance and hegemony.

7. *The Politics of Popular Islamic Texts*

thought and a habit of inquiry are also blessed with material progress" (5).

Mawdudi is clearly articulating a view of power that emerges in Western theory after Antonio Gramsci, who had clearly outlined a view of power's dominant and hegemonic role. Mawdudi is also preceding Foucault in articulating the inherent connection between power and knowledge. In a certain sense, then, it will not be odd to suggest that Mawdudi here is functioning as an organic intellectual who aims to educate his people about the nature of their material conditions and their intricate connection with the functioning of power itself. For Gramsci, power functions in the following two ways:

> [T]he supremacy of a social group manifests itself in two ways, as "domination" and as "intellectual and moral leadership". A social group dominates antagonistic groups, which it tends to "liquidate", or to subjugate perhaps even by armed force; it leads kindred and allied groups. A social group can, and indeed must, already exercise "leadership" before winning government power (this indeed is one of the principal conditions for the winning of such power); it subsequently becomes dominant when it exercises power, but even if it holds it firmly in its grasp, it must continue to "lead" as well.
> (57-58)

This explanation of power certainly refers to what has come to be understood as the dominance and hegemony model of the functioning of power. Hegemony, for Gramsci, is achieved through various means but depends largely on "the 'spontaneous' consent given by the great masses of the population to the general direction imposed on social life by the dominant fundamental group; this consent is 'historically' caused by the prestige [. . .] which the dominant group enjoys because of its position and function in the world of production" (Gramsci 12).

I am not suggesting here that Mawdudi had read Gramsci; in fact Gramsci's work was published and translated many years after Mawdudi had produced these commentaries. But, strikingly, Mawdudi seems to be theorising power with the same political acuteness as Gramsci, and on the larger scale of colonial politics. Also important to note is that this power (both psychological and political) has its particular locus in the West; it therefore makes it imperative on the native intellectual to seek the causes of its success, and more importantly, the causes of the failure of the primary culture (in this context, Indian Islam) in the face of such an onslaught. An analysis of power imposed from without already presupposes an inward gaze, which in this case drives Muslim thought to its own historical sources in order to articulate a resistant ideology. Because of the history of its textual richness, and Islam's specific identity as a text-based religion, all aspects of the Western intellectual mandate had to be tested against a purely Islamic criterion; this is exactly the case with Mawdudi's explanation of Western power and its impact on Indian Islam. Mawdudi also attempts to explain the causes of what could be termed an expression of the willing "spontaneous consent" (to use Gramsci's term) given to British hegemony by Indian Muslims themselves.

There is no doubt that for Mawdudi the rise of Western political power and its affective value (in creating two kinds of Muslim subjugation) is rooted in the rise of Western knowledge. To some extent, then, the rise of the West is not merely material but is also inextricably connected with the power of the West's capacity for knowledge production. It is this power-knowledge nexus, Mawdudi observes, that must be criticised and challenged in order to create a more viable and resistant Muslim identity. Mawdudi extensively analyses the rise of Western intellectual power. He explains the state of affairs of the global Muslim community of his time, specifically focusing on Indian Islam, in the following words:

> The Muslims of today are caught in this dual slavery: In some places they are under the sway of both intellectual and political slavery, and in other places the degree of mental

7. The Politics of Popular Islamic Texts

> slavery is higher than that of political slavery. Unfortunately, there is not even a single Muslim community in the world that is completely free, intellectually or politically. Wherever they are politically free, they are still mentally enslaved. Their schools, offices, bazaars, societies, homes, and even their bodies, symbolise the power of Western thought, Western knowledge, and Western know-how. They think with a Western mind, see with Western eyes, and walk, consciously or unconsciously, on the paths created by the West. In all it has been imprinted on their minds that truth is what the West considers truth, and false is what the West considers false. (6)

It is important to note here that this passage is not simply a critique of the West, but also of the prescriptive and discursive power of Western knowledge over the very minds and bodies of Muslims. Deeply embedded in this indictment of Westernised Muslims is an attempt at retrieving a Muslim ideal itself, seen through the will to master the modern world without compromising what, for Mawdudi, constitutes true Muslim self-hood. This distrust of the West and its system of knowledge stems from its immediate threat to the Muslim way of life, and eventually is normalised in the text as a corrupting influence. As this power-knowledge affect is produced within a colonised space, the distrust of anything Western then becomes a main default position for religious reformers. In the case of Islam, considering the vast corpus of its own rules for everyday life, any Western concept and practice that is introduced by the British or adopted by Muslims themselves must pass a test of acceptance. Anything that can be accepted as inherently Islamic and, within the range of acceptability of Islamic *Shariah*, can be normalised and accepted; however, anything that is purely Western and can not be normalised within the context of Islamic *Shariah* becomes a threat to both the body and spirit of Muslims.

Juxtaposing one's own historical views with colonial intellectual and social influences is not only pertinent to the Muslims of British colonial India. Even ostensibly secular Indian nationalists attempted to retrieve a purely Indian national past from the effects of colonial domination. Partha Chatterjee explains this tendency in the context of Bengal as follows:

> In colonial society, the political domain was under alien control and the colonized excluded from its decisive zones by a rule of colonial difference [. . .] the nationalist response was to constitute a new sphere of the private in a domain marked by cultural difference: the domain of the "national" was defined as one that was different from the "Western". In this aspect of the political domain, then, the hegemonic movement of nationalism was not to promote but rather, in a quite fundamental sense, to resist the sway of the modern institutions of disciplinary power. (75)

In the case of secular nationalism, which for Chatterjee still had a predominantly "Hindu" (74) character, the cultural and private sphere becomes the place of native dominance, a space the colonisers cannot penetrate. For Chatterjee, the rise of Indian nationalism can be genuinely traced only within the context of this cultural domain. But Islam, as Chatterjee also acknowledges, could not be contained within this paradigm: as opposed to a purist Hindu past, "[it] had its own alternative classical tradition" (73).

This classical tradition, I suggest, was inherently supranational and deeply political in its view of the colonisers, and it is this political aspect of the colonial power structure that finds itself expressed in Mawdudi's essays. As is obvious, Mawdudi can only argue against the colonial power structures in the realm of politics; it is political power, born out of the Western ascendancy in knowledge, which has materially and intellectually vanquished Muslims both internationally and in India. In explaining the rise of Western modernity, Mawdudi dis-

7. The Politics of Popular Islamic Texts

cusses the rise of scientific rationalism and its clash with Christian or metaphysical explanations of the world:

> The cradle of philosophy and science in which Western civilisation was nourished has been moving, for the past six hundred years or so, towards a path of atheism, secularism, and materialism. It would be right to say that the current Western civilisation was born of the clash between religion and reason. (8)

Hence, for Mawdudi, for Muslims to emulate and internalise the precepts of Western civilisation, they must also go through the same processes of inexorable secularisation. A movement into the Western system of thought, then, presupposes a certain degree of detachment from religion, which for Mawdudi, of course, is completely unacceptable for a Muslim way of life. Mawdudi also traces the various stages of the bifurcation between the religious and philosophical paths in Western thought and praxis. It must be noted that the purpose of this particular historical account of the rise of Western civilisation is to prove to his audience that if Muslims uncritically follow the same trajectory, then they will also end up reaching the same kind of future: a future in which religion is *relegated* for the preeminent interests of reason and science. For Mawdudi, an uncritical following of Western ways of thought is the most potent intellectual threat to the Muslims of his time living under colonial rule, and also by extension, to those living in later postcolonial, successor nation-states. The war of ideas in the history of Western civilisation, according to Mawdudi, "was first between the proponents of free thought and the clergy, but as the clergy were fighting the free thinkers in the name of religion, it soon morphed into a fight between Christianity and free inquiry" (9). Hence, for Mawdudi, what could have easily been termed as a contest between two modes of reason (secular and metaphysical) turned into a war between, on the one hand, freedom of thought, and on the other, religious dogma. It is this signification of this medieval European contest that, in Mawdudi's analysis, culminated in the extreme response on both sides of the argument, making it imperative on the proponents of free thought to "declare all those methods unscientific that relied on a supernatural explanation of the world" (9).

It is in the eighteenth century, Mawdudi suggests, that it became obvious to Western civilisation that the "method of inquiry that relegated God in the name of scientific inquiry about the universe would culminate in an atheist and faithless world" (11). The teleological movement of the conflict between reason and faith that Mawdudi observes always results in the annihilation of faith by science. For Mawdudi, in the nineteenth century "materialism reached its ultimate perfection" and philosophers like "Vogt, Buchner, Comte and others privileged matter over all else" (12). Mawdudi goes on to produce his succinct explanation of the debates of Western philosophy, science, and religion, and his discussion also includes a brief reference to the importance of Darwinian thought.

There is, certainly, a reason for Mawdudi to provide a long (albeit cursory and descriptive) list of the main currents of Western philosophy. He concludes his discussion of the movement of Western thought with the following declaration about the outcome of the Western civilisation being proffered to Muslims under colonial rule:

> This is that philosophy and science that produced the Western civilisation. It neither has room for God nor does it offer any weight to the revealed wisdom provided through the prophets. There is no life after death and no accountability for one's life after death [. . .] this is a purely materialistic civilisation. Its whole system is void of all those ideas upon which the edifice of Islam stands. Its ideology is completely opposite to that of Islam and its path is in exactly the opposite direction to that of Islam. (13)

This declaration at the end of a long list of major markers of Western intellectual and religious history is instructive in understanding Maw-

7. The Politics of Popular Islamic Texts

dudi's stance on the adoption of Western values by Muslims. Note that the declaration does not come simply as a statement; it is provided after presenting a brief itinerary of the progress of Western civilisation. It is only after Mawdudi has proved, within the logic of his essay, where a blind following of the development of Western knowledge leads – the death of religion – that he makes his final statement about the degree of difference between Islam and Western civilisation. In the conclusion, he provides some sense of a well-thought-out position, derived from a dialectical argument, according to which the leading paradigms of Islam and the West are revealed as being completely incompatible.

Having given his verdict about the nature and trajectory of Western civilisation, Mawdudi then links this conclusion to the plight of the Muslim world at the time. He writes:

> It can be called nothing other than our bad luck that in the very century [the nineteenth] in which this new civilisation reached the height of its materialism and unfaith most of the Muslim nations were subjugated by the West. Muslims were invaded by the Western pen and the sword simultaneously. The minds that had already succumbed to the political dominance of the West quite easily also became impressed by Western knowledge. The situation was worst for the nations that were directly dominated by Western political power. (13-14)

For Mawdudi, the rise of the West did not just initiate the fall of the Islamic world, but it also caused the fall of the Islamic way of thought and life and replaced it with what he calls the intellectual and political slavery of the Islamic world. The main cause for the fall of Islam, then, is not just the loss of political power but the partial erasure of a purely Islamic explanation of life and the cosmos, caused by the secular and atheistic mode of thought introduced by the West and impressed upon new generations of colonised Muslim subjects. As far as

Mawdudi is concerned, the greatest loss in this encounter is not necessarily material but spiritual, and it is this spiritual deficit that keeps them subjugated and colonised. For any Muslim reform or resistance movement to succeed against the coloniser, a complete break from the Western mode of thinking and a complete immersion into what is considered an Islamic way of life becomes a precondition. Mawdudi writes about this aspect of Muslim struggle in "The Right Method of Reconstructing the *Millat*," which is the second essay from *Tanqihat* included in my discussion.

Having explained the main cause of the Muslim troubles, Mawdudi then goes on to discuss the possibilities of a Muslim revival. He starts this essay with an incisive critique of the revolutionary method of change. Within the context of Mawdudi's essay the revolutionary method is expressed by the Urdu word *Inqalab*, which literally means revolution. Generally, Mawdudi uses it to imply any method of change that uses physical violence in replacing one system with another. As he mentions the Bolshevik revolution as one of his examples in this essay, it is safe to suggest that by *Inqalab* he means something akin to the Russian revolution. Differentiating between a reformer and a revolutionary, Mawdudi comments:

> There is no doubt that often a reformer has to perform the same function as that of a revolutionary, for both of them attempt to slice off any tumors in the body politic. The difference is that the reformer first diagnoses the particular part that needs such invasive surgery and then uses his surgical instrument and has the soothing balms right beside him for application after the removal of the unwanted part. The revolutionary, on the other hand, in his passion uses the blade indiscriminately and in the process ends up destroying even the parts that he could have easily used. (116)

It is obvious in this surgical analogy that for Mawdudi selective reform is a preferred mode of change, as opposed to a revolutionary

7. The Politics of Popular Islamic Texts

mode of change that must destroy the whole structure in order to build a new one. Another important flaw that Mawdudi points out in the revolutionary method is its reliance on these "new forms as opposed to those associated with the old" (117), an approach which necessitates a total replacement of the traditional view by something different and new, even though imperfect. To highlight his point, Mawdudi cites two major outbreaks of such radicalism from European history: the French and the Bolshevik revolutions. Both these movements, Mawdudi suggests, accomplished a total upheaval of the old systems but had to fall back to a more moderate approach in devising their eventual political systems. The revolutionary method, for Mawdudi, is inherently extremist in its nature and must bring extreme suffering that can only be alleviated after a long period of trial and error.

This discussion of the two methods is explicitly connected by Mawdudi with the question of Islam and colonialism:

> I have said all this because Indian Muslims have also reached a revolutionary crisis, and I want that before the negative aspects of this revolutionary crisis manifest themselves, we should attempt to invite both the revolutionary and the traditionalist reform groups to think and contemplate together.
>
> (118)

While Mawdudi does want to change the state of Muslim consciousness under the British, his approach is one of cautious reform rather than revolutionary change. It is this selective method of change and revival, termed "gradualism" by one of his critics (Ahmad 217), that he privileges as a larger mode of resistance that he believes will eventually assist the Muslims in breaking out of the intellectual and political hold of the West. Even though Mawdudi had previously discussed the trajectories of Western civilisation and Islam as two diametrically opposed currents of history, his approach to the Islamic revival is neither so exclusive, nor so binary. He articulates his philosophy of religious reform in the following terms:

> The edifice of Islamic *Millat* was constructed on the following successive foundations: The *Qur'an*, the *Sunnah* of the Prophet Muhammad, and the *Ijtihad* of Muslim scholars. But unfortunately this arrangement has been completely reversed, and the new arrangement first takes into consideration the scholarly *Ijtihad*, then the *Sunnah* and then the *Qur'an*. It is this new arrangement that has made Islam into an ossified and unmoving thing. (119)

There are certain terms in this particular passage that need explaining before the whole passage is unpicked for analysis. The *Qur'an* obviously is the sacred text of Islam; the Sunnah is a religious compendium essentially comprised of the authenticated sayings of the prophet Muhammad's about various aspects of Islamic life. *Ijtihad* in general is the opinion of a scholar or a group of scholars about any issues of Islamic *Sharia* or way of life; it signifies a particular spirit of argumentative inquiry. It is important to note that *Ijtihad* invariably requires knowledge of the *Qur'an* and the *Sunnah*, and only a scholar can think beyond them (a practice called *Qiyas*, or analogy, if there is no clear explanation for a concept or question in the *Qur'an* and the *Sunnah*. Therefore, when Mawdudi criticises the privileging of the *Ijtihad* over the two traditional sources of Muslim *Sharia*, he is actually criticising the official usage of the various schools of Muslim jurisprudence as markers of Islamic sectarianism, as opposed to the *Sunnah* and the *Qur'an* that are uncontested and equally sacred to all Muslims.

This return to the original source text is a direct response to the established practices of Indian Islam, which was deeply entrenched in the methods and practices of the medieval Islamic schools of interpretation, rather than the core texts of Islam itself. The four major Sunni schools of interpretation upon which later Muslims built a certain system of fellowship are named after the four major Sunni scholars from tenth-century Islam. They include: Imam Abu Hanifa, Imam Shafa'i, Imam Malik, and Imam Ahmad ibn Hanble. The major

7. The Politics of Popular Islamic Texts

Imam Malik, and Imam Ahmad ibn Hanble. The major Shi'i jurist is Imam Ja'far Sadiq. In the Indian context, the commentaries written by these scholars had in themselves become didactic texts, and as a result the Muslims of India were divided along the lines of their works; almost all major schools also believed that there was no longer any need for new interpretations as following the paths described by Imams (a practice known as *Taqlid*) was in itself sufficient. Therefore, most of the Islamic reform attempts of the nineteenth century, and even present-day movements, must first convince their audiences of the possibility of opening up the Islamic canon for a re-reading and re-interpretation.

While discussing the reforming role of Shah Waliyu'llah, one of the most important of the eighteenth-century Indian Muslim reformers, Barbara Metcalf comments about attempts at reaching back to the more authentic (and arguably, more substantive) sources of Islamic jurisprudence:

> Shah Waliyu'llah argued that unquestioning adherence to late compilations of legal decisions was an inadequate guide to religious truth. He blamed this dominant approach to the law, known as *Taqlid*, for laxity in religious matters and for differences among the law schools. Were learned Muslims to study revelation, they could unite in obedience to authentic teachings. He argued that the "door to *Ijtihad*," in the classical phrase, was not closed, and that those skilled in traditional sciences had the right and indeed the responsibility to consult original sources. (37)

Obviously Mawdudi was not the only thinker insisting on a return to the original and more authentic sources; however, unlike Waliyu'llah, his immediate context now included the politically charged situation of Indian Muslim life under the rule of the British. His insistence on *Ijtihad* now had far more urgency, for it is needed to prepare Muslims to seriously contest the "corrupting" intellectual and political influences of Western thought, filtered through colonial rule. Mawdudi was clearly opposed to revolutionary modes of change, as seen in his comments on the French and Bolshevik revolutions; he preferred a more reform-oriented movement, but one which was very particular in nature and took into account both the needs of Muslim society and the state of its subjugation to British colonial rule. He reminds his readers that

> [w]e should not forget that we are in a state of subjugation. We have no need for a revolutionary movement, as there is no fear of a strong and powerful opposition to our reform agenda. And even if we were to launch a revolutionary movement, we are not sure how long it would take this movement to reach a state of moderation and equilibrium. In fact, an unending revolutionary movement would only harm the larger edifice of Muslim society itself, for if we destroy the larger edifice of a subjugated Muslim society in the name of revolution, then where will it lead the whole Muslim community? It is because of this that we are forced to oppose the revolutionaries instead of the traditionalists. (122)

Thus ruling out the possibility of a revolutionary mode of change, Mawdudi concludes his essay by a brief reference to his preferred mode of Islamic reform. Note that this reform is offered as a moderate solution to the Muslims of India in the hope that it will create a larger Muslim consensus:

> The real remedy for our troubles is to right the arrangement of our knowledge that has been reversed. The *Qur'an* should be granted its original role as a guide, the *Hadis*, sayings of the prophet should be accorded the same respect as during the time of the prophet himself, and the opinions of the scholars should be graded as they were graded and accepted by their contemporaries. We need not to change everything they have

left us, but we should also not consider everything they have left us as unchangeable [. . .] if we reinitiate this arrangement, then the stalled train of Islam will start moving again, for the main cause of its failure to move was that we had relegated the driver from the front to somewhere in the rear of the train.

(123)

We have now briefly discussed two of Mawdudi's essays, both dealing with the state of Indian Muslims under colonialism. It is evident that Mawdudi traces the main cause of Muslim's subjugation to their intellectual slavery, and hence, his remedy is also inherently intellectual. This intellectual remedy aims to retrieve the best-suited knowledge from within Muslim tradition to offset the pernicious influences of Western knowledge consumed by an uncritical and captive colonised and subjugated Muslim audience.

These two brief occasional pieces published in an Urdu journal in the 1930s also capture the Muslim response to colonialism at a stage when the Indian nationalist movement had reached its maturity and when the Muslims of India were themselves defining their own place in the rising spirit of nationalism. These essays are also instructive in tracing the importance of Islamic political thought within the contemporary Muslim world. It is these aspects of these essays, their effective value in the present, that I will touch upon in the concluding part of this chapter. What Mawdudi discusses in these essays is not a new debate, nor is it specific only to his immediate historical context. This debate had been a part of the reformist discussion before him (as my reference to Shah Waliyu'llah suggests) and even goes on in our own times. For Example, Fazlur Rahman in his book *Islam and Modernity* suggests "a sort of passive and inept carrying on with the educational systems of the colonial period" (90) as one of the reasons for the lack of "creative education" (90) in Muslim societies.

What makes Mawdudi's work more compelling is the context of his intervention, and the mode of representation of his ideas. He is writing, as pointed out earlier, at the height of the Indian nationalist movement, and his writings are published in *Tarjuman-Al-Qur'an*, a popular Islamic Urdu journal sponsored by both Mawdudi himself and his organisation. Thus, his argument is not articulated within the confines of a limited academic space or the mosque, but proffered and consumed as popular writing in the most accessible language available. It is this immediate and popular mode of representation and its affective value on the Muslim masses that makes Mawdudi's intervention so unique and so politically potent.

More importantly, Mawdudi is not just a regional Indian scholar; due to the availability of his works and the extensive range of his expertise on a variety of religious issues, he was also able to achieve an international following, during his life and long after his death. In fact, despite certain clear intellectual limitations, Mawdudi's works, according to his biographer Seyyid Vali Reza Nasr, have "influenced revivalism from Morocco to Malaysia, leaving their mark on thinkers such as Sayyid Qutb [. . .] and have influenced the spread of Islamic revivalism in central Asia, North Africa, and Southeast Asia" (3-4).

Certainly this brief discussion of two of Mawdudi's essays is not meant to represent the totality of Islam in a crystallised form, nor is it an attempt at providing a cohesive argument for the universality of his thought to the Islamic reform movements. What we learn, in a nutshell, is that for Muslims encountering a modernity enforced by the colonial powers, the path was much harder and problematic. Having a deep sense of their own tradition and textual history, they could not just accept Western ideas on face value alone: these ideas had to be filtered through a tradition of Muslim acceptability. That is precisely what Mawdudi, and so many other Muslim reformers, tried to articulate. For Islam to accept modernity, the modern ideas must somehow be made commensurate with existing ideas of Muslim piety and faith; an uncritical following of Western thought, against the backdrop of Islamic knowledge production, can lead to the intellectual and political subjugation of Muslims. This tendency to view the West from the filter of the Islamic *Sharia* and the Islamic system of good and bad is prevalent even today. On the whole, having discussed two of Mawdudi's essays, it can be said that Islam's interface with modernity is quite nuanced and complex, and only a complex view of this experience will render a better understanding between Islam and the West.

Works Cited

Ahmad, Aziz. *Islamic Modernism in India and Pakistan, 1857-1964.* London: Royal Institute of International Affairs and Oxford University Press, 1967.

Chatterjee, Partha. *The Nation and its Fragments: Colonial and Postcolonial Histories.* Princeton: Princeton University Press, 1993.

Gramsci, Antonio. *Selections from the Prison Notebooks.* Trans. and ed. Quintin Hoare and Geoffrey Smith. New York: International Publishers, 1971.

Mawdudi, Abu'l-A'la *Tanqihat : Islam aur Maghrabi Tehzeeb ka Tasadum aur us se Paida Shuda Masail per Mukhtasar Tebsare* [*Investigations: Brief Commentaries on the Problems Caused by the Clash of Islam and the Western Civilisation*]. Pathankot, India: Maktaba Jama'at-i-Islami, 1939.

___. *Islami Riasat* [*The Islamic State*]. 1967. Lahore, Pakistan: Islamic Publications, 2000.

___. "Hamari Zehni Ghulami aur us ke Asbab" ["Our Intellectual Slavery and its Causes"]. Mawdudi, *Tanqihat* 5-15.

___. "Millat ki Ta'meer-e-nau ka Sahi Tariqa" ["The Right Method of Reconstructing the *Millat*"]. Mawdudi, *Tanqihat* 116-23.

Metcalf, Barbara. *Islamic Revival in British India: Deoband, 1860-1900.* Princeton: Princeton University Press, 1982.

Nasr, Seyyed Vali Reza. *Mawdudi and the Making of Islamic Revivalism.* New York: Oxford University Press, 1996.

Rahman, Fazlur. *Islam and Modernity: Transformation of an Intellectual Tradition.* Chicago: University of Chicago Press, 1982.

8. Memoirs of Maharanis: The Politics of Marriage, Companionship, and Love in Late-Colonial Princely India

Angma Dey Jhala
Tufts University

This chapter examines the memoirs and biographies of five Hindu Maharanis who lived during the height of British colonial rule in India. They reveal a fascinating glimpse into the courtly universe of sequestered, royal women, who have been largely neglected in the study of modern South Asian history. Mythologised by Orientalist literature as lascivious and sensual and reconstructed by nationalist discourse as silent and secluded, the courtly Indian woman has invariably been depicted as the object of male desire and devoid of agency. A dependent and victimised creature, bejewelled and dressed only for the eyes of her male kin, she is the screen upon which both colonial and nationalist imaginary play themselves out in forming conceptions of the Indic "traditional" or indigenous. This chapter reveals a picture of much greater cultural cosmopolitanism and paradox.

Despite the secluded boundaries of *purdah*, royal and courtly Indian women lived within three spheres. They navigated the inner realm of the domestic, familial world and the wider arena of the royal court through a familiarity with dynastic politics. They crossed between the regional seclusion of what was termed the "native states" and the major cities of British India such as Calcutta, Bombay and Delhi; and they travelled between Europe and Asia in an era when few Indian women (or men for that matter) made such journeys. Benefiting from a far more heteroglossic and cosmopolitan education than scholars have earlier suggested, they were instructed both in Indic forms of learning (e.g. Sanskrit, regional languages, Hindu customary religious practice) and European disciplines, including British literature, language, history, and mathematics. They served as regents or rulers in their own right, resisting and manipulating British political officers, and, in postcolonial India, a number of erstwhile Maharanis have attained high elected office.

This eclectic group of women was recognised for their influence and contribution to education, politics, religion and historical preservation. Maharani Chimnabai II (1872-1958), wife of the progressive Sayajirao Gaekwad of Baroda, wrote an important treatise, *The Position of Women in Indian Life* (1911), which addressed concerns regarding labour, professional life and gender relations. Maharani Sunity Devi of Cooch Behar (1865-1932), the first Indian woman to write her autobiography in English, travelled often to England, where she was a favourite of Queen Victoria; she also wrote folktales and short stories. Maharani Indira Devi of Cooch Behar (1892-1968), daughter of Chimnabai and daughter-in-law of Sunity, went to boarding school in England; one of the first Indian Maharanis to marry for love, she served as a regent and contributed to the social and political life of her state.

Her daughter Maharani Gayatri Devi of Jaipur (b.1919) studied at Shantiniketan in Bengal and at boarding schools in Switzerland and England, eventually marrying the Rajput Hindu ruler of Jaipur. After her marriage, she was influential in opening schools for *purdah* girls during the 1940s, participated in the All-India Womens' Conferences, aided in wartime relief during WW II, and after 1947, ran for Parliament and served as Minister of Tourism in Rajasthan. Maharani Vijaya Raje Scindia (1919-2001) attended university in Benares and Lucknow, married into the powerful Hindu Maratha kingdom of Gwalior, later ran for election and became one of the most powerful and senior members of the Bharatiya Janata Party (BJP).

The memoirs of these Indian princesses suggests a far more nuanced picture of British India, which brings out of the archive both a history of the private domestic sphere and the political universe of royal Indian women. They comment on the affairs of family, on marriages, courtship and love, as well as the relationship between Indian indigenous rulers and British paramountcy. In certain instances, it was British political agents and tutors who facilitated the marriages of these women, influenced their education and engendered their political involvement in the princely state and later the postcolonial republic.

A brief history of princely India

Most South-Asian historians of the colonial period have focused exclusively on the social, cultural and political developments of what was termed "British India." Nineteenth- and twentieth-century historiography has eclipsed the rich and vibrant legacy of what was dubbed the "native states" of princely India, some six hundred semi-autonomous kingdoms of varying geographical, religious, ethnic and linguistic diversity. Before 1947, two fifths of the subcontinent and one third of the population belonged to these native states, which spanned the foothills of the Himalayas to the southernmost tip of the Indian peninsula (Copland 8). Many princely states maintained *zenanas* or "women's courts." Architecturally, the *zenanas* were the sequestered women's quarters of the palace or home, where wives, mothers, sisters and courtesans of the ruler lived with their extended female relations and attendants behind *purdah*. More generally, the term relates to the socio-cultural world created by courtly women, with its ensuing traditions of marriage, politics, material culture, and aesthetics.

After Britain emerged as the single paramount power in the subcontinent, it determined not to directly rule the whole of India, but only those areas which were financially profitable and politically expedient. For the remaining terra incognita, which included many "princely states," the British implemented a policy of indirect rule. Indian rulers held full authority in internal matters of state governance such as taxation, state revenue collection, criminal and judicial law, and the development of educational and cultural institutions, but could not conduct foreign relations with other nations (Ramusack 2; Ashton 7). After 1857 it became evident that Indian princes were a vital component in

Britain's policy of indirect rule (Ramusack 87). According to Lord Canning, first Viceroy of India, certain "patches" of the native states proved to be "breakwaters in the storm" which would have otherwise "swept away" the British (Government of India).

Thereafter, the princes were "accorded a permanent position as part of the British Empire" (Ashton 17). From the 1860s onwards, a system of personal relationships between Indian rulers and their British sovereigns began to emerge. The adoption and giving of Imperial honours, such as medals, gun salutes, seating placement at durbars, orders, and knighthoods further tied Indian princes to their colonial masters. Royal Indian women were included in this process of "ornamentation" (Cannadine 90).

In 1921 the princes founded their own body, The Chamber of Princes, which provided a forum for dialogue and cultivated "an environment in which good government became more fashionable" (Rudolphs 6-7). As modern statesmen, they attempted to combine indigenous *rajadharma* with British models of good governance. However, the differences between the princes proved to be too great to create a united political force. Rajput Kshatriya kings in Jaipur and Jodhpur looked down upon the Sudra-descended Maratha kings of Gwalior and Indore, as well as the Jat-Sikh kings of Punjab, and vice versa. This lack of cohesiveness led to the wane of the princely order and its weakened place in Indian politics by the mid-twentieth century. The princes were generally characterised as the losers in the battle for power between the British and the Indian nationalists with the resolution of Partition in 1947 (Ramusack, *Princes of India*, xv).

At independence, the princely states lost their autonomous identities. Rulers were stripped of their executive rights and their territories merged with the new democratic republic. Under Indira Gandhi in 1971, the erstwhile princes further lost their last major entitlement, their constitutionally granted income (the Privy Purse) which was based on an annual percentage of the revenue from their former kingdoms. Nonetheless, many of these former sovereigns remained active in public life, and a number of courtly and royal women emerged from *purdah* and entered democratic politics.

In contrast to arguments that the colonised woman literally "disappears" (Spivak 306) from lived historical experience between patriarchy and imperialism, tradition and, modernity or that the public and private spheres of male and female discourse are separated through a construction of *bahir* 'the world' and *ghar* 'home' (Chatterjee 120), these memoirs reveal heteroglossic women who crossed both the inner and the outer spaces of governance, both colonial and postcolonial. Neither silent nor silenced figures, their lives provide new readings on the roles of women in *purdah* in colonial India. In this chapter, I will analyse the ways in which the colonising process influenced their motivations for politically based unions of alliance.

The use of the biography as text and source

In part, these memoirs and biographies reflect the richness of the archive available for historians of British colonialism in South Asia. Non-literary material which was earlier disqualified from scholarly investigation (oral histories, interviews, lyric etc) are becoming increasingly accessible to academics, and to groups previously marginalised from this discourse, such as women. Social anthropology, literary criticism, psychoanalysis, and history have challenged the emphasis once placed on "high culture" print forms, articulated by dominant, (often white, male) empowered elites (Scott). In addition, literary sources which have earlier remained exclusively within the domestic sphere, such as women's memoirs, diaries, letters, poetry and fiction, are being incorporated into socio-political histories. As Antoinette Burton points out in *Dwelling in the Archive:*

> What counts as an archive? Can private memories of home serve as evidence of political history? What do we make of the histories that domestic interiors, once concrete and now perhaps crumbling or even disappeared, have the capacity to

yield? And, given women's vexed relationship to the kinds of history that archives typically house, what does it mean to say that home can and should be seen not simply as a dwelling-place for women's memory but as one of the foundations of history – history conceived of, that is, as a narrative, a practice, and a site of desire? (4)

These biographies of *zenana* women from the late nineteenth and twentieth centuries provide rare descriptions of experiences (familial, political and private) of women's lives through their own eyes. As a number of these women who wrote autobiographies were also interrelated through marriage or birth, they thus shed light on a whole generation of elite women across India.

It is important to mention both the advantages and limitations of personal historical narratives as source material. Mary Chamberlain and Paul Thompson note in their introduction to *Narrative and Genre* that with the move from deconstruction to postmodernism, advocated by a small but influential group of radicals in the 1980s, the autobiography became interpreted as a purely literary and subjective genre, "in which there was no longer a biographical self capable of reflection, or a biographical reality upon which to reflect [. . .] reflection itself was merely ideology; and autobiography totally fictional" ("Genre" 3).

This observation highlights autobiography's nebulous place between fact and fiction. Chamberlain and Thompson ask, "how far should it [autobiography] be read as a narrative of real experience, and how far as a form of fiction?"(3). The memoir can be read both as history and as literature; it is neither infallible nor objective, and a scholar must be aware of the subjectivity of these personal histories. On the other hand, nearly every life is heightened by colourful anecdotes. Who can legitimately be the writer of a categorical truth? If the memoirist cannot tell her tale without some embellishment, no one can. Lucy Moore observes that Gayatri Devi herself admitted in a letter to Lord Mountbatten that her autobiography was full of mistakes,

8. Memoirs of Maharanis

as it had been too hurriedly put to print before she could properly revise it (Moore 287).

In particular, these memoirs reveal the politics of the private for women who inherently led public lives. As Maharanis, these women had innately politicised roles, being the daughters and wives of ruling princes. For them marriage was perhaps the most significant event of their lives, both in a private context and as a political institution of alliance making, and it often shaped the future course of their involvement in public life. The late nineteenth and twentieth centuries in particular brought radical change to traditional concepts of marriage within Indian aristocratic circles, in large part because of the active participation of the British in making marriage alliances, but also due to the introduction of Occidental ideas of romance, and new definitions of partnership.

British matchmaking in late-colonial India: The case of Sunity Devi of Cooch Behar

The Victorian Age was one characterised by an almost obsessive urge to commemorate events and life stories through the written word. Queen Victoria herself published her memoirs and accounts of her time as a queen and mother, which she gave to official guests (Moore 57). Like her friend and contemporary Queen Victoria, Maharani Sunity Devi of Cooch Behar was a keen memoirist and writer. Her married life from its inception was a reflection of the period for it was deeply influenced by Victorian attitudes in regards to companionship, family and friendship.

Sunity Devi was an unusually educated woman for her day. She claimed to be the first Indian woman to write her autobiography in English in 1921 and was one of a handful to attend university in Calcutta (Sunity Devi 11, 1). She promoted female education in Cooch Behar and all over Bengal when she was Maharani and later as a Rajmata (dowager queen). She was born in 1865 as the daughter of the

Kshatriya Bengali Hindu reformer, Keshub Chandra Sen, who was considered to be the Martin Luther of Hinduism, for his advocacy of a dynamic policy of social reform and a "superstition-free" Hindu spirituality. He endorsed monogamy and a theistic belief in one omniscient and omnipresent God and supported the eradication of caste distinctions and greater education for women. His views were encapsulated in his lifelong mantra, "One God, One Life, One Wife" (Moore 55). He argued that women who were learned would make better spouses and mothers and in 1872 urged the British government to pass legislation, known as the Brahmo Marriage Act, which increased the minimum marriage age for girls to fourteen and boys to eighteen (Moore 55-58).

Sunity grew up in a household influenced by such views, which encouraged women's learning and agency and promoted classical Indian culture. Intimately connected with the family of Rabindranath Tagore, the Sen home was full of music, song and theatre. Sunity Devi often heard open-air theatricals, such as the *jatra* performed nearby (Sunity Devi 29). In addition, Sunity was skilled in the English language, literature and music. In the eyes of the British, her progressive and anglicised upbringing made her an ideal bride for the eastern Indian princes they wished to influence. In 1878 the British tutors of the Maharaja of Cooch Behar approached her father with this in mind. The Maharaja of Cooch Behar, Nripendra Narayan Bhup Bahadur, was a minor and ward of the British Government; he was being carefully "educated" into a model ruler (Sunity Devi 49). His English tutors wanted the young prince to attend public school in England, but his mothers and other female relations would not consent to his voyage unless he was first married in India.

In search of an enlightened and educated Hindu bride who was no longer in *purdah*, the Cooch Behar contingent pursued Sen, believing his reformed view of Hinduism, with its emphasis on a theistic philosophy and the abolition of caste, was closer to an Occidental, Christian sensibility. The Maharaja's British advisors, Dalton and Kneller,

8. Memoirs of Maharanis

arranged the meeting between the two families and prospective partners; it was their approval that sanctioned the union. As Sunity Devi noted in her *Autobiography*, her first interview was performed by Mr. Dalton. She describes their meeting in her father's house in Calcutta:

> Then I was taken to the drawing-room, where Mr. Dalton and the Bengali officials awaited me. Mr. Dalton looked kind but critical.
>
> "Won't you play for me?" He asked.
>
> I obediently sat myself at the piano and played a simple piece of music. Dalton scrutinized me as I went up to the piano with my back to my seat and as I talked to him; and wrote a descriptive letter to the Maharajah afterwards.
>
> "Very nice," he said, in such a charming way that I did not think he was examining me. He seemed favourably impressed, and so it proved, for in one of his letters to my father he wrote: "I thought your daughter a very charming young lady, and in every way a suitable bride for the Maharajah."
>
> (54-55)

The Maharaja's British advisor served as matchmaker, overruling the position normally taken by family members (particularly the mother) or indigenous state advisors. Only after Dalton found the girl to be "a suitable bride" did the young Maharaja proceed to meet his bride-to-be. In this case, the colonial government subtly influenced perceptions of conjugal love and social mores. In addition, it affected religious practice in the kingdom, for the marriage was agreed upon only on the condition that Cooch Behar would perform Brahmo rites and rituals and that the young Maharaja would accept the practice of monogamy. In 1878, the young prince wrote this reply to his future father-in-law, as Sunity Devi noted in her *Autobiography*:

> My Dear Sir,
>
> I have been asked to let you know what my honest opinion is on the subject of polygamy.
>
> In reply, I beg to inform you that it has always been my opinion that no man should take more than one wife, and I can assure you that I hold that opinion still.
>
> I give below a statement of my religious views and opinions. I believe in one God and am in heart a Theist. (58-59)

By marrying this eastern Kshatriya ruler to the daughter of a Bengali reformer, the British-Indian government hoped to lead the native state one step closer to modern progress and Western enlightenment. Even members of the British aristocracy and royal family became involved in the politics of arranged marriages for Indian princes, and their ideas of companionate relations changed the motivations for personal unions. This alliance expressed the linking of two parts of India: the autonomous princely states and the suzerainty of the paramount power, based in Calcutta. It also reveals how disparate and distinct communities and regions of the sub-continent could be joined under the unifying banner of the Imperial Raj, for these were families which ordinarily would not have intermarried.

Queen Victoria served as a godmother to the children of several Indian rulers and was on close terms with a number of *zenana* ladies. She had met Keshub Chandra Sen in 1870, when he visited her at Osborne House, the Queen's residence on the Isle of Wight. At their meeting, he presented her with a portrait of his wife. The Queen was "so pleased" by the gift, as he wrote of their meeting, that she requested his portrait and gave him two inscribed copies of her books, *Early Years of the Prince Consort* and *Highland Journal* (Moore 57).

The Cooch Behar family in particular enjoyed a close relationship with British royalty. Arriving in London for the Queen's Golden Jubilee in 1887, they were soon caught up in the functions of the season. They attended dances, receptions, and garden parties, dined with the

8. Memoirs of Maharanis

Prince of Wales, and resided in a luxurious gilt bedroom during their stay at Windsor Castle. Sunity Devi was well liked by the English royal family and was on familiar terms with Princess Mary, who later became Queen Mary, the Duchess of Teck and Alix, Princess of Wales. At her formal presentation to the Queen in Buckingham Palace, Sunity Devi was the only woman whom Victoria kissed in greeting that day; a rare sign of favour. A few months later when Sunity Devi became pregnant, the Queen immediately stepped in as the future godmother of her son, Victor, who was born in May 1888. Such close association with the British upper classes would continue when the Maharani returned to India. Sunity and her family feted leading Victorian and Edwardian aristocrats, who regularly made visits to Cooch Behar for shooting and other recreational activities (Moore 103-08).

Just as British officials were instrumental in arranging marriages for Indian princes, so were members of the British royal family. Famously, Queen Victoria was instrumental in proposing an alliance between her favourite, the deposed Sikh ruler Duleep Singh of the Punjab, and the Hindu princess Victoria Gourrama from Coorg in the South. The young Maharaja Duleep Singh, son of Maharaja Ranjit Singh, the "Lion of the Punjab," was deposed by Governor-General Dalhousie when the kingdom of Punjab was annexed in 1849. The boy-king was quickly made a ward of the British Empire, converted to Christianity, and sent to England for schooling, where he became a favourite of Queen Victoria. In England, Duleep Singh was given a comfortable allowance, worthy of a nineteenth-century British gentleman, and kept away as much as possible from the influence of his former Sikh subjects and relatives in India. Although later in his life Duleep Singh would convert back to Sikhism and long to return to the Punjab, his story is a case in point of the Anglicisation of Indian royals by the British. Taking a personal interest in Duleep Singh, Queen Victoria wrote: "What he might turn out, if left in the hands of the unscrupulous Indians of his own country, of course, no one can foresee" (qtd. in Campbell 47).

Known as a domineering grandmother among European royals, arranging unions between her younger relations from Russia to France, Queen Victoria showed similar interest in her godson. She saw the prospective alliance with the princess of Coorg as one of compatibility between personalities, culture, and religion for "they are both religious, both fond of music, both gentle in their natures" (qtd. in Alexander and Anand 63). While the Queen suggested the marriage, she did not deny the value of love and choice. In a letter from Charles Osborne to Lord Login, Victoria Gourrama's guardian, he describes the Queen's intents:

> I know that the Queen thinks that this would be the best arrangement for their happiness *provided that they were to like each other* – of course, without this no happiness could exist. Of course the Queen takes a great interest in the little princess, as Her Majesty considers Herself as *more* than a Godmother to her. (Ibid.; italics in the original)

Duleep Singh, on his part, was surprised to find himself involved in an arranged marriage, and in the West at that. He believed such calculated proceedings were "not the European way" and was determined to remain a bachelor (Alexander 64). Later, he cited Victoria Gourrama's indiscreet, flirtatious nature as reason for his rejection, noting she would make an inappropriate wife (77). However, when Duleep Singh expressed passionate interest in a young English aristocrat, the Queen and her advisors adamantly opposed that liaison (81). Obviously, she did not favour miscegenation.

Not only did English officials and royals become players in the marriage market, but European perceptions of love and romance also instigated marriages. As Dipesh Chakrabarty has noted with regard to domesticity in nineteenth-century Bengal:

> The British in India [. . .] promot[ed] the idea that husbands and wives should be friends/companions in marriage [. . .] It reflected the well-known Victorian patriarchal ideals of

"companionate marriage" which the British introduced into India in the nineteenth century and which many Bengali male and female reformers embraced with great zeal. (51)

During the height of Empire, the British Raj influenced the personal lives of Indian courtly women, and disseminated Westernised attitudes regarding conjugality, love and family relations. From subtle to overt practices, the colonial government helped to reshape the nature of marriage among Indian royals, even while advancing and refashioning certain allegedly traditional practices. The lives of Sunity Devi's daughter-in-law, Indira Devi of Baroda, and her granddaughter, Gayatri Devi of Cooch Behar, are examples of royal women who chose love marriages – radical acts for the early twentieth century.

Breaking with the old: Marriages of love in the lives of Indira Devi of Baroda and Gayatri Devi of Cooch Behar

Daughter of the progressive Maratha ruler, Maharaja Sayajirao Gaekwad of Baroda, Indira Devi (1892-1968) grew up within a strict *zenana*. Baroda was one of the preeminent Maratha princely states; her father Sayajirao was a forward-looking, modern ruler, much admired for his efficient and enlightened administration of his state and for supporting the education of Dr. Ambedkar, a dalit who would later become one of the writers of the Indian constitution. Sayajirao is well remembered for his subtle resistance to colonial dominance, most notably in the 1911 Delhi Durbar when he famously turned his back on the English monarchs, King George and Queen Mary; he refused to wear his Order of the Star of India, the greatest award given to an Indian prince by the British government (Bhagavan 61). That he did this even though he was constrained by the rubrics of British paramountcy was a strong act of opposition. Indira Devi's mother Chimnabai was a singularly impressive female figure of her generation. The Vicereine, Lady Minto, when she visited Baroda in 1909 described Chimnabai as "very pleasant and hospitable, and [...] clever, taking a great interest in politics, and playing a prominent part in the affairs of the State" (qtd. in Moore 97).

After travelling to Europe and America, Chimnabai published *The Position of Women in Indian life* (1911), which contrasted the roles of Indian and Western women. By her own admission, her objective was to "awaken [her] Indian sisters from their lethargy of ages, to enable them to take their proper place in Indian public life" (viii). Chimnabai's encyclopaedic text glosses many thinkers and ideas; she discusses the role of women across the world and through time, examining women in hunter-gatherer communities, the Arab countries, the heroines of Sanskrit epics and those of ancient Egypt and Greece. She analyses European women as government leaders, professors, and salon intellectuals; describes Winston Churchill's views on women; catalogues great women rulers (from the Maratha princess Ahilya Bai to Queen Victoria) and discusses women's education in India.

The chapter headings of the book are illustrative of the Maharani's broad interests. They include sections on professions for women, agriculture and land ownership, the arts, intellectual calling, philanthropy, business, domestic science (husbandry and cooking), women inspectors, money-lending, rescue women, and women's interests such as issues of labour and work; she concludes with a chapter on the position of women in Japan, a country she had visited. Emphasising the importance of cultural relativism when comparing societies, she argues that the West is not paramount to the East, and certain Indian customs are inimitable and admirable:

> Some of the projects will no doubt appeal to them, but it would nevertheless be well for them to bear in mind the need to guard against too slavish an imitation of Western notions. Every country by intelligent observation can learn something from other lands, but at the same time each should strive to preserve its own racial characteristics, just as each sex should endeavor, not to ape the other but to make the most of its own

peculiar distinctions of character. There should be no hasty adoption of customs essentially foreign to our nations. In the words of Bacon the great English philosopher: "It were good that men into their innovations would follow the example of Time itself, which, indeed, innovateth greatly, but quietly, and by degrees scarce to be perceived." (xiii-xiv)

Indira Devi grew up in just such a progressive and culturally relative environment. Her parents, like the Cooch Behar family, were close associates of the English royal family but they had more stringently traditional attitudes towards marriage. At a young age, her parents arranged her marriage to the Scindia monarch, a member of a fellow Hindu Maratha state that shared the same princely order, caste and community. Her union with the Gwalior Maharaja would have been one of a "business arrangement as well as a romance" (Moore 15). During negotiations for the ensuing marriage, Scindia sent his aide to inform Indira of their future daily schedule as husband and wife. It was a highly pragmatic proposition. They would ride together on Monday mornings and he would visit her rooms on Thursday nights. The other evenings would be kept aside for his other wives and mistresses (15). Indira, who had a mind of her own, found this unacceptable and broke off the engagement. She decided to marry the younger brother of the ruler from the lower-ranked, Kshatriya state of Cooch Behar instead.

This marital choice was greatly influenced by her Anglicised education. Indira Devi first met her future husband, Jitendra Narayan Bhup Bahadur of Cooch Behar (later the Maharaja), at the 1911 Delhi Durbar. She was introduced to him by Pretty and Baby, his sisters, who had studied with her in boarding school at Eastbourne in England. They immediately took to one another and contrived to meet clandestinely during respites between festivities and ceremonies. When Indira broke off her engagement to the Gwalior Maharaja, her parents, Sayajirao and Chimnabai, refused to allow her to marry the Cooch Behar prince. In a desperate attempt to dissuade their daughter, they embarked upon a tour of Europe only to have Jitendra follow them (9-23). Indira subsequently had a covert courtship in Europe, which most likely affected her perceptions of romance and marriage. In 1913, she eloped with Jitendra to England, which created an uproar for both families and was considered inexcusable. As Barbara Ramusack notes, "Indira had scandalized her parents who were known as social reformers and the princely elite by breaking her betrothal to the ruler of Gwalior, a Maratha state equal in status to Baroda, to enter a love marriage which crossed caste, regional and religious categories" (Ramusack, "Fairy Tales" 9).

She was described as the "premier Princess of India, who was giving up everything" for love by the popular press (Moore 139). For several years, her mother Chimnabai would not see her. Few Indian women – let alone royal Indian women – made love matches at that time, and Indira Devi flouted convention in doing so; it took several years for the Baroda family to acknowledge their daughter's choice of a husband. They particularly disliked the highly Anglophile culture of Cooch Behar, especially the "mixing with Edwardian society and entertaining streams of Western guests, ranking from royalty down" (Gayatri Devi 28). They were also uncomfortable with the fact that the Cooch Behar royals were Brahmo (and thereby not orthodox Hindu) and had intermarried with the women of tribal kingdoms (Moore 11).

As a young woman, Indira "attracted more than attention, for to describe her beauty as ravishing would by no means be using an overworked cliché. Reporters flocked to [see her], endless photographs were taken" (139). Her marriage with her husband was written of in romantic terms as one of "perfect joy, of happiness, and bliss" (141). But life was not always placid, and in the early years of her marriage she was financially dependent on Cooch Behar state funds, having been cut off by her parents and without an allowance from her husband. Years later she would advise her granddaughters to maintain their own finances, rather than ask "your husband for money for sanitary towels" (qtd. in Moore 156). By 1922, she was a widow with five

8. Memoirs of Maharanis

children, but she did not retire from public life, serving as Regent in the minority administration of Cooch Behar State and leading a colorful life in India and Europe, where she had no dearth of suitors. She mixed with Hollywood glitterati, leading European royalty, and the great musicians of her day (183).

Like her mother Indira, Gayatri Devi chose a love marriage. As the granddaughter of Chimnabai and Sunity Devi and an inheritor of their social, political, and intellectual legacies, it seems only natural that Gayatri Devi would turn to writing her own autobiography, *A Princess Remembers* (1995). Like her ancestors, she also made a substantial commitment to public service, as a Maharani and later as a Swatantra Member of Parliament and Tourism Minister of Rajasthan.

As a young princess of Cooch Behar, Gayatri Devi had a free and open life; she did not observe *purdah*. One of three sisters and two brothers, she grew up under the guidance of her mother and grandmothers (her father and grandfather being deceased) in what was a matriarchal household. Her own mother was her principal role model. She described her mother as "an unparalleled combination of wit, warmth and exquisite looks" (Gayatri Devi 19). Indira Devi's marriage challenged Indian social norms, which prescribed a life of reflection and severe asceticism for widows. In contrast, she "proved that a woman, a widow at that, could entertain with confidence, charm and flair without being in the protective shadow of a husband or father" (57). Emulating her mother, Gayatri Devi took on a new public role when she too became a widow. Tutored at home in English history and literature, French, mathematics, Indian history, Bengali, and Sanskrit, Gayatri Devi also learnt how to shoot (she shot her first panther at age twelve), play tennis, ride, and manage her own money (71-72). In July 1934, the Cooch Behar princesses were sent to Shantiniketan; Gayatri Devi passed her matriculation exam first class and continued on to finishing school in Europe in March 1936 (Kanvar 27-29). She attended the Monkey Club in London and Brillantmont in Switzerland, as well as the London College of Secretaries (Gayatri Devi 119, 126, 129).

Gayatri Devi married Maharaja Sawai Man Singh II of Jaipur on April 17, 1940, a few months before she turned 21 (142). Originally, he entered her life as a friend of her mother's, when she was twelve; by the time she was fourteen, he was inviting her to dinners in Calcutta (which she attended supervised) (102). During her time in Europe, the Rajput ruler continued to court her. As she remembered their romance:

> It was so important to be able to talk to Jai [the maharaja's nickname] without somebody eavesdropping each time. I used to go to this small cubicle where I would try to conceal myself while making my phone calls! Very often he would ask me out and I would happily agree. In order to hide the fact that we were meeting regularly, Jai would park his Bentley in Wilton Crescent. I would walk to that place, get into the waiting car and we would drive off!
>
> Those times were much more fun than an ordinary approved courtship would have been. We were constantly trying to outsmart our elders, arranging clandestine meetings and finding a system of posting letters to each other without our ADCs and other staff getting any wiser. Once in a while we also managed to go boating and on long drives in the country and have dinner at Bray. We formalized our relationship by buying gold rings with our names engraved on the inner surface. I, of course, had to save my pocket money to be able to buy one for Jai. It was a lovely and intoxicating time. (Kanwar 41)

Their marriage was unconventional, for it was between two dynasties which did not intermarry: the eastern Kshatriya kingdom of Cooch Behar in Bengal and the western Rajput princely state of Jaipur in Rajasthan. Nonetheless, there had been an earlier precedence of a Jaipur-

8. Memoirs of Maharanis

Cooch Behar marriage during the reign of the last Maharaja Man Singh I, who had served as a general to the Mughal emperor in the sixteenth century. There was no formal objection from the Jaipur nobility to Gayatri Devi's paternal family; however, they were hesitant of her suitability as a bride due to her Maratha connections (Rajput-Maratha couplings were rare) (Jhala ch. 4, 71).

Indira Devi was initially as apprehensive about the marriage as the Rajput nobility, but for different reasons. She was concerned that her daughter would be entering into a household that still practiced *purdah* and polygamy, as the third and youngest wife (Kanwar 41). Despite these objections, the Jaipur Maharaja was determined to marry Gayatri Devi; having already married conventionally, he desired a companion who could stand by his side as the public face of a modern Jaipur. As Sher Ali Pataudi observed, Gayatri Devi was an "attractive modern princess with a most attractive family, well connected and with the kind of upbringing he wanted – modern, European, and yet belonging to the same fraternity" (Moore 205). Ironically, Gayatri Devi entered a *zenana* environment of *purdah*, very similar to the one her mother had so obstinately rejected earlier, when breaking off with the Gwalior Maharaja.

The Jaipur *zenana* Gayatri Devi entered housed as many as 400 women, including widowed relatives, daughters, ladies in waiting and their staffs, the Rajmata (queen mother) and other wives of the former ruler, as well as two of her husband's own co-wives (Gayatri Devi 167-170). Accustomed to the informal social environment of Cooch Behar, she found it difficult to adapt to the strict *zenana* hierarchy; she would "plead with the ladies in the *zenana* who spoke English to talk freely with me, to argue with me, even just to call me Ayesha [her nickname] in private, but they would smilingly, deferentially, ignore my requests" (179).

During the 1940s, she slowly began to emerge out of the *zenana*. She opened girls' schools in Jaipur and attended meetings of the All-India Congress of Women (like her Baroda grandmother before her);

she went to Red Cross work-parties where she met women who were "teachers, doctors and wives of government officials" and whose company was "far more stimulating than that of the *purduh*-ridden palace ladies" (202). In 1943 she opened the Maharani Gayatri Devi School in Jaipur, to educate Rajput girls from noble *purdah* families in Jaipur. At first, it was difficult to find families who would enroll their daughters; in time it became a pre-eminent institution for girls.

After independence in 1947, her husband was stripped of his executive powers, and was briefly given the position of Rajpramukh or "Head of State" of the new Rajasthan Union whereby he would have the "overall supervision of the administration of the entire province" during the interim years of integration (241). At the same time, Gayatri Devi began increasingly to participate in public life; in 1952 she attended the meeting of the All-India Congress of Women, which introduced certain rights for Indian women such as legal provisions for divorce. In 1957 she was asked by the Chief Minister of Rajasthan to stand for Parliament on a Congress ticket. She was surprised by the unexpected invitation; the "request that I – of all people – should start to play a role in Indian politics" (255). Later she would be elected as a Member of Parliament on the Swatantra ticket and spend several months in Tihar jail as part of Indira Gandhi's incarceration of opposition members during the Emergency of 1975; she also served as Tourism Minister for Rajasthan and championed architectural preservation and wildlife conservation in the state.

The traditional marriage of alliance reconstructed:
Vijaya Raje Scindia of Gwalior, the Maharani as politician

Traditional marriages were affected by both Western concepts of conjugality and British-sponsored intermarriage between dynasties. Just as Rajput Hindu princely states married other Rajputs, most other royal houses, whether the Marathas, the Sikh kingdoms of Punjab or the east Indian principalities, also married within their own caste and

8. Memoirs of Maharanis

community. However, as ideas of India changed, so did perceptions of appropriate alliance. The life of Vijaya Raje Scindia exemplifies this trend.

Vijaya Raje was born on 12 October 1919 (the same year as Gayatri Devi) (Scindia 20). The daughter of a Rajput nobleman and the aristocratic Rana family of Nepal, which had connections with the Nepalese Crown, she had little thought that one day she would marry a Maratha ruler. Her mother's family had been earlier expelled from Nepal and was still trying to establish itself in India.[1]

She grew up surrounded by educated and empowered women; her mother was the first Nepalese woman to pass the university matriculation exam (she married a petty Rajput nobleman but died in childbirth) (*Scindia* 16). Consequently, Vijaya Raje was brought up by her maternal grandmother, a Rana widow. Like Gayatri Devi, she saw that it was possible for woman to acquire power independent of her husband; and she observed the reverence and respect given to a widow within her own family.

Vijaye Raje's grandmother shaped her religious identity, which would influence her throughout her life and drive her politics. She was drawn most to religion over her studies, and became a Krishna *bhakt*, confessing that "Krishna who played the flute, tended his cows, stole butter from irate housewives and slew dragons, became my private god" (27). She sang the devotional songs of Mirabai, a sixteenth-century Rajput princess who had relinquished her husband to become a Krishna devotee and follow the wandering life of an ascetic. This admiration for a Rajput royal woman who had given up family for her

---

[1] The connections to the Nepalese crown continue in the family to this day. Vijaya Raje Scindia's granddaughter, Devyani Rana, has been associated as the love interest of Crown Prince Dipendra of Nepal, who in 2001 allegedly assassinated his parents and numerous members of the royal family in Kathmandu on the grounds that they would not accept her as his choice for a bride.

beliefs may have influenced Vijaya Raje's later decision to choose her allegiance to the Bharata Janata Party over her ties to her son.

Originally home-tutored, she later studied in Vasantha College, Benares, and Isobella Thoburn College, Lucknow ("Vijayaraje Scindia"). After university, her family began to look for possible marital partners. Following four proposals, which for various reasons were unacceptable, she was married to Jivajirao Scindia, Maharaja of Gwalior, a large Maratha state in Madhya Pradesh in February 1941 (Scindia 131).

The Ranas of Nepal claimed descent from the Sesodia Rajputs of Mewar in India, the Nepalese court having exiled Vijaya Raje's family to India. Ranas living in India wed other Rana families or married Rajput clans with whom they had earlier marital connections (Scindia 18). Vijaya Raje went through several marriage propositions, each successively of higher status than the last. The first came from a Rajput nobleman who worked in the Indian Civil Service, while the second was from a Rajput Lieutenant in the King's Commissioned Officers of the Indian army; both proved inauspicious (36; 48-49). The third offer came from the brother of the ruler of Tripura, a Kshatriya Hindu state in eastern India. Through this introduction to the Tripura royal family, her uncle was able to facilitate an engagement with the much higher-ranked, larger Maratha state of Gwalior; she married Jivajirao Scindia on 21 February 1941 (50-57; 131). The successive proposals demonstrate the upwardly mobile aspirations of her family in procuring the most advantageous match.

Vijaya Raje first met her husband at the horse races in Bombay, and the subsequent negotiations for their marriage took place in the Taj Mahal Hotel. The Scindias were the most prominent Maratha rulers in mid-twentieth-century India, and except for her Rajput mother-in-law, Vijaya Raje was the only non-Maratha to marry into the family. As she noted in her memoirs, "Caste and clan considerations made it obligatory for [Maratha rulers] to find their brides from among their own people, and from within a hundred or so families which possessed the proper origins and ancestries" (120). This union represented a newly expedient alliance. In post-Independence India, Vijaya Raje, as did Gayatri Devi, would play a significant role in national politics. Like Gayatri Devi, she was imprisoned in Tihar jail during Indira Gandhi's emergency. A stalwart of the Hindu nationalist Bharatiya Janata Party, she went on to serve as one of its vice presidents; her political legacy continues with two daughters, a son and a grandson in Indian politics.[2]

Conclusion: The marriage of drawing room etiquette

At a broader level, the accounts of these memoirs reflect the growing dissemination of occidental views on marriage making among Indian families during the late-colonial period. The adoption of the English drawing room as an architectural space and social venue was widespread. Marriages were settled within the setting of the drawing room from the late nineteenth-century alliance of Maharani Sunity Devi of Cooch Behar to the early mid-twentieth-century marriage of Maharani Gayatri Devi of Jaipur. Sunity Devi had been approved by her husband's British advisor in her father's Calcutta sitting room. Similarly, Gayatri Devi was courted by her husband, Sawai Man Singh of Jaipur, in finishing schools, Calcutta restaurants, and London parties. Vijaya Raje Scindia first met her husband at the Turf Club in Bombay, and details of her future marriage were settled within the social setting of the British-styled Taj Mahal Hotel (Scindia 62-66). In such a manner, royal marriages became motivated by a political vocabulary of etiquette, prestige and status building, modelled on the social decorum established by the anglicised drawing room, in a form of colonial mimicry.

---

[2] Her daughters Vasundaraje (the present Chief Minister of Rajasthan) and Yashodaraje (current Minister of Tourism for Madhya Pradesh), her son Madhavrao Scindia (who was a senior minister in the earlier Congress government) and her grandson, Jyotiraditya Scindia, are all active politicians.

During the height of Empire, the British Raj influenced marriage, spreading Western ideas of conjugality, love and family relations. From subtle to overt practices, the colonial government helped to reshape marriage among Indian royals, even while advancing and fashioning certain traditions. This fundamentally influenced their role as public and politicised beings, both before and after Independence. The spread of love marriages within royal Indian circles in the late nineteenth and early twentieth century mirrored the emerging idea of India (developed under the Pax Britannica), which encouraged novel forms of political marriage, often with British complicity, between dynasties which ordinarily did not intermarry.

As sources for new readings on British India, these memoirs reveal the cosmopolitanism of Indian courtly women during the height of Empire. The lives of these Maharanis contribute to a richer portrait of domestic life in colonial India. These women crossed between private and public spheres within the *zenana* and the larger mechanisms of power inside the Hindu kingdom, the confines of the princely state to the wider perimeters of British India, and finally from South Asia to a larger global conversation of cultural exchange. Their histories are an intriguing lens into the influence of Anglo-European mores on reshaping traditional Indian conceptions of marriage, conjugal love, and religious practice.

Works Cited

Alexander, Michael, and Shushila Anand. *Queen Victoria's Maharajah: Duleep Singh, 1838-93*. London: Weidenfeld and Nicolson, 1980.

Ashton, S. R. *British Policy towards the Indian States, 1905-1939*. London: Curzon, 1982.

Baroda, Maharani Chimnabai. *The Position of Women in Indian Life*. Delhi: Neerag, 1981.

Bhagavan, Manu. *Sovereign Spheres: Princes, Education and Empire in Colonial India*. Oxford: Oxford University Press, 2003.

Burton, Antoinette. *Dwelling in the Archive: Women Writing House, Home and History in Late Colonial India*. New York: Oxford University Press, 2003.

Campbell, Christy. *The Maharajah's Box: An Imperial Story of Conspiracy, Love and a Guru's Prophecy*. London: Harper Collins, 2001.

Cannadine, David. *Ornamentalism: How the British Saw Their Empire*. Oxford: Oxford University, 2001.

Chakrabarty, Dipesh. "The Difference-Deferral of a Colonial Modernity: Public Debates on Domesticity in British Bengal." *Writings on South Asian History and Society*. Essays in Honour of Ranajit Guha. Ed. David Arnold and David Hardiman. Subaltern Studies 8. New Delhi: Oxford University Press, 1994. 50-88.

Chamberlain, Mary, and Paul Thompson. "Genre and Narrative in Life Stories." Introduction. *Narrative and Genre*. Ed. Chamberlain and Thompson. London: Routledge, 1998. 1-22.

Chatterjee, Partha. *The Nation and Its Fragments: Colonial and Postcolonial Histories*. Princeton: Princeton University Press, 1993.

Copland, Ian. *The Princes of India in the Endgame of Empire, 1917-1947*. Cambridge: Cambridge University Press, 1997.

Devi, Gayatri. *A Princess Remembers: The Memoirs of the Maharani of Jaipur*. Calcutta: Rupa, 1995.

Devi, Sunity. *Autobiography of an Indian Princess: Memoirs of Maharani Sunity Devi of Cooch Behar*. New Delhi: Vikas, 1995.

Government of India, Foreign Department, Despatch No. 43A to S/S, 30 April 1860, PCI, 1792-1874, Vol. 85.

Kanwar, Dharmendar. *Rajmata Gayatri Devi: Enduring Grace*. New Delhi: Roli & Janssen, 2004.

Jhala, Jayasinhji. "Marriage, Hierarchy and Identity in Ideology and Practice: An Anthropological Study of Jhala Rajput Society in

Western India, against a Historical Background, 1090-1990. A.D." Diss. Harvard University, Anthropology Department, 1991.

Moore, Lucy. *Maharanis: The Lives and Times of Three Generations of Indian Princesses*. London: Penguin, 2004.

Ramusack, Barbara. *The Indian Princes and Their States*. Cambridge: Cambridge University Press, 2004.

___. *The Princes of India in the Twilight of Empire: Dissolution of a Patron-Client System, 1914-1939*. Columbus: Ohio State University Press, 1978.

___. "Fairy Tales, Soap Operas, or Expressions of Individuality: Autobiographies of Indian Princesses." 1987. Unpublished paper.

Rudolph, Lloyd I., and Susanne H. Rudolph. *Essays on Rajputana*. New Delhi: Concept, 1984.

Scindia, Vijaya Raje. *The Last Maharani of Gwalior: An Autobiography*. Albany: State University of New York, 1987.

Scott, Joan Wallach. "Women's History." *Gender and the Politics of History*. By Scott. New York: Columbia University Press, 1988. 15-27.

Spivak, Gayatri. "Can the Subaltern Speak?" *Marxism and the Interpretation of Culture*. Ed. Cary Nelson and Lawrence Grossberg. Urbana, IL: University of Illinois Press, 1988. 271-313.

"Vijayaraje Scindia dies." *Rediff on the Net*. 25 Jan. 2001. 1 Aug. 2007 <www.rediff.com/news/2001/jan/25raje.htm>.

9. The Reception of Marie Corelli in India

Prodosh Bhattacharya
Jadavpur University

As early as 5 October 1895, Methuen & Co. in London published evidence of Marie Corelli's Indian connection, advertising her forthcoming novel, *The Sorrows of Satan,* in *The Athenæum.* The advertisement also deals with the eighteenth edition of Corelli's previous novel *Barabbas* published on 21 September 1895, listing all the foreign editions of the book and ending with the following:

> **IN HINDUSTANI ... ...** Translated by KUNIVAR SHIVANATH SINGH (Barrister-at-Law), and published at the State Press, Lucknow, India.
> **IN GUJARATI ... ...** Translated by M. C. MURZBAN, and also published in Lucknow.
> (Federico 18, fig. 1)

On 7 September 1911, Methuen published Corelli's latest novel, *The Life Everlasting.* To this work, Corelli appended an "Author's Prologue" analysing her own literary career, in the course of which she proudly acknowledged the impact *Barabbas* had had on Europe and India:

> Within a few months it was translated into every known European language, inclusive even of modern Greek, and nowhere perhaps has it awakened a wider interest than in India, where it is published in Hindustani, Gujarati, and various other Eastern dialects.[1] (*Life* 24)

---

[1] See appendix for translations and adaptations.

About three years later, there would be a gratified response from the colonised Indian intelligentsia. A letter of Corelli, professing her "great sympathy for India" and her respect for Oriental religious and philosophical texts, which she claims to read frequently, would be translated at the end of a literary-cum-biographical notice in the Bengali periodical *Bharatbarsha*. The Bengali writer Anilchandra Mukhopadhyay would add the comment that this was "most certainly a matter of joy and pride for us" (Mukhopadhyay, "Kalpataru" 149-50.[2] Earlier, the same notice not only mentions [*The*] *Sorrows of Satan* and *The Life Evrelasting* [sic] as novels still being perused with respect and affection by "our readers," but also gives a translated list of thoughts selected from Corelli's novels. This reminds us of larger anthologies of quotations from her, like *The Marie Corelli Calendar*.

Marie Corelli's popularity in India is attested not only by any list of translations into various Indian languages or biographical-cum-literary notices in Indian periodicals, but also by the fact that most of her fiction as well as some of her non-fiction was reprinted in the late 1950s and the 1960s by Wilco Books in what was then Bombay.[3] In fact, a large number of her works in the National Library of India in Kolkata happen to be Wilco reprints. Both British and Indian editions of her

---

[2] All translations from Bengali originals are mine, except for the translations from the preface to the Bengali translation of *Joseph Wilmot* by Reynolds. Corelli is credited in this notice with eighteen novels in addition to non-fictional works and short stories, although the actual number of Corelli's fictional works up to 1914 is twenty-three. Excluded from this count are *Jane* (1887), *My Wonderful Wife* (1889), *The Silver Domino* (1892), which was published anonymously, *The Devil's Motor* (1911), and *Innocent*, which, though published in the year 1914, may have come after the notice was written or may not have been available or known to the writer. The notice is followed by similar entries on Hall Caine and H. G. Wells. I am indebted to Sudeshna Datta Chaudhuri for this information.

[3] See the appendix. Corelli's admirers included Queen Victoria and Edward VII, as well as the Maharajah of Kartarpur (Hallim 8).

9. The Reception of Marie Corelli in India

works can often be found on the shelves in educated Indian households. Amitav Ghosh made the following observation about his grandfather's library:

> The books that were prominently displayed were an oddly disparate lot – or so they seem today. Some of those titles can still be seen on bookshelves everywhere: Joyce, Faulkner and so on. But many others have long since been forgotten. Marie Corelli and Grazia Deledda for instance, names that are so little known today, *even in Italy*...[4] ("March"; my italics)

Priya Joshi records how she "wept over Miss Letty and Robert D'Arcy-Muir in Corelli's *Boy* in a dusty backwater town in central India" in the 1970s which sported a "dank circulating library" (Joshi xvi). Subsequently, as a scholar researching "what British novels Indians read for pleasure in the nineteenth century," she discovered "what I had already known by the time I reached ten. My forebears too had been reading the very same novelists I had as a girl: Reynolds, Corelli, Crawford" (xvii).

There was, however, a general lack of awareness in the British intellectual establishment about the reading habits of Indians. Joshi notes how the eminent writer of Indian novels in English, Mulk Raj Anand, horrified Virginia Woolf by telling her of the influence on his style of George W. M. Reynolds – whom Woolf had never heard of – and Rider Haggard "and Marie Corelli and Charles Garvice" (36). Woolf may have been ignorant of Reynolds, but she certainly knew (and violently disliked) Corelli. Corelli's commercial success was to Woolf "as damning an indictment of Victorian taste in one way as the Albert Memorial is in another. Of these two excrescences, perhaps that which we call Marie Corelli is the more painful (Woolf 97). Leonard Woolf, whom Joshi calls the other "tropical" in the room, spoke at this point

---

[4] The last three words are misleading because Marie Corelli was a thoroughly British writer, with the real name of Mary (Minnie) Mackay, who merely adopted the Italian-sounding nom-de-plume.

to reassure his wife regarding her ignorance of Reynolds with the explanation: "hardly ever mentioned here ... the fodder on which the subalterns chew the cud in the cantonments of the empire," an explanation which Joshi describes as being typical of "the inadvertent arrogance of conventional wisdom about the Subcontinent: if anyone read there, they read unimaginatively whatever came their way in much the way that cows did, without exercising much discrimination of taste or distinction of choice" (37).

A webpage dealing with the premier Bengali novelist Saratchandra Chattopadhyay claims with regard to two early novels of his, *Abhiman* and *Pashan*, which unfortunately are lost:

> Abhiman was based on **East Lynne** – the 1861 English novel of the [sic] English middle-class life by Ellen Wood (better known as Mrs. Henry Wood, 1814-1887) which sold over half a million copies in those days and was dramatised repeatedly. Pashan was written following the theme of the then spectacularly popular English novel **Mighty Atom** by Marie Corelli (1855-1924). Corelli's novels were said to be extravagantly romantic. Can one consider [Saratchandra's own novel] Debdas in the same light? ("Sarat")[5]

Evidence of how such interest in Corelli continued is proved by the *The Oxford Companion to Indian Theatre*, according to which Sachindranath Sengupta's Bengali play *Naradebata*, "Man-God" (1935) is adapted from Corelli's *Temporal Power*. The entry adds that it is among those of Sengupta's plays which "reflected contemporary Indian reality and politics" (432). Anecdotal evidence suggests that adaptation and appropriation of Corelli was widespread. The eminent Bengali novelist Gajendra Kumar Mitra once told Taradas Bandop-

---

[5] *Debdas* is one of Saratchandra's most popular novels, with its figure of the pathetic hero drinking himself to tuberculosis and death when separated by paternal intransigence from his childhood beloved Parbati.

9. The Reception of Marie Corelli in India

adhyay, son of the novelist Bibhutibhushan Bandopadhyay (of *Pather Panchali* fame) that Bibhutibhushan's novel *Debjan*, with its account of the main characters moving in literally metaphysical regions after death, was probably influenced by Corelli's account of the narrator-heroine in *A Romance of Two Worlds* travelling in extra-terrestrial regions when Heliobas sets her soul free from her body.[6]

Outside the area of adaptation, Corelli was widely translated into Indian languages; the appendix includes titles in the catalogues of the National Library of India in Kolkata. Before concentrating on a few specific translations, some valuable statistical data provided by Priya Joshi needs to be mentioned. On the basis of the extant catalogues of fourteen public libraries in the six Indian cities of Allahabad, Chennai (formerly Madras), Delhi, Kolkata, Mumbai and Patna, she lists twenty-two authors "most consistently available to Indian readers [. . .] between roughly 1850 to 1901" (64-65). Among these twenty-two, two novelists, Scott and Bulwer-Lytton, appear in all fourteen catalogues; a further three, Dickens, Disraeli and Thackeray, are present in thirteen catalogues. Another eight novelists, Corelli, F. Marion Crawford, Dumas, George Eliot, Kingsley, Marryat, Reynolds, and Taylor are to be found in twelve out of the fourteen catalogues.

Bengali translations of Corelli show considerable variety of approach, intention, and quantity. At one end is Bhubanchandra Mukhopadhyay's 1903 translation of *The Sorrows of Satan*. It seems to read like a verbatim rendering of the original. This is not to suggest that Mukhopadhyay's translation is ideologically neutral. As a colonial subject, he seems to select for translation those British works which expose the defects of British society.[7] Before Corelli's 1895

---

[6] I am grateful to Tathagata Bandopadhyay, Bibhutibhushan's grandson, for telling me about this.

[7] A descriptive list of Occidental intellectuals published in the periodical *Bharatbarsha* in 1913 has Bernard Shaw followed by Corelli as a name known to all in modern English literary circles ("Paschatya Vidvamandali").

novel he chose (in 1889) to translate G. W. M. Reynolds's *Joseph Wilmot* (1853-1854), a translation to which he added a preface, explaining his choice of Reynolds:

> I wish to compare the progress of civilization in this country and abroad. As the English spread their rule and their civilization in this country, while they proclaim the defects of Hindu customs and behaviour, when they ask us to bring these in line with their civilization, at this juncture, it is surely not irrelevant to take an impartial look at the stench that is being spread in the atmosphere by some leaders of this same civilization in their own country. (Mukhopadhyay, *Bilati Guptakatha*)[8]

The Oriental Other has made itself into the Self vis-à-vis the Occidental, which has itself been transformed from its self-appointed position into the Other. Of even greater interest with regard to Mukhopadhyay's translation of *The Sorrows of Satan* (made fourteen years later) is the following sentence from the same preface: "There are those in this country who imagine that the English [are] without any of the contamination of *Kaliyug* [. . .] but the upshot of the tale is that the gods are few and the devils many."[9]

Like Reynolds, Corelli in her novel "goes after Victorian society with both barrels," to quote Federico (83). Regarding the main narrative, some howlers aside, Mukhopadhyay does produce a faithful rendering of the original; terms like penny and shilling are glossed. The translator coins Bengali compounds for concepts like "New fiction" which he calls *nabanyas* and "New Woman" which he designates on

---

She is also lauded for having "exposed the defects of European society in merciless but well-argued language" in her *Free Opinions Freely Expressed*.

[8] This translation is from an unpublished paper on Reynolds by Sajni Mukherji of Jadavpur University, Kolkata.

[9] *Kaliyug* may be translated as "era of decadence"; *shaitans*, the Bengali word used for 'devils' here, is cognate with the English 'satan.'

9. The Reception of Marie Corelli in India

two different occasions with the two compounds *nabakamini* and *nabanari*.[10] In his faithfulness to his original he manages to retain Corelli's evocation of what Sharon Crozier calls "desperate lust" and other features of decadence, and her simultaneous absolution of her readers "of any possible guilt" in having indulged in such things through "her constant moralizing."[11] Lady Sibyl's speeches on decadent Victorian society, the marriage market, and the corruption of young women through the prurience of contemporary journalism and fiction are rendered faithfully, as are passages dealing, in the words of Max Beerbohm, with "the love of horror and all unusual things" (qtd. in Federico 78). Mukhopadhyay makes the novel particularly relevant to his readership through faithful renderings of passages, like the one in which Lucio comments on how the English ape the French in religion and dress. This would have an obvious resonance for the middle-class Bengali in 1903 Calcutta, with his newly-acquired Western education and desire to emulate English manners and dress.

On the other hand, there are later translations which are heavily abridged but still have similarly ideological intentions. Kumaresh Ghosh published his translation of Marie Corelli's 1887 novel *Thelma* in the 1960s.[12] The translator's preface declares that

---

[10] A memorable howler occurs where Corelli's Satan, "a creature formed of translucent light undefiled, with all the warm rose of a million orbs of day colouring his bright *essence*, and all the lustre of fiery planets flaming in his eyes" (53, ed. Keating; italics mine) becomes in Mukhopadhay "a radiant figure, a lotus blooming joyously in the rays of ten lakh suns, beautiful in hue as well, with a captivating *smell*, the shining planets gaining radiance from his eyes" (107). Until recently, the Bengali word for 'essence' was synonymous with 'perfume.'

[11] Reynolds, whom Mukhopadhyay translated earlier, used the same formula of titillation and restraint (although the titillation in Corelli is feeble when compared with that in Reynolds).

[12] Published by Bharat Book Agency (Calcutta); undated. Entered in the National Library, Kolkata, on 12 Feb. 1965.

Occidental society is today [inclined towards] brash progressiveness. And our oriental society is busy with blind imitation of that. At this [critical] juncture [of time/social change], Thelma, a girl from those countries, is made to stand in front of our girls through the medium of this delicate and beautiful novel by the able authoress Marie Corelli. It is hoped that, if they must imitate, may Thelma be their role-model. (n. pag.)

This may sound innocuous. Oriental society is being misled into imitating certain negative aspects of Occidental society. Therefore, an alternative Occidental role-model – "delicate and beautiful" rather than brashly progressive – is offered through the fictional personage of Thelma. However, the publishers' advertisement, appended at the end of the work, reveals the aim of the translation project to be far more complex and ideologically loaded. Addressing the reader directly, the publishers claim that he or she will be "enchanted and overwhelmed [*mugdha*] by reading [the reflection of] Hindu ideals and culture in the character of this Norwegian girl, Thelma" (n. pag.).

The premise seems to be what Sadik Jala al-'Azm calls "Orientalism in Reverse," in which "the Orientalist essentialistic ontology has been reversed to favour one specific people of the Orient" (231). Both Ghosh and his publisher suggest that the Oriental Self has been corrupted by an Occidental "Other." To counter this negative influence they do not turn to Oriental texts. Brash progressiveness, especially on the part of girls, has traditionally been associated with popular culture. Therefore, Ghosh and his publisher select a text which once belonged to the ranks of English popular fiction. They declare that the Oriental ideals will, paradoxically, be found in this text which has been produced by a different constituent of that same Other. In effect, the Self of the Orient is seen to permeate the Other so deeply as to be able to nullify any anti-Oriental influence emanating from it. This seems to be a remarkable case of reverse domination.

9. The Reception of Marie Corelli in India

A close examination of Corelli's translations bears this out. Ghosh's translation was used to promote certain so-called Hindu ideals and values (a purpose totally alien to Corelli). The method seems to be to retain, at one level, the distinction between the Western "Other" and the Eastern "Self" in the shape of Thelma, showing how she embodies and practices values which Eastern women are in danger of losing through their slavish imitation of Western culture. This distinction between East and West seems to be obliterated, as the translator implies that Thelma is more Eastern than the eastern women who are the translator's actual contemporaries. This is evident in the translation of passages where (in Corelli's original) Thelma opposes the assertive and aggressive role nineteenth-century women were accused of having in relation to their husbands. A conversation between Lady Winsleigh and Thelma confirms that Thelma will not allow herself to doubt her husband's fidelity (to do so would make her unworthy of his love), and even if his unfaithfulness were proved, she would not blame him. Complaining that Thelma's devotion and loyalty to Philip are excessive, Lady Winsleigh tells her:

> Thelma, you're the oddest creature going – a regular heathen child from Norway! You've set up your husband as an idol, and you're always on your knees before him. It's awfully sweet of you, but it's quite absurd, all the same. (418)

Ghosh translates this as:

> Clara: You do look upon your husband like a god, but is it right to do so in this age?
> Thelma: What can I do, that is the traditional upbringing of our country. We worship our husbands [*bhakti kori*], we can never think of them as servants to carry out our orders.
> (Ghosh 134-35)

The choice of the Bengali word *bhakti*, with its connotation of 'worship,' rather than *shraddhaa,* which is a more neutral word for 'respect,' is deliberate. While Ghosh suppresses all negative references to idolatry (which is central to Hinduism), he uses the suggestive *bhakti* to show the desired image of Oriental devotion to the husband in the Bengali reader's mind. Thelma is not a pagan (although her father is so), she is a Roman Catholic. However, her attitude towards her husband is identified by Lady Winsleigh as excessively outdated, which she expresses through the image of pre-Christian idol-worship. To Corelli, she is an "Other" who embodies values which she regards as desirable, but absent for so long that they appear alien to London society. The use of the pagan image should have held a special appeal for the Bengali translator of the novel, as he is presenting Thelma as an ideal to Hindu women. His abridgement of the exchange between Lady Winsleigh and Thelma, however, is curiously muted.

Given how Ghosh's translation is used to promote Hindu ideals, his omission of Lorimer's sarcastic reference to "a fellow in London who writes poetry on Indian subjects and who, it is said, thinks Buddhism might satisfy his pious yearnings, – but I think Odin would be a personage to command more respect than Buddha" (83) is understandable. In other words, paganism (tolerated by Corelli) must be European, not Oriental (Lorimer's equation is Hindu/India/Buddha). A derogatory reference to India generally and Buddhism specifically would subvert the purpose of this translation which purports to show how a Western text actually embodies Eastern values. This is nothing less than judicious editing – even censoring – of the original text where it would subvert the translator's purpose.[13]

In the 1960s the Bengali *Thelma* preached what Begum Rokeya Sakhawat Hossain in the preamble to her 1922 translation of Marie

---

[13] Most Bengali translations of Corelli omit Indian references, even when laudatory. Thus, Sudhindranath Raha's translation of *The Secret Power* omits crucial references not only to the non-Bengali Calcutta scientist Sir Ronald Ross, but also to the renowned Bengali scientist Sir Jagadish Chandra Bose.

9. The Reception of Marie Corelli in India

Corelli's *The Murder of Delicia* (1896) had identified as the Indian (male) writer's motivated propagation of "the ability of the powerless heart to endure" gender-based oppression. This preamble also notes the "remarkable similarity between the story of Delicia and [that of] women in our society" (Hossain 115). Hossain goes on to display the Oriental woman's "essentialism" regarding her Occidental Other, declaring, "what kind is the life of an English woman? We think they are independent, educated/intellectually equal with men, respected in society" (115). However, such essentialist distinctions between the Oriental Self and the Occidental Other are soon demolished, as she observes that "[i]n the land of civilisation and independence, London city, hundreds of 'Murders of Delicia' are acted out daily. Alas! Women are powerless everywhere on earth" (115).

Hossain's device to drive home the parallels between Occidental and Oriental women is to choose a "representative" of oppressed Indian womanhood she names "Majluma." The dialectic between the oriental translator and the occidental text (which in the Bengali *Thelma* is only explicit in the translator's preface and the publishers' advertisement), pervades the entire translation of *The Murder of Delicia*. Delicia, Hossain says, is independent, belongs to the ruling race, and is not confined indoors. Majluma has no independence, belongs to a subjugated race, and is imprisoned for the great sin of being born a woman (115). Delicia is an educated intellectual, whereas Majluma is illiterate. However, the only *real* difference between Delicia and Majluma, as Hossain's comments make clear, is in the *manner* in which they react to gender-based injustice. This translation is interspersed with the translator's commentary; Hossain singles out the moral courage of Delicia in freeing herself from her faithless husband, despite opposition from society and the law. He also suggests that Delicia would have separated from her husband, even if she were penniless. Delicia's education and economic independence make her aware of her own value as a human being; she threatens to shoot her philandering husband, should he dare to touch her against her will.

Majluma, says Hossain, can only throw herself at her oppressor's feet and beg for his mercy, and be repeatedly kicked while drenching his feet with her tears (116). The end is, however, the same for both; they are both killed by gender-based injustice and oppression.

In *The Murder of Delicia*, Corelli rewrote the *Thelma*-story with the important difference that Delicia's husband is actually unfaithful to his wife and exploits her both economically and emotionally.[14] Like Thelma, Delicia at first ignores rumours regarding her husband's affair, in this case with the danseuse La Marina. Unfortunately, going to a jeweller to buy her husband a wedding-anniversary present, Delicia sees a beautiful pendant which the unwitting jeweller tells her has been reserved by Lord Carlyon for La Marina. Delicia's reaction shows how Corelli's attitude towards worshipping one's husband like an idol has changed in the nine years between *Thelma* and *The Murder of Delicia*:

> "I have loved him too much," she said half aloud. "I have made him the idol of my life, and I am punished for my sin. We are all apt to forget the thunders of Mount Sinai and the great Voice Which said, 'Thou shalt have none other gods save Me' [. . .] I made of my beloved a god; he has made of me – a convenience!" (104)

---

[14] Corelli's biographers have suggested that *The Murder of Delicia* was her reaction to the discrimination and injustice she suffered as a popular but critically derided novelist and independent woman. Her half-brother Eric Mackay who lived on her (just as Lord Carlyon lives on Delicia) pestered her to have his poems published and, envious of her popularity, told outsiders that her novels were actually written by him. In 1914, Corelli rewrote the story again in the novel *Innocent*. The eponymous heroine, once again a successful novelist, dies of heartbreak after being emotionally abused by her lover Amadis de Jocelyn. This was a reflection of the emotional abuse inflicted by the artist Arthur Severn (a married father of five children) on Corelli; see Ransom 89-90, 172, 190.

9. The Reception of Marie Corelli in India

The translator of *Thelma*, Kumaresh Ghosh, planning to show in Corelli's occidental heroine the reflection of Hindu culture and values, discreetly endorsed her idolising of her husband, who, let us remember, unlike Delicia's husband, is worthy of her love. As a Muslim sharing the Judeo-Christian antipathy to idolatry, Hossain's translation of *The Murder of Delicia* enthusiastically seizes on this passage and comments on it. A translation back into English of the important parts of this section in Hossain is essential:

> "I loved him so much – I thought him an idol to be worshipped. This is punishment enough for my sin [of idolatry]!"
> [. . .] The bewitching idol that Delicia had established – adorned with the priceless gems of worship – on the throne of her heart, God shattered to pieces before her eyes. Delicia! Do not pick up the broken pieces of that doll.
>
> When idolators worship an earthen image, they have the faith that a deity is inhabiting it. At the end of the act of worship, when they feel that the deity has returned to its own abode, they immerse the image in water. Who would worship a doll, knowing it to be a mere piece of clay? If the worshipper comes to know that instead of a deity, a ghost or vampire is in the image, then? Can he [or she] then worship it? Not only that – that a vampire has been worshipped by being mistakenly taken for a god, such a thought, such shame is unbearable. (125)

This remarkable passage shows an understanding of the principles underlying the rituals of a religion and a culture alien to the translator. The English translation of Hossain's commentary is feeble when compared with the original. Hossain uses the word *pauttalikata* from Sanskrit for idolatry. The Sanskrit word *puttalika* is the origin of the Bengali word *putul* ("doll"). The suggestion of utter triviality contained in *putul* and its Sanskrit original is missing in the English "idolatry," which is why, when possible, the translation has used "doll," which manages to convey the intended sense of contempt for triviality.

Why was a radical novel like *The Murder of Delicia* translated in pre-Independence India, when the 1960s saw the translation of a decidedly reactionary novel like *Thelma*? A simplistic explanation would be that pre-Independence India was open to Occidental influences which were making the educated Indian aware of the shortcomings of Oriental society and its values. Hence Hossain's translation of *The Murder of Delicia* both lauds and displays the problems associated with the economic and intellectual independence of women. By the 1960s, following over a decade of independence, a conservative reaction had naturally set in, accounting for the choice of *Thelma* for translation. In *Reorienting Orientalism*, Chandreyee Niyogi suggests that "Ghosh's choice of *Thelma* for a Bengali readership may have been motivated by a recent reprint of *The Murder of Delicia* from Mumbai in 1963" (21), that it was a conservative reaction to the appearance in India of a novel showing the radical side of Corelli. However, 1922, the year of Hossain's *Delicia-Hatya*, also witnessed the appearance of *Mriter Pratishodh*, "Vendetta of the Dead," the earliest translation of *Vendetta* into an Indian language that can be found in the National Library at Kolkata. The Bengali version is heavily abridged, but the translator, Manomohan Roy, retains Corelli's virulent misogyny, who wrote:

> We know [. . .] that the infidelity of wives is [. . .] far too common for the peace and good repute of society. Not so common is an outraged husband's vengeance; not often dares he take the law into his own hands, – for in England at least, such boldness on his part would doubtless be deemed a worse crime than that, by which he personally is doomed to suffer. But in Italy [. . .] the verbosity and red-tape of the law, and the hesitating verdict of special juries, are not [. . .] considered sufficiently efficacious to soothe a man's damaged hon-

9. The Reception of Marie Corelli in India

our and ruined name. And thus, – whether right or wrong, – [. . .] strange and awful deeds are perpetrated [. . .] which, when brought to light [. . .] are received with surprise and incredulity. (1960 edition, v)

Roy also adds the following comments, not in Corelli, which are translated back into English here:

> The mental weakness, adulterous nature, selfishness, cruelty, cunning, lasciviousness and grotesque sensual thirst of the female race have been accepted as indisputably proven truths from the beginning of creation [. . .] If husbands who have been betrayed and have had their hearts broken by women had taken revenge on their adulterous and wayward wives in accordance with the misdeeds of the latter, perhaps the all the waters of the seven seas would have been stained with blood.
> (n. pag.)

Corelli's comment that the "boldness" of a husband in avenging himself on his adulterous wife "would doubtless be deemed a worse crime than that, by which he personally is doomed to suffer" (v) is altered by Roy into the claim that avenging husbands are rare because "compared with women, men have greater fear of social discipline and show greater obedience to the rule of the law." Roy amplifies Corelli's misogyny in the Bengali version of the preface.

Radicalism and reaction have always co-existed. With the spread of Western education for women in the nineteenth century came the lament of the poet Ishwarchandra Gupta (1821-1859) that they would now, having learnt A B (i.e. the English alphabet), dress up as *bibis* (Westernised women), and insist on speaking *biliti* (i.e. English) words. Would they ever again, he wonders, recite traditional chants to

(Hindu) gods and goddesses and maintain traditional (Hindu) rituals?[15]

Marie Corelli herself took up contradictory stances regarding women's issues (e.g. the different attitude towards husbands in *Thelma* and *The Murder of Delicia*) throughout her life. While she advocated economic independence for women and claimed that they were intellectually equal (if not superior) to men, she vehemently opposed giving women the right to vote – a position which she later recanted.[16] If *The Murder of Delicia* reads like a feminist attack on patriarchal and male chauvinist society, her most successful novel, *The Sorrows of Satan* (1895), through the character of Lady Sibyl Elton, unambiguously condemns the New Woman as promiscuous and spiritually as well as intellectually barren.[17] Also, the novel of Corelli most frequently translated into Indian languages is her second, and misogynistic, work *Vendetta*.[18]

---

[15] Paraphrased from a poem by Gupta quoted by Hemendra Kumar Roy in "Nutan Banglar Pratham Kabi" (283-89). Roy associated Gupta with "new" Bengal in spite of his backward-looking views simply because, according to Roy, no previous Bengali poet had dealt with the phenomenon of Bengali men and women picking up Western habits of dress, food and speech (283).

[16] See *Free Opinions Freely Expressed* and *My Little Bit*. Both books were reprinted by Wilco Publishing House in Bombay in 1962. On suffrage, see her *Woman, or – Suffragette: A Question of National Choice* and "Is All Well with England?" (reprinted in *My Little Bit*).

[17] Bhubanchandra Mukhopadhyay's 1903 translation of *The Sorrows of Satan* into Bengali is the earliest Corelli translation in the National Library of India. The publishers of the Bengali *Thelma* claimed in their advertisement that a second translation of *The Sorrows of Satan* by Kumaresh Ghosh was in progress; I have verified from Ghosh's family that this translation was not published.

[18] The National Library stocks the following translations: Bengali – Roy, Manomohan, *Mriter Pratishodh* (*Vendetta of the Dead*), Calcutta: 1922; Hindi – Koti, Baijanath, *Pap ka Pratikar* (*Atonement for Sin*), Delhi: 1954; Oriya – Mahapatra, G., *Raktapata* (*Bloodshed*), Brahmapur: 1963. It was translated at least once again in Bengali, by Sudhindranath Raha in the 1970s, in the popu-

9. The Reception of Marie Corelli in India

Mukhopadhyay largely adheres to the original text with occasional editing out of details and leaves Corelli's attack on Victorian society to have his intended effect on the colonised Indian reader's mental image of the colonising race. Hossain's translation explicitly addresses both Oriental women and men. Her intention is to urge the former to rebel against gender-based oppression (as Delicia did), and to shame the latter into changing their attitudes.[19] Ghosh prefers to let his doctored version of *Thelma* have its intended effect on his audience without any explicit commentary outside his preface and the publishers' advertisement. His engagement with the original text is far more intrusive as he edits and suppresses elements which might impede his intention of influencing his readership. A final case of Ghosh's censoring needs to be mentioned. There is no marriage between the middle-aged Lorimer and the sixteen-year old daughter of Thelma at the end of the Bengali version; 1960s middle-class Bengalis might have found it hard to accept such a union. Instead, Lorimer seems to be avuncularly affectionate towards the teenager, in a deliberately ambiguous declaration:

> "So, at last I have been caught in her hands!"
> "Mad little girl!" said our old Thelma, the mother, with a mild smile. (Ghosh 213)

---

lar magazine *Nabakallol*, published in Calcutta by Deb Sahitya Kutir. This translation simply retained the original title, *Vendetta*. *The Oxford Companion to Indian Theatre* (268) lists a Sindhi dramatisation, revived in 1920, by Nanik Ram Dharamdas Mirchandani, entitled *Farebi Fitno* (*Deceitful Brawl*).

[19] Hossain also addresses Indian men. Corelli's original text asserts that "if truth, fidelity and devotion are virtues, then dogs are certainly superior to men; if selfishness, cunning and hypocrisy are virtues, then men are certainly superior to dogs!" (*Delicia* 171); Hossain translates this and adds the following comment: "what does the society of our Bengali brethren have to say in reply to this? This comment is made by an English lady. It is beyond the abilities of the powers-that-be in this country to say anything to her [. . .] then what will you do, brethren? Shed tears in silence!" (Hossain 133).

As Susan Bassnett-McGuire explains (80-81), the translator first reads/translates in the source language, and then, through a further process of decoding, translates the text into the target language. Translation and interpretation do not remain mutually exclusive processes, as the interlingual translation is bound to reflect the translator's own creative interpretation of the source language text.

Works Cited

Anukriti.net. 1 Aug. 2007 <http://www.anukriti.net>.

Bassnett-McGuire, Susan. *Translation Studies*. Rev. ed. London & New York: Routledge, 1991.

Crozier, Sharon. "The Voices in the Making and Unmaking of History: Arnold Bennett, Marie Corelli, and Single Women in Late Victorian England." *Electronic Journal of Australian and New Zealand History*. From a Conference held by the History Department, University of Newcastle, 3 July, 1998. Looking Ahead: New Directions in Postgraduate Historical Research. 6 Sept. 2000. 1 Aug 2007 <http://www.jcu.edu.au/aff/history/conferences /newcastle/crozier.htm>.

Federico, Annette R. *Idol of Suburbia: Marie Corelli and Late-Victorian Literary Culture*. Charlottesville: University Press of Virginia, 2000.

Ghosh, Amitav. "The March of the Novel through History: The Testimony of my Grandfather's Bookcase." *Kunapipi: A Journal of Post-Colonial Writing* 19.3 (1997). *Kenyon Review* 20.2 (Spring 1998). 10 Sept. 2003 <http://www.amitavghosh.com/essays_html_indv.php?essay_no=53>.

Hallim, Robyn. "Marie Corelli: Science, Society and the Best Seller." Diss. University of Sydney, Department of English, May 2002. 28 Sept. 2004 <http://ses.library.usyd.edu.au/bitstream/2123/521/2/adt-NU20030623.11115902whole.pdf>.

Jalal al-'Azm, Sadik. "Orientalism and Orientalism in Reverse." *Orientalism: A Reader*. Ed. A. L. Macfie. Edinburgh: Edinburgh University Press, 2000. 217-38.

James, Louis. "The View from Brick-Lane: Contrasting Perspectives in Working-Class and Middle-Class Fiction of the Early Victorian Period." *The Yearbook of English Studies* 2 (1981): 7-101.

Joshi, Priya. *In Another Country: Colonialism, Culture and the English Novel in India*. New York: Columbia University Press, 2002.

Lal, A., ed. *The Oxford Companion to Indian Theatre*. New Delhi: Oxford University Press, 2004.

Mukhopadhyay, Anilchandra C. "Kalpataru." *Bharatbarsha* 2.1 (June-July 1914): 149-50.

Niyogi, Chandreyee, ed. *Reorienting Orientalism*. New Delhi: Sage, 2006).

"Paschatya Vidvamandali" ("Occidental Intellectuals"). *Bharatbarsha* 1.2 (Dec. 1913-Jan. 1914): 155-56.

Ransom, Teresa. *The Mysterious Miss Marie Corelli: Queen of Victorian Bestsellers*. Gloucestershire: Sutton, 1999.

Roy, Hemendra Kumar. "Nutan Banglar Pratham Kabi" ("The First Poet of New Bengal"). *Hemendra Kumar Roy Rachanabali* (*The Writings of Hemendra Kumar Roy*). Calcutta: Basumati Sahitya Mandir, n. d. 283-89.

"Sarat Chandra Chattopadhyay (Chatterjee)." Bengali Greats Series: The Immortal Wordsmith of Bengal. *bengalonline.sitemarvel.com*. 3 Jan. 2006 <http:/bengalonline.sitemavel.com/saratchandra.html>.

Woolf, Virginia. "The Dream." *Listener* 15 Feb. 1940. Rpt. *Collected Essays*, by Virginia Woolf. Vol. 4. London: Chatto & Windus, 1966-1967. 97-100.

Appendix

A. Novels of Corelli translated into Indian languages

(The items marked * came into existence in Corelli's lifetime; see above)

Barabbas.
1. *By 1895: Hindi translation by Kunivar Shivanath Singh (Lucknow: The State Press). Source: the advertisement, dated 5 Oct. 1895, in *The Athenæum*, reproduced as fig. 1 in Federico (18).
2. *By 1895: Gujarati translation by M. C. Murzban (Lucknow). Source: the advertisement, dated 5 October, 1895, in *The Athenæum*, reproduced as fig.1 in Federico (18).
3. 1954: Oriya translation *Barabbasa* by Subhadra Nandan (n.p. Dasa Praphulla Chandra). Source: *Anukriti.net*.
4. 1955: Malayalam translation by Z. M. Parett (Kottayam: Sahitya Pravarttaka, C. S. Ltd.). In the National Library of India, Kolkata.

The Murder of Delicia.
Into Bengali (*Delicia-Hatya*), *1922, trans. Begum Rokeya Sakhawat Hossain, in *Matichur*, vol. 2, rpt. in Abdul Quadir (ed.), *Rokeya Rachanabali (Complete Works of Begum Rokeya Sakhawat Hossain*) (Dhaka: Bangla Academy, 1973, new edition, 1999), 115-33.

A Romance of Two Worlds.
Into Urdu (*Do Jahana ki Saira* [see Anuk*riti.net*]), trans. Saghar Akbaradi (Ferozapur: Faiz Baksh Agency, n. d.).

The Secret Power.
Into Bengali, trans. Sudhindranath Raha (Calcutta: Deb Sahitya Kutir, rpt. 1995, date of first publication not given).

9. The Reception of Marie Corelli in India

The Soul of Lilith.
1. 1962: Kannada translation *Mahaparayoga* by Vellala Satyam (Bangalore: Ananda Prakashana). Source: *Anukriti.net*.
2. Urdu translation *Ruh-I-Laila* by Saghar Akbaradi (Ferozapur: Faiz Baksh Agency). Source: *Anukriti.net*.

The Sorrows of Satan.
1. *1903: Bengali prose translation *Santapta Saitan* (*Penitent Satan*) by Bhubanchandra Mukhopadhyay (Calcutta: Basumati Karyalaya). In the National Library of India, Kolkata.
2. 1958: Gujarati translation *Setanano Santapa* by J. P. Maheta (Bombay: Vora & Co.). In the National Library of India, Kolkata.
3. 1960s: Bengali prose translation *Shaitaner Shok* by Kumaresh Ghosh (Calcutta: Bharat Book Agency). Advertised in the Bengali translation of *Thelma* (see below). Not certain whether actually published.

Temporal Power.
1. *1917: Marathi translation *Alla ho Akbar* by N. S. Phadke. Source: Professor Ananda Lal, Department of English, Jadavpur University, Kolkata. On *Anukriti.net* the date mentioned is 1944, although it is not claimed that this is the date of first publication.
2. 1935: Bengali dramatisation *Naradebata* (*Man-God*) by Sachindranath Sengupta. Source: *The Oxford Companion to Indian Theatre*, ed. A. Lal 432.

Thelma.
1. *1911: Marathi dramatisation *Kamala* by Y. N. Tipnis. Source: Prof. Ananda Lal, Department of English, Jadavpur University, Kolkata.
2. 1960s: Bengali prose translation by Kumaresh Ghosh (Calcutta: Bharat Book Agency). In the National Library of India, Kolkata.

The Treasure of Heaven.
1. *1915: Marathi translation *Premaparikshana* by A. Hari Gadre (Poona). In the National Library of India, Kolkata.
2. 1936: Kannada translation *Niskama Prema* by Ullala Mangesaraya (Mangalore: Bala S. Mandala). In the National Library of India, Kolkata.
3. 1947: Gujarati translation *Prabhunun Dhana* by Chandrashekhar Shukla (Bombay: N. M. Thakkar Ni Co.). Source: *Anukriti.net*. The website does not specify the Corelli title. That it is translated or adapted from *The Treasure of Heaven* is guesswork on my part, based on the second word in the Gujarati title, which may be translated into English as *Treasure*. There is a similar problem with *Premapanth* (see last paragraph below).

Vendetta.
1. *c.1920: Sindhi dramatisation, *Farebi Fitno*, "Deceitful Brawl" by Nanik Ram Dharamdas Mirchandani. Source: *The Oxford Companion to Indian Theatre*, ed. A. Lal 268.
2. *1922: Bengali prose translation *Mriter Pratishodh* (*Vendetta of the Dead*) by Manomohan Roy (Calcutta: Union Press). In the National Library of India, Kolkata.
3. 1954: Hindi prose adaptation *Pap ka Pratikar* (*Atonement for Sin*) by Baijnath Koti (Delhi: Bharati Bhavan). In the National Library of India, Kolkata.
4. 1963: Oriya translation *Raktapata* (*Bloodshed*) by Godabaris Mahapatra (Brahmapore: Das Brothers). In the National Library of India, Kolkata.
5. 1970s: Bengali prose translation *Vendetta* by Sudhindranath Raha (Calcutta: Deb Sahitya Kutir). In the magazine *Nabakallol*.

Wormwood.
Into Urdu (*Kahani Aashiq*), trans. Mirza Mohammad Hadi Ruswa (Patna: Nimatullah Educational Society, 1987), mentioned on p.

10 of Robyn Hallim's "Marie Corelli: Science, Society and the Bestseller").

The website *Anukriti.net* lists *Premapanth* by Himmatlal Tunara (Baroda: Jivan Sahitya Mandir, 1950) as a Gujarati translation or adaptation from Corelli, without giving the title of the English original. The alleged adaptation of *The Mighty Atom* into the Bengali *Pashaan*, (*Stone*) by the premier novelist Saratchandra Chattopadhyay in the early years of the twentieth century is a piece of literary folklore unsupported by any hard evidence.

Finally, I must mention my mother, Mrs Suprobhat Bhattacharya's hand-written Bengali translation of *The Life Everlasting*, which she entitled *Saswata Jiban*. She made it after seeing my interest in Corelli, so it must have been written sometime in the 1970s.

What emerges from the tables is:

a. *Vendetta* is the most frequently translated of Corelli's novels, with five translations into four Indian languages. It has been translated twice into Bengali.
b. *Barabbas* comes next with four translations, each into a different Indian language.
c. *Thelma, Vendetta*, and *Temporal Power* have been dramatised, each in a different Indian language: Marathi, Sindhi and Bengali, respectively. All three novels have also been translated as prose fiction: *Thelma* into Bengali, *Vendetta* into Bengali (twice), Hindi, and Oriya, and *Temporal Power* into Marathi.

B. Indian reprints of Corelli's works

The following is a list of Wilco reprints of Marie Corelli:
Address: Wilco Publishing House, 33 Ropewalk Lane, Rampart Row, Bombay – 1.

1958: *Vendetta* (2nd ed., 1960)
1958: *Thelma*

March 1959: *The Sorrows of Satan* (rpt. 78 times)
1959: *Love and the Philosopher*
1959: *A Romance of Two Worlds* (2nd ed., 1962)
1959: *Ziska* (2nd ed., 1961)
1959: *Innocent* (2nd ed., 1962)
1960: *Temporal Power*
1960: *The Treasure of Heaven*
1960: *The Mighty Atom*
1960: *The Soul of Lilith*
1960: *Open Confession* (non-fiction)
1960: *Boy* (rpt. 1965)
1960: *The Secret Power* (National Library catalogue: 1959)
1961: *Barabbas*
1961: *The Life Everlasting*
1962: *Ardath*
1962: *God's Good Man*
1962: *The Master-Christian*
1962: *Free Opinions* (non-fiction)
1962: *My Little Bit* (non-fiction)
1963: *The Murder of Delicia*
1963: *Wormwood*
1963: *Cameos*
1968: *Jane*

The fly-leaf of *Jane* also mentions *The Silver Domino*, *The Young Diana*, *The Devil's Motor*, and *The Love of Long Ago and Other Stories* under "Other Books by MARIE CORELLI" without specifying whether they are available as Wilco reprints.

C. Primary texts by Marie Corelli

Novels

Barabbas: A Dream of the World's Tragedy. 1893. Bombay: Wilco, 1961.

9. The Reception of Marie Corelli in India

Boy: A Sketch. London: Hutchinson, 1900. Bombay: Wilco, 1960, 1965.
Innocent: Her Fancy and His Fact. London: Hodder & Stoughton, 1914; rpt. Bombay: Wilco, 2nd ed., 1962.
The Life Everlasting: A Reality of Romance. London: Methuen, 1911, 1954.
The Murder of Delicia. 1896. Bombay: Wilco, 1963.
A Romance of Two Worlds. 1886. Bombay: Wilco. 2nd ed. 1962.
The Sorrows of Satan, Or, The Strange Experience of One, Geoffrey Tempest, Millionaire. 1895. Ed. Peter Keating. Oxford World's Classics. Oxford and New York: Oxford University Press, 1998.
Thelma: A Norwegian Princess. 1887. London: Methuen, 1929.
Vendetta!: or The Story of One Forgotten. 1886. Bombay: Wilco. 2nd ed. 1960.

Non-fiction

Free Opinions Freely Expressed on Certain Phases of Modern Social Life and Conduct. 1905. Bombay: Wilco, 1962.
The Marie Corelli Calendar: A Quotation from the Works of Marie Corelli For Every Day in the Year. Selected by E. M. Evans. London: F. Palmer, 1913.
My Little Bit. 1919. Bombay: Wilco, 1962.
Woman, or – Suffragette: A Question of National Choice. London: C. Arthur Pearson, 1907.

D. Other Primary texts

Reynolds, George, W. M. *Joseph Wilmot; or, the Memoirs of a Man-Servant.* (1853-1854).

Bengali Primary texts

Bandopadhyay, Bibhutibhushan. *Debjan.* 1944.
Chattopadhyay, Saratchandra. *Debdas.* 1917.
Ghosh, Kumaresh, trans. *Thelma.* Calcutta: Bharat Book Agency, n. d.

Hossain, Begum Rokeya Sakhawat. *Delicia-Hatya* (*The Murder of Delicia*). 1922. In *Matichur*, vol. 2, rpt. in Quadir, Abdul (ed.), *Rokeya Rachanabali* (*Complete Works of Begum Rokeya Sakhawat Hossain*). Dhaka: Bangla Academy, 1973, new ed. 1999. 115-33.

Mukhopadhyay, Bhubanchandra, trans. *Bilati Guptakatha* (*Joseph Wilmot*). Calcutta: 1889.

Mukhopadhyay, Bhubanchandra, trans. *Santapta Saitan* (*The Sorrows of Satan*). Calcutta: Basumati Karyalaya, 1903.

Raha, Sudhindranath, trans. *The Secret Power*. Calcutta: Deb Sahitya Kutir, rpt. 1995, date of first publication not given.

Roy, Manomohan, trans. *Mriter Pratishodh* (*Vendetta*). Calcutta: Union Press, 1922.

The prefaces to *Thelma* (*Delicia Hatya*), *Bilati Guptkatha* and *Mriter Pratishodh* are integral parts of the respective texts, or have no pagination, or are numbered in an obsolete style, which I cannot decipher.

10. "The Sahib try to kiss me": The Construction of the Queer Subaltern in J. R. Ackerley's *Hindoo Holiday*

Shafquat Towheed
Open University

> If he had sexual relations whilst in India, he left no record of the fact. (Parker 74)

Framing an era that systematically criminalised same-sex desire, J. R. Ackerley's (1896-1967) heavily autobiographical and keenly ironic work presents a fertile corpus for postcolonial and queer theorists. From his first work, the explicitly homoerotic play *The Prisoners of War* (1925) to his posthumously published and astonishingly honest account *My Father and Myself* (1967), Ackerley's work consciously transgressed the socially constructed English niceties of the discrete, the conventional, and the legal. His life and writing has become a synecdoche for English homosexuality in this period.

And yet, Peter Parker in his otherwise excellent biography of *Ackerley* assumes that because little or no documentation exists from his five-month stay in India (December 1923 - April 1924), it was unlikely that he engaged in any meaningful sexual encounters there. Parker's sweepingly improbable assumption of sexual continence begs the question: what kind of written record is Ackerley, or more pertinently, his semi-literate or illiterate sexual subjects, supposed to have kept? This spuriously geographical/cultural separation is particularly implausible considering Ackerley's own compulsive cruising and the apparently homonormative sexual licence that life in the Chhatarpur court offered. Parker's reading of Ackerley's five-month "Hindoo Holiday" presents as normative an enforced metanarrative of foreclosure, excluding the testimony of non-documented sources or counternarratives, and disavowing Ackerley's own implicated and anomalous position in the politics (sexual and otherwise) of the Chhatarpur court.

This approach has been mirrored by other commentators[1] on Ackerley's sexuality who seemingly endorse this splicing and policing of the construction, practice, and literature of same-sex desire between metropolitan core and colonial periphery, between the *grand récit* of master narrative and the often (un)written colonial counter-narrative of oral testimony, between the (over)determined cultural and pathological construction of the Western homosexual and its assumed, putative homonormative Oriental "other," the contingent, sexualised, unwritten (and underwritten) Asian subaltern.

Discussions of homosexuality in the context of postcolonial theory have often mirrored the narrative of colonial dominance, closing down, rather than opening up, fissures, intersections, and interpretations. Leela Gandhi has noted that "both empire and its antagonist, the anticolonial nation" are "profoundly heteronormative projects that founded their competing authorities on the categories of sex – that is, on a closed, masculine signifying economy" (89). Drawing upon this idea, I want to investigate whether queer readings of this explicitly homoerotic colonial text necessitate a universalising homonormative outcome; does the act of re-inscribing a defined, pathologised, Eurocentric same-sex desire onto the text effectively efface and silence the viewpoint of indigenous subjects? Ackerley's memoir, tangentially poised between competing narratives of Western homosexuality and Indian nationalism, and yet distanced from both by his keen autonomy and irony, offers the ideal locus for this discussion. Using Gandhi's axiom, I also want to examine whether a postcolonial reading of this "queer" text voices or silences sexual identity and choice.

I want to offer two distinct readings of *Hindoo Holiday*: a postcolonial reading of the subaltern, and a queer theory reading of homosexual desire. The gaps, fissures, discontinuities, and congruities between postcolonial and queer theory offer the critic imaginative space denied by the rhetoric of either discourse alone; that there is a repeated en-

---

[1] See Bristow 146-53; McHugh; and Whisnant.

gagement in ideas, but curious lack of intimacy between these two approaches mirrors Ackerley's own predicament, caught between desire and intimacy, arousal and fulfilment, gratification and deferral, and between the mutually imbricated, ritually mediated, cultural constructions of English "repression" and Indian "licence."

I Can the (homo)sexual subaltern speak?

Drawing attention to Gramsci's enforced substitution of the term 'subaltern' for 'proletarian' in his prison diaries, Gayatri Chakravorty Spivak has defined the subaltern as an explicitly subordinated individual or collective position, "persons or groups cut off from upward – and, in a sense, 'outward' – social mobility" ("New Subaltern" 235). In fashioning a critical space for retrieving subaltern consciousness, whether resistant or compliant, Spivak has noted the inadequacy of mapping gender on to subaltern status without appreciating the internal displacement that this invites. "Within the effaced itinerary of the subaltern subject, the track of sexual difference is doubly effaced," she has observed, arguing that if the "subaltern has no history and cannot speak, the subaltern as female is even more deeply in shadow" ("Can the Subaltern Speak?" 287). Spivak's work has demonstrated the potential agency for the "collective ideological refusal" (286) of the subaltern within the structures of power that define her. This retrieval and reinscription of subaltern consciousness is refashioning Indian colonial historiography and has been taken up by the Subaltern Studies group.[2] Spivak recognises the "irretrievably heterogeneous" nature of the "colonized subaltern *subject*" and acknowledges that several of her chosen subjects (e.g. the Rani of Sirmur, Bhubaneswari Bhaduri), do not conform to Gramsci's subaltern, but suggests their "claim to subalternity" is due to their "muting by heterogeneous circumstances" (*Critique* 308).

---

[2] See the work of Ranajit Guha, Dipesh Chakrabarty, Vinayak Chaturvedi, and others in the Subaltern Studies collective.

Spivak's work has dealt with the subaltern as female, but it could equally include the poor, juveniles, the illiterate, and adivasis. Her inscription of subalternity is not entirely gendered female; commenting upon the hegemonic structures of power at play in the practice of *sati*, she notes that "the few male examples cited in Hindu antiquity of self-immolation on another's pyre, being proofs of enthusiasm and devotion to a master or superior, reveal the structure of domination within the rite" ("Can the Subaltern Speak?" 300). Male immolation is glanced at in *Hindoo Holiday*. Babaji Rao presents an essentialist, heteronormative defence of male gendered self-immolation, declaring that "when a king died, not only his wives but his servants and household goods [. . .] went with him into the fire, so that he should not lack in the next world anything to which he had been accustomed in this" (140).[3] Spivak's reading of female *sati* has opened up the interstices between competing and mutually legitimising discourses; her acknowledgement of the existence of instances of male immolation only serves as a marker that reinforces the hegemonic absolutism of the practice of the Hindu rite (see Mani 86-126). How was the male-gendered, subaltern subject of self-immolation constructed? Did he denote a space analogous to, or radically different from, that of the officially legitimised, socially sanctioned widow sacrifice? Was his marginalised subaltern position, the virtue of his silencing, denoted through his sexuality (whether contingent and pragmatic or essential and normative) as well as the other obvious demarcations: his class, caste and economic status? And was his self-immolation an act that reinscribed or effaced the heterogeneous circumstances of his construction as a potentially sexualised subject?

Acknowledging Spivak, John Hawley has asked "whether the *gay and lesbian* subaltern can speak," inviting us to investigate the "effects of colonisation and neo-colonialism on the sexualities and sexual relations both of those designated elsewhere as subalterns," and of

---

[3] References in parentheses are to the 1952 edition, reprinted 1983.

10. The Queer Subaltern in J. R. Ackerley's Hindoo Holiday

"those whose position as members of the ruling class persisted or persists regardless of their own possible deviant status within their own cultures" (13-14). I want to engage Hawley's proposition, while offering two further caveats. First, discussing Ackerley's interaction with male subaltern sexualities in *Hindoo Holiday*, I want to avoid using the culturally constructed, historically, socially, and ethnographically constricting term 'gay,' a term which in the context of the stratified (and largely moribund) hegemonic structures of the princely state of Chhatarpur in British colonial India in the 1920s carries neither substantive weight nor legitimacy. Second, I want to question Hawley's assumption that the (homo)sexual subaltern subject permanently maintains a position of subalternity and is always denied the possibility of social mobility; the politics of the Chhatarpur court, and Ackerley's own involvement in it, suggest otherwise. Instead, I investigate the contingencies that create and maintain the (homo)sexual subaltern, and the means by which his voice is silenced and misrepresented, often through the enabling intervention of a male hegemonic narrator.

Hindoo Holiday, Ackerley's thinly fictionalised memoir of a five-month stay in the princely state of Chhatarpur (now part of Madhya Pradesh) presents both the reality and the fiction of British "indirect" rule in the 1920s. Chhatarpur had been carved out of the Bundelkhand by Kunwar Sone Shah Panwar in the last decades of the eighteenth century; his rule had been formalised by British sanction (the first recorded direct intervention in the territory) in 1806. By 1854, after the death of the incumbent Maharajah without issue, the state was confiscated by the British, who placed the late ruler's adopted son, Jagat Raj Bahadur, on the throne; from this point on, despite the legal fiction of indirect rule, the system of royal succession in Chhatarpur was mediated through (and legitimised by) British intervention. After Jagat Raj Bahadur's untimely death in 1867 (believed poisoned by his mother), his fourteen-month-old son Vishwanath Singh Bahadur (1867-1932) was confirmed as the heir apparent by the resident political agent; the Dowager Rani acted under British nomination as the putative regent until the child reached his majority. When Ackerley arrived in Chhatarpur in December 1923, he found that the openly homosexual, philosophically inclined, and comically eccentric Vishwanath Singh Bahadur was again a source of both Imperial concern and complicity.

At the time of Vishwanath Singh's accession to the *gadi* in 1887, Sir Leppel Griffin, the agent to the Governor General of Central India, had expressed grave doubts about his competence. "He is singularly weak [. . .] and I cannot believe that he will ever prove an independent or energetic ruler," he concluded, an opinion supported by the *de facto* administrator of the territory, the resident political agent Lt. Col. F. A. Wilson, who recorded his opposition to the Prince "being entrusted at first, with full powers in the administration of the state" (BL OIOC Chhatarpur Archive).[4] Both correspondents also noted Vishwanath Singh's obvious homosexual inclinations, observing that he was "exceedingly boyish for his age" and "liable too easily to make favourites".

Vishwanath Singh's sexual proclivities complicated the Chhatarpur succession and troubled successive resident political agents. In 1921, just before the death without issue of the Maharani, the Maharajah took a second wife. Despite the Maharajah's proclivities and his impotence (caused by venereal disease), she miraculously produced a son just months later, thereby guaranteeing an apparently legitimate succession. In reality, Vishwanath Singh had ordered two of his barbers to impregnate the new Maharani; this was known to the British.[5] Imperial policy towards the Chhatarpur court was based on its historical

---

[4] BL OIOC, Internal and Political Branch A, 1887, investiture, 10R/1/1/785, File 1A, dated 27/04/1887. Both correspondents considered Vishwanath Singh's effeminacy as justifying a greater than usual degree of direct intervention. For Indian "effeminacy" used as a justification for direct rule, see Sinha.

[5] BL OIOC, Internal and Political Branch, first cycle, 1922, recognition of the legitimacy of the heir, 10R/R/1/1/1356 File 584-P(S), especially TS 1-2, TS 4. The barbers named in the Jujharsinha petition as "Barosa" and "Bahora" are fictionalised in *Hindoo Holiday* as Sharma and his unnamed brother.

10. The Queer Subaltern in J. R. Ackerley's Hindoo Holiday

loyalty to British rule (it hosted the garrison at Nowgong), especially during 1857; official correspondence insisted upon a narrative of foreclosure, rather disclosure. Any attempt to force an enquiry into the succession by Vishwanath Singh's disgruntled cousin, Jujharsinha, was to be avoided, as it would be "as distasteful to Government" as it was "to His Highness."[6] The political circumstances of the Chhatarpur court at the time of Ackerley's arrival can be described as a series of direct British interventions masquerading as non-intervention: an enabling fiction emanating from discontinuous crisis management that provided the illusion of normative narratives of both governance and legitimacy.[7] The structures of power and control in Chhatarpur replicated and parodied the wider structures of Imperial India; Ackerley, who took up his post as personal secretary under the recommendation of E. M. Forster, was aware of this.

Ackerley's own position within the negotiated power structures of Chhatarpur was shaped by complicity and deference. Employed as a "personal secretary," but effectively little more than a paid companion, Ackerley's status was determined by his proximity to the Maharajah, whose own powers were policed and legitimised by the British resident agent. Ackerley's authority over his Indian "subjects" was negotiated through the same hegemony as that of the much-derided garrison British, from whom he conspicuously distanced himself. By his own admission, Ackerley flinched from the same instances of perceived Indian "disrespect" as the resident British, the only difference being in his interpretation of perceived slights. Ackerley views Sharma's refusal to take off his shoes in his presence (69) with the same disdain as Mrs Montgomery does to being touched (22) or Miss Gibbins to the apparent insolence of a cultivator (11); but while the British as a group perceive these isolated acts of disobedience as con-

---

[6] Ibid., letter dated 3/12/1921.

[7] Vishwanath Singh Bahadur's legitimacy was officially sanctioned by the award of the KCIE in 1928; see Chhatarpur papers, Internal and Political, Honours Records, dispensation warrant, 10R/L/PS/15/66, File H56/1928.

stituting a potential collective (and therefore ideological) refusal of authority (i.e., an act of *insurgency*), Ackerley views them as individual (and therefore personal) refusals of his authority.

The composition and publication of *Hindoo Holiday* mimics the official discourse between the Chhatarpur court and the British in insisting upon a narrative of foreclosure, even when ostensibly claiming to be one of disclosure.[8] Ackerley's understanding of the political necessity of discretion meant that the initial publication of *Hindoo Holiday* was held back until April 1932; at the insistence of his publisher, Chatto and Windus, excisions were made to the text in order to avoid prosecution for libel.[9] The death of Vishwanath Singh Bahadur on 4 April 1932 had again raised the issue of the legitimacy of the Chhatarpur succession; the British were determined to avoid the accusation that they had authorised a succession that was neither legally nor socially acceptable in favour of political expediency.[10] Printed after both the deaths of most of its fictionalised protagonists and Nehru's abolition of royal succession, Ackerley's preface to the revised 1952 edition of *Hindoo Holiday* remarked that as the "State of Chhokrapur" had "dissolved away in the new map of India" he could now "restore most of the omissions" that he had been forced to make to the 1932 edition.

There is one excision – a conversation between Ackerley and Narayan about the Maharajah's use of Sharma to impregnate the Maharani, and Sharma's own reluctance to penetrate the Maharajah – which was not returned to the text, and has not appeared in any published edition

---

[8] See the Dewan's annual administrative reports; Chhatarpur Papers, Administrative report, 1909-1927, 10R/V/10/943.

[9] See Parker 159-62. Readers and censors of the manuscript included E. M. Forster, Henry Fielding Jones, Harold Nicolson and Charles Prentice.

[10] See Chhatarpur Papers, Political Branch Files, 1932, 10R/R/1/1, 2262(1) & 2262(2). The 1932 political agent's advice mirrors that offered in 1867; the Maharani should not be allowed any political influence, and her illegitimate son by the Maharajah's valet should be recognised as the heir and placed under the control of the resident political agent.

10. The Queer Subaltern in J. R. Ackerley's Hindoo Holiday

of *Hindoo Holiday* (see Braybrooke 334-35). Despite the relaxation of obscenity laws and the increasing social tolerance of homosexuality, Ackerley made no attempt to return this excised passage to the text. Despite Ackerley's awareness of the mutually legitimising effect of different taxonomies of knowledge (Narayan's aural/oral gossip vs. the political agent's reports), *Hindoo Holiday* is shaped as a narrative of foreclosure, drawing as much attention to what it does not say, as to what it does say. By refusing to bring his private conversation with Narayan about Sharma's alleged sexual preferences (information retrieved by and mediated through Narayan himself), into the public space of the printed text, Ackerley locates in an apparent instance of an individual subaltern's hesitance a point of alterity which the official taxonomy of knowledge can acknowledge, but not accommodate. In perpetuating Narayan's secret that Sharma is "the father of little Raja and the girl baby," Ackerley demonstrates its legal veracity, and in locating Narayan's non-literate, personal testimony (Sharma's twice-effaced, illiterate consciousness) outside of the policed confines of the official publication, he establishes the accuracy and efficacy of the unrecorded. Ackerley attempts to voice privately what Foucault would deem "subjugated knowledge" (Sharma's intimate feelings, mediated through Narayan) outside of the confines of the text; he presents a counter-discourse of equivalence and offers the possibility that the dominant narrative is always inscribed by its resistance. Ackerley's fascination with recovering the material and personal history that constitutes subjugated knowledge is evident in his account of his fruitless search in the Public Record Office to find documentary evidence of his father's possible homosexual relationships with several older men in his youth, related at length in *My Father and Myself*.

Ackerley's perennial problem with fiction (particularly characterisation and interiority) is self-evidently demonstrated in his presentation of the text as a first-person "Indian journal" pieced together from his recollection, drawing attention to its immediacy and veracity as a historical document. It also highlights the inextricable problem of voicing

253

(or ventriloquising) subaltern consciousness and conveying it to his metropolitan readership. There are three examples of such a process of capturing and mediating the consciousness of male-gendered, sexualised subalterns in *Hindoo Holiday*: the guest house clerk Narayan; the royal valet Sharma; and the unnamed child entertainer, dubbed by royal prerogative and without his knowledge or consent, "Napoleon the Third."[11]

Of the three, Narayan offers the most complex narrative trace. It is indeed arguable whether he ought to be viewed as a subaltern subject or referred to by that rather more implicated and less resistant term, "native informant" (Spivak, *Critique* 270). Narayan's position differs from those of Sharma or "Napoleon the Third" by virtue of his caste (a Brahman, like the Dewan), his potential social mobility in the court, his knowledge of English (which facilitates some self-representation, seen inside and outside the foreclosed narrative), his official and publicly articulated commitment to heteronormative patriarchy and religious orthodoxy, and his competition with Ackerley and the Maharajah for the ownership of Sharma.[12] As the signifying determinant in maintaining Sharma's subjection, Narayan is committed to the structures that create and sustain Chhatarpur subalternity; despite his privileged complicity, Narayan is subject to the same forces of effacement, erasure and marginalisation. Even more intriguingly, he offers a narrative trace replete with acts of individual refusal and official complicity

---

[11] Even more systematically effaced subalterns glossed in the text are the Indian women subject to both Chhatarpur and British suzerainty: the Maharani, Narayan and Sharma's child wives, Narayan's childless widowed sister (surely a candidate in the absence of *Pax Britannica* for sati?), the Maharajah's newborn daughter, and the small shrines valorising sati scattered across the countryside.

[12] Narayan's caste is superior to Babaji Rao (*Vaiśya*), his lover Sharma (*Śudra*) and the Maharajah (*Kshatriya*); it is debatable whether this privileges his voice in the narrative. Narayan espouses heteronormative patriarchy; if his widowed sister were to bring shame upon their family, "he would let his sister kill herself sooner than stretch out a hand to her in her disgrace" (230).

10. The Queer Subaltern in J. R. Ackerley's Hindoo Holiday

directed at both Ackerley and the Maharajah; whether this should be interpreted as ideologically radical or reactionary remains a matter of conjecture.

Narayan's act of individual refusal towards Ackerley is his refusal to initiate or reciprocate the kiss on the mouth, despite having exchanged photos and acknowledged his love for him. "I want to love you very much," Narayan tells Ackerley, "but you will go to England and I shall be sorry" (218), he realistically observes. When Ackerley reciprocates Narayan's kiss on the cheek with a kiss on the mouth, he flinches back in disgust ("Not the mouth! You eat meat!") before accepting a second kiss on the mouth, without drawing back. Narayan's revulsion reinforces both his caste identity, cathected in the form of Ackerley's meat-eating pollution, and his agreement with the Dewan's Brahmanical and patriarchal reading of sexuality: "a kiss on the mouth is a very big thing; it is a completed sexual act" (221). Whether Narayan's participation in the second kiss confirms or refutes the event of a "completed sexual act" remains open to debate, but as far as the Dewan is concerned, the kiss on the mouth legitimises real sexual relations that would otherwise go unrecognised; whatever "illicit lovemaking" did "go on in the State, there was *no* kissing upon the lips" (221), he declares. In the light of the enforced, almost exclusively homosexual service demanded by the Maharajah, the Dewan's foreclosed reading of the sexual practices of the Chhatarpur court allows "illicit love-making" to flourish unrecognised and uncriticised. That Narayan has an instinctive sympathy for the Dewan's reading of the "kiss on the mouth," but is unable to ignore or escape the sexual attention of both the Maharajah and Ackerley, further complicates his individual act or refusal; despite his strongly amorous feelings towards Sharma, Narayan insists that he only kisses his cheek and never his mouth, "but publicly, never in private" (243).

Sharma's position as Narayan's "bearer" (244) and caste inferior is reinforced by his total subjection to Narayan's emotional and sexual needs. "You are my God, my friend and brother" Sharma declares, replicating the enforced rhetorical devotion of the male-gendered self-immolator for his master: "What can I do but die too?" (244). The construction of the subaltern is always relational, and here Narayan replicates rather the constricting hegemonic structures of the Chhatarpur court.

Narayan is steadfast in his refusal to satisfy the Maharajah's sexual desires or to encourage Sharma to act in his place; this is glanced at in the narrative and recorded in its margins (the excised passage and Ackerley's correspondence). He refuses to accede to the Maharajah's demand to "see him naked" (225), despite the threat of exile from the State. The excised passage notes Narayan's open disapproval of the Maharajah's sexual demands ("It is bad, wrong"), and Sharma's submission to them ("He is half-made"), as well as his own relative powerlessness as a subaltern subject to stop it (Braybrooke 335). Ackerley's correspondence is more explicit. Narayan is "a constant source of irritation" to the Maharajah because he "steadfastly refuses to participate in these affairs"; Ackerley views his individual act of refusal as resistance that undermines royal authority: the Maharajah "still attempts to break his resistance [. . .] uneasy perhaps at such virtue in a servant" (*Letters* 12). Narayan's resistance is often indirect or coded. Forced to order Sharma to satisfy the Maharajah, he touches Sharma's foot with his own and shakes his head to convey his disapproval. Narayan's subaltern resistance is stymied by his own unquestioning commitment to patriarchy. Ackerley notes that Indians are "blindly obedient" to "the power of authority [. . .] whether it proceeds from their parents, their chief, or the conquering European" (*Letters* 13).[13]

Ackerley's dominant discourse disables the effectiveness of Narayan's functionally ambiguous resistance even while attempting to represent it. He interprets Narayan's refusal in essentialist terms; if he "had not an inherent aversion for such practices," Ackerley deter-

---

[13] Ackerley concedes that Narayan's refusal had left him "without the smallest hope of any advancement" in Chhatarpur (*Letters* 13).

10. The Queer Subaltern in J. R. Ackerley's Hindoo Holiday

mines, "he would have quietly submitted years ago [. . .] he has no real rebellion in him" (*Letters* 13). And yet, Ackerley concedes that Narayan is the only person that had openly expressed criticism of the Maharajah during his five months in Chhatarpur. Even at the point of inscribing subaltern agency, Ackerley undermines it; Narayan's objection is not principled, but constitutional, it is not a conscious exercise of autonomous self-hood, but instinct. In the enforced homonormativity of the Chhatarpur court, one that cathects the homosexual service of minors towards the Maharajah as both "duty" and "reward," Narayan's acts of individual refusal have a social and political price. Despite his attempts at autonomy, his marginalisation from the main source of political power serves only to re-inscribe him as a subaltern subject.

Sharma's inability to articulate his own position and Narayan's obligation to speak for him is consistent in the narrative. While ostensibly resisting the discourse of command, Narayan's voice, by enforcing Sharma's silence, replicates and reinforces it. Paradoxically, Narayan's complicity in enforcing a discourse that denies the ability of the subaltern to provide consent helps record the discontinuous assertions of his own refusal to give consent (his mouth to Ackerley, his body to the Maharajah). Narayan's narrative traces subaltern resistance against hegemonic power, albeit always framed, shaped, and historically represented by the dominant signifying discourse.

The "fair, but unreadable" sixteen-year-old Sharma, dubbed "the White Sphinx" by the Maharajah, had already been in his personal employ for two years at the time of Ackerley's arrival. His primary duty was to satisfy, *per anum*, the fifty-seven year old ruler's still considerable sexual appetite, a situation that the Maharajah cryptically alludes to repeatedly with the proverb "no man can be a hero to his valet" (30, 127). Ackerley's first encounter with Sharma is initiated at one of the Maharajah's famous evenings with the "Gods," the troupe of boy entertainers bought to gratify his aesthetic, religious and erotic sensibilities. His first glance is both titillating and discomforting; at the Maharajah's order, Sharma is brought out, "motionless, expressionless," for his "inspection" and he is instantly made aware of the subjection of the boy to the sexual demands of his master: "I couldn't manage that – sitting there studying him as though he were a slave, so I hurriedly murmured my satisfaction" (38). Despite Ackerley's discomfort, his appreciation of Sharma's physical appearance ("he was young and tall [. . .] his face was strikingly handsome – fairer than usual") and his realisation of Sharma's status initiates a reciprocal relationship with the Maharajah: he engages in an economy of exchange with him over his valet, requesting him as a Hindi tutor. Sharma's worth is negotiated between the two hegemonic adults; the denial of the juvenile subaltern's consent in this discourse of power is cemented through a legitimising classical allusion. "[T]aking advantage of some remark of his on Zeus and Ganymede," Ackerley asks the Maharajah "whether I might not have his valet to teach me" (46).

Sharma's first appearance in Ackerley's guest house inscribes his mute powerlessness. Ackerley the master-narrator becomes both the temporary master of Sharma and the putative narrator of his mediated, translated consciousness. Denied the capacity for self-representation, or even comprehension, Sharma's subaltern status is confirmed by his physical discomfort, denoted both through acts of respect – "he shuffled his laceless European shoes from his bare feet" – and fear of possible physical or sexual violence – he "pulled the curtain right back so that the open doorway was revealed" (47). Lacking a common language, Ackerley's first private encounter with Sharma limns the failure of comprehension between the master-narrator and his fugitive subject. Ackerley's recourse to sketching, a channel for his erotic desire for Sharma, fails: "I could not get him to sit still" (48). Whether Sharma's restlessness suggests peevishness or the refusal of consent is a matter for conjecture. Ackerley's grasping at signs is mitigated by the arrival of Narayan, who serves as mediator, interpreter and censor of his consciousness for the remainder of the narrative. When Ackerley asks what the reason for Sharma's "agitation" is, Narayan replies,

10. The Queer Subaltern in J. R. Ackerley's Hindoo Holiday

"he is much frightened" (48). Narayan's presence serves to re-inscribe Sharma's perennially subordinate position.

Sharma's voice is always mediated through and effaced by Narayan, and in some cases by the Maharajah, who also translates and ventriloquises his valet, before being presented by Ackerley; retrieving an authentic voice for Sharma is impossible. The axiomatic explanation for Sharma's fear of Ackerley in their first encounter is offered by the Maharajah. "He told me [. . .] that you would beat him," the Maharajah declares, while confessing that he has had to beat Sharma "very much" and that for the British (like or unlike Ackerley?) inflicting systematic violence upon servants was expected: "no servant could be expected to be faithful [. . .] until he had cuts on his back two fingers deep" (51-52). All of the instances of Sharma's disobedience and the violence and/or repentance that they precipitate are recounted by the Maharajah and then narrated by Ackerley. Sharma's voice is doubly effaced, and the speech acts are reconstructed, invariably to justify the necessity of the acts of discipline. Examples of this include Sharma's alleged "impertinence" towards the palace sentries, which results in the Maharajah striking him with a cane (64); his refusal of a ten-rupee gift, which results in his temporary banishment from the court (81-82); his refusal to massage the Maharajah's stiff legs (88); and his eventual repentance, signalled through his renewed acceptance of the Maharajah's gifts (92). These encounters mark Sharma's disobedience and demonstrate how a dominant discourse records the resistance it faces, but it does not make the question of interpreting his actions any easier.

In relation to Sharma, the Maharajah, Ackerley and Narayan exist entirely within a signifying discourse of command, reiterated repeatedly in the absence of his comprehension, complicity, consent, or often, his presence. Narayan maintains that it is his "duty" as Sharma's friend, mentor, caste superior, and lover, to "slap him [. . .] many times, in many places" if he "were in fault" (194). Ackerley notes that Narayan's "possession" of Sharma, the fact that he "reflects, like a mirror, all his moods and variations," makes him "indifferent to the handsome body and contemptuous of the childish mind" (244). Incapable of penetrating or clearly representing Sharma's consciousness, Ackerley's text marks Sharma's incomprehension, rather than his own. Repeatedly, he draws attention to Sharma's ignorance of English and mimicry of Narayan's behaviour: "Sharma, who understands nothing that is being said" Ackerley observes, "sits and watches me with round eyes, ready to laugh at any moment should Narayan lead the way" (229). Sharma's inability to voice his consent from inside a discourse that refuses to recognise his ability as a juvenile, low-caste subaltern to offer such consent, leads Ackerley to reinscribe Narayan's dominance over Sharma. He legitimises Narayan's claim to be able to speak for his friend; "Sharma never does anything without Narayan's consent" (244), Ackerley concludes. This abrogation clearly includes offering his body, particularly the most significant orifice in Indian sexuality (the mouth), as an object of gratification. Near the end of the memoir, Narayan declares that he has given Sharma permission to reciprocate Ackerley's kiss:

> "He tell me 'The sahib try to kiss me'."
> "And what did you say?"
> "I say he must kiss you if you want." (252)

Narayan's equivocal, semi-fluent articulation places the discourse of command ("he must") above the ambiguous discourse of consent ("if you want" – but to which "you," Ackerley or Sharma, does he refer?); there is no record of Sharma's opinion or consent. Consent is further complicated by language. Distinguishing between formal *ap* and informal *tum* ("you"), the original Hindi conversation would enable a definitive answer to who Narayan privileges; this is impossible in English. Narayan's command ordering Sharma to reciprocate Ackerley's kisses is unequivocally noted in Ackerley's correspondence: "he ought to have kissed the sahib if the sahib wanted it" (*Letters* 13). We do know the outcome of Narayan's command: "*You* get much love

10. The Queer Subaltern in J. R. Ackerley's Hindoo Holiday

Sharma one time" (252), he tells Ackerley. In the history of a subaltern subject, this is certainly an unacknowledged, measured silence.

Ackerley's depiction of Sharma offers an example of the heterogeneous means by which the subaltern's ability to voice consent is constantly obscured and effaced. Shaped by the conflicting demands of the Maharajah, Narayan and Ackerley, and despite (or perhaps because) of his ability to perform the active sexual role, Sharma is commodified and exchanged within a signifying discourse that re-inscribes caste and economic dominance. His own permanent subordination, as a (homo)sexualised subaltern and the illiterate, non-English-speaking son of a barber, is determined within these structures. Sharma's periodic fits of disobedience, his sporadic, discontinuous, individual acts of refusal are constantly categorised and normalised in the narrative as the actions of a child, a "half-made fool-boy"; his consent is suppressed through the use of systematic, and largely legitimised symbolic violence (the Maharajah's cane or Narayan's threat to slap him) usually directed at children. Sharma's subaltern position, like that of "Napoleon the Third," mimics the wider social construction and management of the subaltern in colonial India: effectively denied social mobility, except on the terms of the source of hegemonic power, denied voice, through the effacing of their point of view, denied reparation, through their lack of access to literacy, and denied a historical record, except when they have acted in the agency of the dominant power.

In his final aesthetic response to Sharma, and at last overcoming the emotional and erotic hesitance he felt when he first viewed him, Ackerley compares the body of the youth to the body of a prize-winning (and holy) bullock, gazing in "wonder and admiration at the huge white marble form and calm majestic eyes," he notes Sharma's absorbed attention, and the "expression of awe in his great silly eyes", before casting his own penetrating gaze beneath "his vest and *dhoti*" to scan the "fugitive lines of his animal body" (253). Ackerley's unvoiced thought, unspoken and yet mediated to us (his English speaking readership), but not to the uncomprehending Sharma, the person with whom he shares this aesthetic experience, is presented as a speech act, even though it is not: "'Ah, my fine young bullocks!' I thought" (253). It is not Sharma's body, controlled as effectively as the bullock despite the lack of a "cord [. . .] through the dark nostrils" that is "fugitive" in the text, but his consciousness. Sharma's importance is recorded in Ackerley's excised passage and in Chhatarpur's history by his non-consensual genitive acts that insure the succession of the ruling family. The subaltern becomes a historically recorded agent only in the service of the hegemonic structures that maintain its silence.

The very first reference to the twelve-year-old orphan child entertainer, dubbed "Napoleon the Third" by the Maharajah, places him within the trade in sexual subalterns and more precisely, within an extant pre-colonial economic activity: bonded child labour. Informed by the "manager of the company," who is also apparently the "boy's uncle," that the price would be "fifty rupees a month for the boy's life" (53), the Maharajah enters into protracted negotiations. The subaltern position of "Napoleon the Third" is determined and enforced through the discourse of economic exchange, not personal consent. The boy's *de facto* guardian makes an "alternative offer for a lump sum of two thousand rupees" (56), which provokes the Maharajah, who has "dreamed of that face, it is entangled in my heart" (57), to threats of violence: "I should like to poison him" (58). When news of the failing health of the "uncle" is brought to the Maharajah's attention, it initiates a contest over the child, now in Cawnpore, based around the right of ownership rather than the responsibility of care. Bewailing a purchase slipping out of his fingers, the Maharajah exclaims: "if he dies *now* I shall lose the boy for ever!" (94). The Maharajah's messenger, dispatched to Cawnpore with five hundred rupees, arrives to find himself enmeshed in an intrigue involving another of the uncles and a hitherto unknown aunt, but his actions are futile: "Napoleon the

10. The Queer Subaltern in J. R. Ackerley's Hindoo Holiday

Third" has already been sold for five hundred rupees to "another company" in Calcutta (97).

Soon "Napoleon the Third" appears in Chhokrapur, "under escort and unpaid for" (101). The Maharajah demands two performances from the kidnapped child; the first, a formal dance at the court for the *Basant* festival, the second, a private function the following night, where he would "dance naked" (127) for the Maharajah's (and Ackerley's) gratification; the narrative relates only the first performance. Soon after the performance, "Napoleon the Third" is given permission to leave; he returns three weeks later, when Ackerley retrieves the exhausted child from Dipra station. There are only two further references to "Napoleon the Third" after his return to Chhokrapur; we are told of an accident with some gunpowder and a mistaken diagnosis of leprosy (254), and later, of the accidental removal of his *choti* (pigtail) by the court barber (273). Typifying discontinuously recorded subaltern history, the rest of his narrative, like his name, remains unwritten and unexamined.

In the very name "Napoleon the Third," the text presents the disjuncture between the nominated, overdetermined signifier (the face that the Maharajah has "dreamed" about for "thirty years") and the effaced, underwritten signified. As an explicitly subaltern object of sexual desire, Ackerley consciously and ironically draws attention to the fact that the boy's name and face bear no relation to one another:

> He was diminutive and dark, with very large eyes and an air of self-possession. A streak of white paint decorated his forehead, a single pearl his nose, and his cheeks were vividly coloured with vermillion. Whether this description bears any resemblance to the real Napoleon the Third I do not know. If I ever saw a picture of that monarch in his youth, I have forgotten it, and so, I imagine, has His Highness. (130)

Although the pursuit of "Napoleon the Third" occupies the Maharajah's mind for most of Ackerley's five months in Chhatarpur and haunts the narrative, his metonymic "name," shadowing the absence of a discourse of consent, remains absent from Ackerley's dramatis personae. More completely than any other male-gendered subaltern subject in *Hindoo Holiday*, "Napoleon the Third" is effaced from the text, his voice entirely muted, his autonomy disregarded, his actions reported, mediated and interpreted for us, his intent and his consent, obscured.

Despite the Maharajah's endless attempts to secure him (reprised through the repeated allusions to Zeus and Ganymede), "Napoleon the Third" is only present in Ackerley's narrative twice. The first instance is the formal *Basant* dance, where Ackerley notes the "tremulous, almost imperceptible movements of the head and hands," and his "discordant and rather fretful" (130) singing voice; there is no description of the second, private, naked performance. Ackerley's second description of the child places him in a different and more revealing context; found with his "uncle" and "aunt" on a lorry at Dipra heading for Chhokrapur, Ackerley is ordered to retrieve him. He finds him in a "very grubby" state, "seated on a pile of dusty blankets" and "wedged" between "the knees" of "his uncle and aunt," his "sore eyes [. . .] lavishly smeared with a thick black paste" (166). "Napoleon the Third" presents a picture of abjection and captivity rather than the aesthetic "air of self-possession" earlier noted. Ackerley's response is revealing: "we rescued him and his uncle [. . .] and stuffed them and their baggage into the back of the car," adding, "the aunt [. . .] we left where she was" (166). Unable to distinguish between animate and inanimate chattel, between the boy and his baggage, Ackerley reinscribes "Napoleon the Third" as a commodified subaltern subject, denied self-hood despite his position as a "court god."

Dominant discourses invariably trace the resistance, refusal or complicity of their silenced, subaltern subjects. Ironically for a child singer and dancer, the direct speech acts of "Napoleon the Third" are entirely absent from the text, but his temperamental outbursts and measured silences are not. After the accidental removal of his *choti* the Maharajah confirms both his distress (he "had burst into lamentations") and the inconsolability of his grief: "we have all tried to comfort him, but he will not speak to any of us [. . .] he is very angry indeed" (273). The Maharajah's awareness of the child's moods, even when mediated through the twin filters of the manager/uncle and the procurer/messenger, is itself a marker of the one point of resistance that even a kidnapped child can realistically offer: silence.

II Queering the text: Sexual difference and cultural relativism in *Hindoo Holiday*

Introducing Ackerley's *My Father and Myself*, W. H. Auden pointedly noted that the central complication of male same-sex relations was often cultural, rather than generational: "those who like 'chicken' have relatively few problems," but when the "desired difference" is "psychological or cultural," he observed, "the real trouble begins" (x). Recent critical attention directed at *Hindoo Holiday*, Ackerley's most consistently "queer" text and one that limns same-sex desire across the borders of race, space, social status, cultural context, and the colonial construction of power, has often been silent on these very differences.

David Bergman's discussion of Ackerley's quest for the "Ideal Friend" assumes Narayan and Sharma's relationship to be that between "best friends, who although married, sleep together, but without sex": a garbled, late twentieth-century, post-sexual-liberation reading (265). Individual choice and mutual consent were in fact often absent in the Chhatarpur court. In judging the "Indian concept of masculinity" (he only sees one, and he doesn't say what it is) as being "warped" by "colonialization and patriarchy" (265), Bergman unwittingly recapitulates colonial arguments documented by Mrinalini Sinha that projected the British as a conquering race who determined the *lack* of masculinity of a subject population through the fact of their subjugation (what consequences such a relational opposition has for the conquering Occidental remains glaringly unexamined by Bergman).

Bergman entirely ignores critical differences between Narayan and Sharma (caste, age, social position, knowledge of English, ability to ensure some measure of self-representation, etc) before coming to a startlingly unsubstantiated conclusion: "Ackerley sees in this relationship the asymmetry that ruins all his own friendships" (265). His analysis is expressed entirely through a liberal humanist late twentieth-century conceit (egalitarian relationships between consenting adults), which is not evident in the text and was not either espoused or practiced by Ackerley, who admitted that he longed for an "animal-man," the "mind" of his bitch Queenie in the "body" of a sailor, "the perfect human body always at one's service" combined with "the devotion of a faithful and uncritical beast" (*My Father and Myself* 282). Bergman is silent about Indian sexualities and how they might inform his analysis of *Hindoo Holiday*; in reading Narayan and Sharma's relationship through the privileged gaze of a liberal humanist, self-identified, and socially recognised Western male homosexual, Bergman offers a totalising commitment to his own cultural values which blinds him to the localised cultural values of the sexual subjects who he apparently scrutinises. In a similar vein, Robert Clark's reading of *Hindoo Holiday*, which deploys critical tropes from both queer theory (performativity) and postcolonial theory (Orientalism), offers a normative and totalising universalism in its reading of homosexuality in the text (Indian sexualities remain glaringly unscrutinised).

Too often, the position of the Western representing intellectual has been hegemonic rather than discursive, constricting rather than liberating, idealistic (and ideological) rather than culturally sensitive and enabling. This normative assumption of the universality of the Western taxonomy of homosexuality, born out of twin nineteenth-century discourses on crime and pathology, enforces the marginalisation of localised, culturally and socially specific sexual practices and identities. Disturbingly, the casual commitment to this universalising and essen-

10. The Queer Subaltern in J. R. Ackerley's Hindoo Holiday

tialist view of sexual identity threatens to silence the often noncompliant colonised subjects apparently under their scrutiny. Even as part of a liberal humanist project that accepts the nature of human sexuality as a constantly shifting continuum ranging from absolute heterosexuality to its putative redefining and reforming other, absolute homosexuality, such sexual determinism runs the risk of replicating the paradigm of colonialism by denying the specificity of a localised culture which may not classify sexualities in the same way (or indeed, *at all*) and thereby undermining the ability of such sexualised or gendered subjects to ever voice or represent themselves.[14]

Before discussing some of the implications of interpreting the sexualities in *Hindoo Holiday*, I need to outline the relevant taxonomies and epistemologies of sexuality extant in colonial India. Indrani Chattarjee has made a cogent argument for viewing sexuality in precolonial India through "the lens of slavery," observing that the "dialectic of *alienation and intimacy*" (61) is visible in the overtly hegemonic codes of both Sanskrit texts and Islamic era verse. She notes that the ubiquity of "beautiful young 'slave' boys in personal proximity" to free adult men during the Delhi Sultanate and the Mughal period denoted the "free nobleman's rank" rather than the individual sexual choices of the youths (as slaves, like women and children, they had limited agency). Chattarjee finds the same privileging of the adult hegemonic male over his sexual subjects in earlier Sanskrit texts, such as the delineation between descriptive and prescriptive categories of sexual acts in Vatsyayana's *Kama Sutra*. The epistemology of description shows oral sex being practiced across genders and social groups. However, the taxonomy of prescription recommended by Vatsyayana is not one predicated by gender, or sex, but by social rank; thus oral sex is prohibited with "married women," but permitted with "female attendants," "serving maids," and "male servants of some men" (67).[15]

---

[14] For an intelligent critique, see Hayes 79-98.

[15] Both categories are depicted on the Chandela temples at Khajuraho.

Chattarjee notes that "particular kinds of sexual activity were imagined and represented in the past as markers of people's status" (65). The defining qualifier was neither an essentialist argument of sexual orientation, nor a socially constructed one of individual choice, but rather the official sanction of sexual practices that did not threaten existing hierarchies of authority. Even existing "discourses of condemnation" (65) in the fourteenth-century Delhi court (such as that of Ziauddin Barani) refused to contemplate any reversal of sexual roles within same-sex attachments, which were always asymmetrically constructed between a hegemonic free man and his slave. The King, Chattarjee observes, is never depicted by Barani as passive, even when he is the subject of political invective.

Ruth Vanita and Saleem Kidwai note the same non-judgmental, socially privileging classification of the hegemonic man's sexuality in the famous Sanskrit work of Hindu Law, the *Manusmriti*: a free man "who sheds his semen" in "nonhuman females, in a man, in a menstruating woman, in something other than a vagina, or in water" i.e., outside of the socially and religiously sanctioned female vagina, must perform a "minor penance consisting of eating the five products of the cow, and keeping a one-night fast" (Vanita and Kidwai 25). The sexuality of the free man is predicated not by any notion of his sexual orientation (the *Manusmriti* does not distinguish between male/female, adult/child, or human/animal), but by the locus of his emission (sanctioned vs. non-sanctioned). Thus an act of oral sex with a female subject (in British taxonomy a heterosexual act) would incur the same small penalty as an act of anal sex with a male subject (a homosexual act, identified and punished under British sodomy laws) and neither would in itself, change the sexual identity or social esteem of the active hegemonic male. Both Hindu and Islamic pre-colonial Indian epistemologies and taxonomies of sexuality consistently ignored sexual binarism, refrained from presenting the often socially sanctioned actions of hegemonic men purely in the language of crime and/or pun-

10. The Queer Subaltern in J. R. Ackerley's Hindoo Holiday

ishment, and even more insistently effaced the sexualities and consents of the subject, gendered bodies available to them.

The *Manusmriti* and the *Kama Sutra* were written for a self-selecting readership (literate, Brahman, and almost always, male) who were responsible for perpetuating a hegemonic structure of classification, justification and control. In the Chhatarpur context, this privileges Narayan and the Maharajah over the illiterate, low caste "bearer" Sharma and the pre-literate, caste indeterminate child, "Napoleon the Third." Before romanticising the often the non-judgmental acceptance of "queer" sexualities in pre-colonial Indian civilisation, we also need to accept the intensely hierarchical and hegemonic manner in which such sexualities are inscribed. Vanita and Kidwai have defended "texts written in the language of the elite, such as Sanskrit, Persian and English" against the charge that they "inherently perpetuate oppressive attitudes to lower castes, tribal peoples and women" (xvii), but this defence is specious. The cultural production of the elite was designed entirely for their own consumption, and the hegemonic discourses of power that they register provide the only extant record of the multiple, effaced sexualities of subalterns in pre-colonial India.

While the *Manusmriti* and the *Kama Sutra* provide a working *vade mecum* of potentially "queer" sexuality for an indigenous male elite, their objective is not to voice the sexuality of the subaltern, even when his or her subjection is a prerequisite for the adult male's sexual gratification. Pre-colonial Indian paradigms for "queer" sexuality are neither repressive nor permissive, but essentially privileging along extant lines of social stratification. Unlike the Western construction of homosexuality, which evolved through a long process of classification and repression, pre-colonial Indian writing about "queer" sexualities does not identify or voice the consciousness of a specific community; instead it shows the widespread practice and social sanction of certain sexual acts by hegemonic men upon social groups deemed to be their class, caste, or gender inferiors.

The first systematic attempt in India at classifying sexuality was the colonial anti-sodomy statute, Section 377 of the Indian Penal Code, introduced as part of Lord Macaulay's sweeping consolidation of Indian law in 1860. The law defined the offence as "voluntarily" having "carnal intercourse against the order of nature" with "any man, woman or animal," punishable by life imprisonment, or a sentence of up to ten years, and a fine (Bhaskaran 15).[16] Suparna Bhaskaran has demonstrated how section 377 was an extension of existing metropolitan statute that was incorporated into colonial legislation and attempted to harmonise seemingly contradictory Indian laws at the time. As part of the universalising impetus of colonial administration, Section 377 placed the onus of criminalisation on the active participant, ignored the issue of consent, and massively raised the tariff of the penalty, now seen as a crime rather than a private sin requiring personal penance. Where pre-colonial India had not subjected the sexual identity of the transgressor to any scrutiny as a result of his actions, the British-imposed statute demanded the classification and punishment of the offender through the metropolitan British filters of the "sodomite" and later, the "homosexual," an enabling violation that, Jeremy Seabrook has observed, created both the consciousness and the institutionalisation of same-sex desire through its repression: a dialectic that had never been a historical reality in India (136). By the time of Ackerley's arrival in the Chhatarpur court, the new Western taxonomy of "homosexuality" (and with it, its relational concomitant, the "normative" ideology of heterosexuality) enshrined in the legal framework of identification, punishment, and identity formation, was in direct competition with existing established Indian sexual practices.

We should not assume that the British imposition of supposed norms of Anglo-Saxon metropolitan sexuality remained either uncontested or dominant in Indian thinking about sexual practice or identity formation. Jeremy Seabrook's informative work has demonstrated the

---

[16] Section 377 remains on the statute in all the successor states to British India.

10. The Queer Subaltern in J. R. Ackerley's Hindoo Holiday

extent to which men who have sex with men in modern India remain for the most part informed and influenced by traditional, pre-colonial ideas about same-sex desire and practice rather than instinctively sharing the universalising assumptions of Western homosexual identity politics. His detailed interviews with seventy-five men who have sex with men in a Delhi Park reveal interesting insights into their sense of self; about 40 percent were married, less than a quarter identified as "gay," only three said they had no desire to marry, and most viewed marriage and parenthood with a "remarkable absence of anxiety" (10, 47). Seabrook observes that "most of those who identified as gay" were of a "higher social status," while for "most of the poorer men, the idea of being gay, or of being homosexual scarcely arose" (46), replicating the absence of a discourse about sexuality or sexual identity amongst subaltern Indian groups.

The prescriptions of the *Manusmriti* and the *Kama Sutra* rather than Section 377 still shape the self-consciousness of same-sex participants in India today. Seabrook admits that his investigation required him to re-examine "what constitutes sex," for many of the men that he interviewed insisted that they had "never had sex" (166). "For many," Seabrook concedes, sex exclusively means only "vaginal intercourse with a woman," and therefore "whatever they did with men [. . .] did not even constitute sexual activity at all" (166) and was euphemised by their participants as *masti* (fun), *ananda karna* (having pleasure) or *khayal* (play). Seabrook observed in Delhi many of the traditional practices of the Indian hegemonic free male, separating sanctioned, marital vaginal sex from non-sanctioned, contingent acts, again refuting the universalising claims of Western sexual politics. Several of his interviewees openly voiced their preference for a local reading of their own sexual practice and identity, rather than the importation of an universalising concept of gay identity, perceived as inferior to the Indian tradition of a "discrete [. . .] effective and civilized way of managing human sexuality" (139). Seabrook's findings suggest that the Chhatarpur court needs to be seen in the context of competing sexual taxonomies, rather than by assuming the universalising and hegemonic validity of a Western homosexuality, fashioned through the narratives of repression and liberation.

To conclude, I want to look at Ackerley's "queer" text with the twin filters of both sexual difference and cultural relativism and examine the extent to which such a reading of *Hindoo Holiday* can avoid simply mapping a reductive, universalising Western homosexuality upon captive, gendered sexual subjects, and fulfil what Samir Dayal has intelligently observed is the ostensible purpose and "shared premise" of "queerness" as a textual and cultural practice: "a queering of the pitch, a displacement of the colonial, heteronormative, or otherwise hegemonic stratifications" allowing the "interrogation, implicitly at least, of the way all subjects" are "interpellated as gendered bodies within a given social space" (Dayal 305).

In his depiction of the complex web of sometimes imbricated, sometimes unreciprocated expressions of same-sex desire in *Hindoo Holiday*, Ackerley explicitly assumes the position of both master-narrator and amateur anthropologist in negotiating a path for a Western, metropolitan reader into his experience of India: here specifically, a "queer" India. Sexual desire in the Chhatarpur court is cathected as "duty" and enforced through financial reward and physical violence; it involves the Maharajah, Narayan, Sharma, "Napoleon the Third," and Ackerley, and is mediated through Ackerley's implicated and erotically charged gaze. I have already discussed the issue of the consent of the male-gendered sexual subaltern in the Chhatarpur court; what is less obvious is the extent to which homoerotic desire maps the same territory.

Homoerotic desire in the text (the Maharajah's and Ackerley's) is always directed at sexual subjects who are unable or unwilling to refuse consent (the partial exception here, both as object and subject, is Narayan). This negotiated structure is replicated in heteroerotic desire, especially the complete erasure of the consent of wives (cathected as "duty") towards their husbands. Shadowing the *Manusmriti*, there is

10. The Queer Subaltern in J. R. Ackerley's Hindoo Holiday

no disjuncture between heteroerotic and homoerotic desire and sexual practice in Chhatarpur. Both are predicated by the position of the adult hegemonic male *vis-à-vis* the sexual subjects available to him (children, women, servants, and lower castes of any gender) rather than by his sexual identity. The Chhatarpur adult hegemonic male enjoys the same sexual sanction outlined by the Sanskrit texts. He may avail himself of his spiritually sanctioned command over his wife (by having penetrative vaginal sex with her, but *not* any other form of sexual intercourse), which she cannot refuse. Both Narayan and Sharma have recourse to this (although whether Sharma's marriage to his twelve-year-old child bride has been consummated is debatable), but the Maharajah does not; his abrogation of this prerogative is both symptomatic and significant.

The adult hegemonic male may also avail himself of other forms of sexual pleasure with his caste inferiors of any gender, as long as he maintains the active role, and perform penance for these minor sins by following the *Manusmriti*'s prescription: eating the five products of the cow and fasting for one night. This supplementary sexual practice may be recreational and contingent behaviour, or it may be an expression of an essential inclination; it does not, however, contribute to the formation of a separate sexual identity. Narayan engages in such activity with both sexes. Ackerley acknowledges that Narayan had "had many affairs with other girls" before his marriage "during his sixteenth year" and that he has had "many since" (250-51), with girls and boys (including Sharma and Ackerley). Recognising his minor sins, Narayan takes the five products as penance (224-45). The Maharajah demands the sexual service of those recognised as his slaves (Sharma, Narayan, and potentially "Napoleon the Third"); unsurprisingly, he admits to taking the five products as penance "every day" (153).

The problem for the Maharajah is his sexual passivity, which undermines the stratified hierarchy of authority that underpins his position; as Chattarjee points out, for a free born man to offer himself for sexual penetration would be equivalent to "acting like a slave" (72), and for a ruler, it would imperil the state. In the terms of pre-colonial sanctioned Indian sexuality, the Maharajah's "queer" use of Sharma for his personal gratification is an abuse of his own highly privileged autonomy, rather than an abuse of a inferior over whom he has complete authority, and whose consent and desire are obscured and irrelevant. However, the Maharajah's attempts to force Narayan (as a Brahman, Sharma's master, an adult and potentially a hegemonic male) to penetrate him in public potentially breaches codes of sexual and political conduct for both actors. For Narayan to concede to the Maharajah's demands would be to deny the authority of the ruler by virtue of his penetrative abjection; for him to refuse would constitute an act of disobedient rebellion. In Narayan's implicated position, between active acquiescence (implying his rejection of tradition and the patriarchal privileges it accords him) and outright refusal (denoting his rejection of the absolute authority of the Maharajah), any exercise of choice becomes a politically freighted act. The gap between Narayan's espousal of traditional sexuality and the Maharajah's championing of an allegedly Hellenistic homonormativity displays the resistance, still evident in India today, towards totalising modes.

Ackerley's depiction of Chhatarpur refutes *both* the universalising impetuses current at the time: the Western epistemology of sexual binarism *and* the concomitant taxonomy of identification and punishment. The locus of rupture in Chhatarpur, the potential entry point for "queerness," occurs not in the choice of sexual partner, but in the choice of sexual role and the ability of the subject to refuse consent. In this respect, the gendered body that warrants the most scrutiny, and offers the most resistance, is that of the "queer" subaltern, Narayan.

Archival Sources

Chhatarpur papers in the Oriental and India Office Collection, British Library:

10. The Queer Subaltern in J. R. Ackerley's Hindoo Holiday

Internal and Political Branch A, 1887, investiture, 10R/1/1/785, File 1A, dated 27/04/1887

Internal and Political Branch, first cycle, 1922, recognition of the legitimacy of the heir, 10R/R/1/1/1356 File 584-P(S), especially TS 1-2, TS 4

Internal and Political, Honours Records, dispensation warrant, 10R/L/PS/15/66, File H56/1928.

Administrative report, 1909-1927, 10R/V/10/943.

Political Branch Files, 1932, 10R/R/1/1, 2262(1) & 2262(2).

Works Cited

Ackerley, J. R. *Hindoo Holiday: An Indian Journal.* London: Chatto & Windus, 1932. Rev. 1952 text, rpt. London: Penguin, 1983.

___. *My Father and Myself.* Introd. W. H. Auden. London: Bodley Head, 1968.

Auden, W. H. Introduction. Ackerley, *My Father* i-xxiii.

Bergman, David. "J. R. Ackerley and the Ideal Friend." *Fictions of Masculinity: Crossing Cultures, Crossing Sexualities.* Ed. Peter F. Murphy. New York: New York University Press, 1994.

Bhaskaran, Suparna. "The Politics of Penetration: Section 377 of the Indian Penal Code." Vanita, ed., *Queering India* 15-29.

Braybrooke, Neville. *The Letters of J. R. Ackerley.* Chatham: Duckworth, 1975.

Bristow, Joseph. *Effeminate England: Homoerotic Writing After 1885.* Buckingham: Open University Press, 1995.

Chattarjee, Indrani. "Alienation, Intimacy, and Gender: Problems for a History of Love in South Asia." Vanita, ed., *Queering India* 61-76.

Clark, Robert L. A. "Queering Orientalism: The East as Closet in Said, Ackerley and the Medieval Christian West." *Medieval Encounters* 5.3 (1999): 336-49.

Dayal, Samir. "By way of an afterword." Hawley, ed., *Post-Colonial, Queer* 305-325.

Gandhi, Leela. "Homosexuality and Utopian Thought in Post/Colonial India." Vanita, ed., *Queering India* 87-99.

Gramsci, Antonio. *Selections from the Prison Notebooks*. Trans. and ed. Quintin Hoare and Geoffrey Nowell-Smith. New York: International Publishers, 1971.

Hawley, John C., ed. *Post-Colonial, Queer: Theoretical Intersections*. Albany: SUNY, 2001.

Hayes, Jarrod. "Queer Resistance to (Neo-)Colonialism in Algeria." Hawley, ed., 79-98.

Mani, Lata. "Contentious Traditions: The Debate on *Sati* in Colonial India." *Recasting Women: Essays in Colonial History*. Ed. Kumkum Sangari and Sudesh Vaid. Delhi: Kali for Women, 1989.

McHugh, Susan. "Marrying my Bitch: J. R. Ackerley's Pack Sexualities." *Critical Inquiry* 27.1 (2000): 21-41.

Moore-Gilbert, Bart. *Postcolonial Theory: Contexts, Practices, Politics*. London: Verso, 1997.

Parker, Peter. *Ackerley: A Life of J. R. Ackerley*. London: Constable, 1989.

Seabrook, Jeremy. *Love in a Different Climate*. London: Verso, 1999.

Sinha, Mrinalini. *Colonial Masculinity: The "Manly Englishman" and the "Effeminate Bengali" in the Late Nineteenth Century*. Manchester: Manchester University Press, 1995.

Spivak, Gayatri Chakravorty. "Can the Subaltern Speak?" *Marxism and the Interpretation of Culture*. Ed. Cary Nelson and Lawrence Grossberg. Basingstoke: Macmillan, 1988. 271-316.

___. "The New Subaltern: A Silent Interview." *Mapping Subaltern Studies and the Postcolonial*. Ed. Vinayak Chaturvedi. London: Verso, 2000. 324-40.

___. *A Critique of Postcolonial Reason: Towards a History of the Vanishing Present*. Cambridge, Mass.: Harvard University Press, 1999.

10. The Queer Subaltern in J. R. Ackerley's Hindoo Holiday

Vanita, Ruth, ed. *Queering India: Same-Sex Love and Eroticism in Indian Culture and Society*. London: Routledge, 2001.
Vanita, Ruth, and Saleem Kidwai, eds. *Same-Sex Love in India: Readings from Literature and History*. Houndsmills: Macmillan, 2000.
Whisnant, Clayton J. "Masculinity and Desire in the works of J. R. Ackerley." *Journal of Homosexuality* 43.2 (2002): 127-42.

11. Cultural Contestations in the Literary Market Place: Reading Raja Rao's *Kanthapura* and Aubrey Menen's *The Prevalence of Witches*

Ruvani Ranasinha
King's College, London

This essay provides new readings of the publication history and critical reception of Raja Rao's *Kanthapura* (1938) and Aubrey Menen's *The Prevalence of Witches* (1947). Written a decade apart, their distinct first novels influence, chronicle, and respond to the shifting aesthetic, cultural, and political contexts and tastes of the metropolitan literary market place during this notable era in world history.

I Raja Rao's *Kanthapura* (1938): Contexts of literary production

Raja Rao (1909-2006) emerged on to the European literary scene during the ferment of Indian nationalist and political struggles. In this context, the spiritual versions of the Indian subcontinent that preoccupied British readers (evinced by the impact of the Theosophical Society, Rabindranath Tagore, and the publications of the *India Heritage* and *Wisdom of the East* series marketing the "essence" of India's wisdom) seemed to Rao and his contemporary Iqbal Singh out of step with contemporary, pressing political realities and therefore of little use to modern Indian and international readers. Particularly invested in the task of nation-building in the lead-up to independence, through a rediscovery and revaluation of India's past and contemporary culture, Rao and Singh sought to secure the publication of new editions and translations of Indian classics, such as Kalidasa's *Shakuntala*, alongside influential nineteenth- and twentieth-century texts by Indian writers who played historic roles in the shaping of the Indian national movement. In 1938 they approached the principal of publishers Allen and Unwin, Stanley Unwin, who had published Gandhi, Nehru and

Radhakrishnan in the decade prior to independence, and had already undertaken to publish Rao's novel *Kanthapura*. Unwin was a Nonconformist and liberal thinker. His views were often reflected in the books he published, such as work by Bertrand Russell, J. A. Hobson, L. T Hobhouse and Ramsay MacDonald, and books about India. His support of Indian writers and his desire to increase understanding of Indian affairs can be seen as an extension of this effort. Promoting local reappraisals of India's past did not, however, necessarily match British readers' interest in "modern" India, and this is likely to have been the reason why Allen and Unwin chose not to publish Singh and Rao's projected series of Indian classics.[1] However, at Rao and Singh's instigation Allen and Unwin published their edition of *Changing India* in 1939. This anthology of writings by modern Indians began with Raja Rammohun Roy, described as "the first of the moderns," and ended with Jawaharlal Nehru, who in the words of Rao and Singh's preface "has given a new and more universal direction to the Indian struggle for social and political emancipation" (9). With the backing of an enlightened publisher, Rao and fellow Indian writers played an extremely influential role in shaping the content of South Asian Anglophone writing published in Britain during this period. What was produced under the sign of India at this time reflects these bilingual, Westernised writers' emergent nationalism.

Given the often patronising, imperialist attitudes of the era, Allen and Unwin was ahead of its time in giving South Asian writers an overtly political platform. This was not, however without political and cultural constraints. With tensions escalating between the Congress and British colonial government in the 1930s, books critical of British rule were subject to censorship. The critical material of Anand's unflinching portrayal of British tea companies' exploitation of plantation workers in a tea-estate in Assam in his novel *Two Leaves and a Bud* (1937) led to its banning in colonial India. This had implications for

---

[1] Allen and Unwin, letter to Rao, 6 February 1939 (qtd. in Ranasinha 28).

11. Rao's Kanthapura *and Menen's* The Prevalence of Witches

Rao's novel *Kanthapura* (1938), a fictionalisation of a small village's participation in Gandhi's 1930-1932 Civil Disobedience movement in the Kara district of Karnataka. The young radical Moorthy influences the caste-ridden villagers to dispel some of their prejudices, spin their own cloth and participate in a non-violent satyagraha in defence of the rights of the "coolie" labourers at the Skeffington Coffee Estate; despite the brutal assaults they suffer at the hands of the British Officers, they remain defiant. In this way the novel dramatises the freedom struggle in terms of its effects on India's vast rural hinterland; it represents the impact of Gandhian nationalism on rural populations and the withdrawal of the collaboration on which colonialism depended. It is for these reasons that Allen and Unwin employed an editor to identify potentially inflammatory material, recommending "the slight toning down of certain passages."[2]

Rao prudently accepted this pre-publication vetting in the interest of the dissemination of his work amongst nationalist intellectuals in India. In 1937, in the immediate context of the banning of Anand's *Two Leaves and a Bud* (1937) by the colonial government in India he wrote: "As I am myself keen that the book [*Kanthapura*] should circulate freely and largely in India, I should be glad to accept all toning down of the text, which would unnecessarily bring down the heavy hands of the Censors on my book."[3] However, Rao was not prepared to allow important parts of his novel to be censored: "[. . .] I must say that it would be difficult with passages which form integral parts of the book. However as you say there are not many passages which need be touched up, such a difficulty would not probably arise."

While it is not clear to what extent passages were "toned down," *Kanthapura* remains a graphic critique of the exploitation of labour by the resident Englishmen at the Skeffington Coffee Estate. The novel

---

[2] Allen and Unwin, letter to Raja Rao, 20 February 1937 (qtd. in Ranasinha 27).

[3] Rao, letter to Allen and Unwin, 24 February 1937 (qtd. in Ranasinha 27).

recounts the way the labourers did back-breaking work in the "heavy piercing" sun for less pay than initially promised, suffering fever and dysentery (54) . The workers are subject to physical beating from the Old Sahib, while the women are later sexual exploited by his nephew, who rapes young girls of seventeen, or withholds the salary of any family who refuses to send him their female relative. He fatally shoots a Brahmin, Seetharam, who refuses to send his daughter, and never pays the family the promised compensation because, as Rao's narrator puts it, the "Red-Man's Court forgave him" (61). This constitutes the very same criticism of colonial courts and British tea companies' exploitation of tea-plantation workers that Anand portrayed in his novel *Two Leaves and a Bud* (1937) which proved so threatening to the colonial government in India and so unpalatable and unbelievable to a British reviewer on publication. Incredulous that the labourers can be as "underpaid, starved, bullied, beaten" as Anand depicts, the reviewer claimed it was "against commonsense" for a company to mistreat the labour on whom it depends for its profit (Moloney 379). Anand becomes an unreliable informant in the reviewer's insistence that "Penny wise, pound foolish is an Indian rather than an English characteristic." Preferring to dismiss the fictionalised possibility that an English-dominated jury would overturn the charges against a British officer, guilty of brutally murdering the protagonist Gangu, and attempting to rape his daughter, the reviewer claims "it is [. . .] unlikely that English jurymen in disregard of their oaths would return a manifestly iniquitous verdict; it is much more unlikely that an English judge would concur."

This myopic nationalism and denial of injustice reappears in a similar response to the Parsi journalist D. F. Karaka's (b.1911) "unreasonable obsession" with "colour prejudice" in his book *I Go West* published by Michael Joseph in the same year as *Kanathapura*. The reviewer suggests Karaka should reflect more on his being elected as the first Indian President of the Oxford Union and comments that "there is too much bitterness, too little thought in this book" (rev. of *I Go*

11. Rao's Kanthapura *and Menen's* The Prevalence of Witches

West). The review dismisses Karaka's critique of the exclusion of Indians from certain European clubs in India and advocates instead the "commonsense reflection" that this "really means no more than that the intimacy of club life is impossible for persons whose ideas of social propriety are wholly different [. . .] for this reason Europeans do not seek admission to orthodox Indian clubs."[4] Such reactions point to some of the prevailing attitudes circulating at this time, giving us a fuller picture of the sociological and ideological conditions surrounding the emergence of these writers.

While these first British critical assessments do not represent the entire spectrum of opinions in existence at the time, they offer influential mediated, fixed, and limited readings of these texts to their putative British readers; I will discuss this mediation in relation to Aubrey Menen in the second part of this essay. For example, the 1938 *Times Literary Supplement* review of Rao's *Kanthapura* euphemistically refers to its depiction of "the troubles in a village in Southern India" with no further analysis ("Review of Novels"). Allen and Unwin's pre-vetting suggests they read the novel in terms of the way it overtly dramatises the struggle to get rid of "the Red-man" (51). Subsequently, it was primarily Indian scholarship that did justice to the novel's richness, providing close readings of the text's remarkable sensitivity to the mood of its time, and its encoding of the decade's tensions and developments that were visible by the time *Kanthapura* was published in 1938; if not entirely obvious, this can be seen as part of the text's political unconscious.[5] The British reviewers' interest was confined to the paradigm of the British Raj in India, rather than the text's representation of the emergence of leaders such as Nehru, who began to mount the ideological challenge of socialist politics that would eventually displace Gandhian ideology in the national move-

---

[4] The identity of this reviewer is being traced by the *Times Literary Supplement*. In tone this review is remarkably similar to the previously cited review of *Two Leaves and a Bud*.

[5] See M. K Naik; C. D Narasimhaiah; and more recently Rumina Sethi.

ment. The challenges posed to Gandhian traditionalism in terms of socialism and large-scale industrialisation is first articulated by Rangamma, a political activists. She talks about "the country of the hammer and the sickle and electricity [. . .] there were women who worked like men, night and day, and when they felt tired, they went and spent their holiday in a palace – No money for the railway, no money for the palace" (Rao 36). The emergence of Nehruvian socialism is more fully articulated towards the end of the novel in Moorthy's letter to Ratna when he writes:

> I have come to realise bit by bit, and bit by bit, when I was in prison, that as long as there will be iron gates, and barbed wires round the Skeffington Coffee Estate, and the city cars that can roll up the Bebbur mound, and gas-lights and coolie cars, there will always be pariahs and poverty. Ratna, things must change. The youths here say they will change it. Jawaharlal will change it. You know Jawaharlal is like a Bharatha to the Mahatma. [. . .] And he calls himself an "equal-distributionist", and I am with him and his men. (183)

While the narrative foregrounds the role of the women of the village as revolutionaries, in Rangamma's advice to the women in *Kanthapura* also articulates Gandhi's ambiguous mobilisation of women in the nationalist movement: he encouraged women to participate in the public sphere but simultaneously naturalised women's roles in the domestic sphere:[6]

> And when our men heard of this [Sevika Sangha], they said: was there nothing left for our women but to vagabond about like soldiers? And every time the milk curdled or a dhoti was not dry, they would say, "And this is all because of this Sevi business",

---

[6] See Forbes and Katrak.

11. Rao's Kanthapura *and Menen's* The Prevalence of Witches

To which Rangamma replies

"Of course, Santamma has to look after your comforts. If we are to help others, we must begin with our husbands" [. . .] and we all say, "We should do our duty. If not, it is no use belonging to the Gandhi group". Rangamma says, "That is right sister." (110-11)

The novel reflects the deterioration in communal relations between Hindus and Muslims in the Othering of the evil "Mohammedan" policeman Bade Khan, the villain of the story. However the details of this textured fictionalised portrait were not easily consumed by the first British readers, as we will see.

Political constraints aside, at this juncture in the British context it was much harder for South Asian Anglophone writers to be taken seriously as writers of fiction rather than as social historians. Rao's novel *Kanthapura* was an exception to Allen and Unwin's broadly non-fictional Indian list. The publication of Anand and Narayan's first novels – founding fictional texts of the Indo-Anglian tradition – was only secured by the advocacy of established English authors E. M. Forster and Graham Greene. From the early part of the twentieth century, most South Asian Anglophone writing published in Britain was broadly anthropological non-fiction. For example, art historian Ananda K. Coomaraswamy's (1877-1947) early publications in Britain focused on Hinduism and Buddhism, alongside interpretations of Hindu culture (*Suttee, a Vindication of the Hindu Woman*), with an emphasis on insurmountable cultural difference (such as *The Deeper Meaning of the Struggle between Englishmen and Indians*). Later fictional narratives would be seen through such an anthropological lens. Such sociological interpretations stem in part from a suspicion as to whether these Indian writers could actually write fiction. While a number of Indians had recently published sociological treatises on village life in India, these early novels mark British readers' first *fictional* encounter with such topics by Indian writers.[7]

The review in the *Times Literary Supplement* I referred to earlier of novels on the "East," which included Rao's *Kanthapura* (1938) and S. Fyzee-Rahamin's *Gilded India* (1938), the story of the life of a Indian woman married against her will as a child to a dissolute ruling Prince, begins by claiming that:

> It is not unnatural that the focussing of public attention on the East at the present time should produce a considerable crop of novels dealing with India and China, although an intimate knowledge of the subject may not go hand in hand with the ability to tell a story well. In the making of a novel, knowledge, no matter how profound, is not enough to guarantee success. ("Novels in Translation")

The reviewer suggests that Rao's and Fyzee-Rahamin's novels are "disappointing books. It is obvious that their authors have comprehensive knowledge of their subject, but have not discovered how to present it in the form of fiction. Both are half fiction, half history." He contrasts these novels unfavourably with Louis Bromfield's "extremely skilful" novel *The Rains Came*, set in Ranchapur, "a progressive state in the Himalayas." This novel's focus on the white inhabitants, the American missionaries, millionaires, and the protagonist Tom Ransome ("part English Aristocrat, part Republican American") no doubt secured "a wide and human interest" for this reviewer. However, his resistance to the Indian writers' novels does not appear to stem from their culturally different content. The reviewer insists both Rao and Rahamin "have vitally interesting material in their books"; instead it is the challenge to the formal and generic expectations of the Anglo-American novel in the 1930s that are contested ("Novels in

---

[7] Such as Mahadev Desai, *Gandhiji in India* (1927) and G. G. Mukhtyar, *Life and Labour in a South Gujarat Village* (1930).

11. Rao's Kanthapura *and Menen's* The Prevalence of Witches

Translation"). This sort of treatment was not uncommon; in his review of Ahmed Ali's *Twilight in Delhi* (1940) for the *TLS*, R. D. Charques claimed that

> [i]t requires an effort to adjust one's imagination to the unfamiliar setting and strange atmosphere of *Twilight in Delhi* and at the end one is not at all sure how rewarding that effort has been. It may be that the failure to discover pattern or significance in this chronicle of Indian social custom springs from an insufficiently attentive or sympathetic reading. On the other hand, it seems possible that Mr. Ahmed Ali in this first novel is as yet too inexperienced to make satisfying use of his material.

Charques's view indicates the response of less well-known reviewers circulating outside the Bloomsbury Group's support of Indian writers.

Other British reviews of fiction at this time confirm a fascination for stories with exotic locations, yet always preferably filtered through the vehicle of European novel. An example of this is the positive remarks on R. P. Russ's *Hussein: An Entertainment* (1938), a tale of the exploits of an Indian boy descended from a family of mahouts which include snake-charming, cheetah-training and political intrigue, alongside Maud Diver's novels in *John O'London's Weekly*. These reviews suggest a desire for difference, but always on prescribed terms, and in a form that will not prove too "difficult for the impatient Western reader to tackle" ("Novels in Translation"). Articulating the rejection of European versions of India voiced by his generation and quoting from a negative review of *Twilight* that is not identified, Anand challenges

> the insanity which leads to the acclamation of another Louis Bromfield novel *Night in Bombay*: 'a spurious scenario P. and O. coloured cartoons of glamorous India [...] the successor in direct descent from Kipling and Yeats-Brown *Bengal-*

Lancer' as a 'great work', and to its choice by The Book Society and the *Daily Mail* Book Club, while so sensitive a narrative as Ahmed Ali's [*Twilight in Delhi*] is dismissed by most of the reviewers with perfunctory notices

in his review of both novels in the literary magazine *Indian Writing*[8] (Anand, rev. of *Twilight in Delhi*). The Book Reviews section of *Indian Writing* served as a space for these South Asian writers to comment on each other's work. This coverage was particularly important in the context of a wider reviewing culture in England that as Anand describes in 1941 had become "increasingly insular, self-centred and chauvinistic since the intensification of this war of rival Imperialisms"

The platform offered to these writers was not, therefore, always on their own terms. As I have argued in my book *South Asian Writers in Twentieth-Century Britain: Culture in Translation*, Rao's editor Malcolm Barnes's ideas of public taste in the book market led him to encourage Rao to minimise the cultural specificity of his Indian material. For instance, Barnes suggested an English title instead of *Kanthapura* (Ranasinha 29-31). Furthermore, he specifically asked Rao to modify his stylistic experimentation with a non-standard English inflected with Kannada cadence, expressions and figures of speech delivered in the colloquial idiom of his narrator, a garrulous village grandmother, evident from her opening description of her village: "High on the Ghats is it, high up the steep mountains that face the cool Arabian seas, up the Malabar coast is it, up Mangalore and Puttur and many a centre of cardamom and coffee, rice and sugar-cane" (Rao 7). Together with the integration of myth, history, realism, and fable, the novel draws on the "rich *sthala-purana*, or legendary history" that Rao describes as the preserve of every village in India. As Shyamala

---

[8] Indian writers Iqbal Singh, Ahmed Ali, K. S. Shelvankar, and Sri Lankan writer Alagu Subramaniam co-edited the literary magazine *Indian Writing* (1940-1945) based at the Indian bookshop "The Bibliophile" in London's Little Russell Street.

11. Rao's Kanthapura *and Menen's* The Prevalence of Witches

Narayan observes, "the narrative structure of *Kanthapura* exhibits many features of the *Puranas* such as the *upakatha* ('subsidiary narrative') which allows the narrator to digress freely" (Narayan 299). The text employs Sanskrit words like *harikatha* and invokes gods and religious texts such as the *dharmasastras*. Empowered by the prior contractual acceptance of this book, Rao steadfastly defended his text through the editorial and publication process and refused to make more than minor adjustments. Yet his experimentation in form and language was not seen as innovation but as "mistakes" and deviations from European literary standards.

In this way the critical reception of the time reveals the gradual emergence of a critical apparatus grappling to evaluate these challenging, "different" fictional texts. Reviewers and publishers both initiate and impede the translation of cultural difference. This kind of conflictual dynamic is evident in the mechanics of book production. The reception and publication history of these early South Asian writers demonstrates the pressure of an indisputable push towards Anglicisation, with the premise that the implied English reader will not be overtaxed.

II Aubrey Menen's *The Prevalence of Witches* (1947):
Writing and mediated readings in post-war Britain

Within a decade, the socio-political and publishing contexts had changed considerably; the Indo-Irish Aubrey Menen (1912-1989) published his first novel *The Prevalence of Witches* in November 1947 in Britain, a few months after India had won its independence. The son of an Indian businessman and his Irish wife, Menen was born in England and educated at the University of London. He worked as a dramatist and in radio before visiting India at the outbreak of World War II, where he spent the next few years broadcasting for the Indian information service; he later worked in the Political Department of the Government of India for several years. Drawing on his experiences as an education officer in a remote part of India, Menen's satire of religion and imperialism, *The Prevalence of Witches* (1947), is set in the mythical Indian state of Limbo, an obscure corner of the former British Empire, where the native community's beliefs in witches thrive and appear at odds with notions of Western morality. The plot turns on the village Chief who claims a witch incited him to kill his wife's demon-paramour. The inflexible course of British justice requires the resident Catullus to imprison him for this homicide, but then Catullus, his friend Bayard Leavis, and the unnamed Education Officer who narrates the tale invent a plan to convince the Judge Chandra Bose that the prevalence of the belief in witches amongst the Limbodians is so great as to mitigate the Chief's sentence. The Judge who subscribes to the Rationalist Society and disputes all this "witchery, flapdoodle" and "fiction" needs some persuasion (Menen 125). The British residents enlist the help of a counterfeit, effeminate, Oxford-educated swami to fake a miracle to convince the Judge that what the Limbodians believe is a real religion. To his great consternation the swami produces a "real" miracle, which in fact has been orchestrated by the villagers who wish to see their chief released. A series of comic reversals swiftly ensue until his escape from jail is secured.

On publication Menen's lively, original novel was described in the *Times Literary Supplement* as belonging to the "neo-Peacockian school of amusing, intelligent conversation and fantastic incident" and thus particularly appropriate to its post-war context: "It is a school which loses pupils in war-time and fills up quickly during the frivolous aftermath" (Richardson 625). Menen's grave, witty and argumentative novel drew further comparisons with Aldous Huxley, Anatole France, Norman Douglas and Evelyn Waugh, and was more akin to European literary traditions than Rao's ground-breaking *Kanthapura*; this evidently facilitated its smoother assimilation into both mainstream literary culture, and wider review coverage.

While Menen was not subject to the pre-Independence political constraints that Rao and Anand faced, in the year before Independence,

11. Rao's *Kanthapura and Menen's* The Prevalence of Witches

his editors at Chatto and Windus had expressed reservations about placing a book about the British in India in the United States market, in view of the prevailing pro-Independence sentiment there at the time. Despite these concerns, Chatto and Windus secured Menen a $750 advance from the American publisher Scribner. The novel sold well in the USA and was published to acclaim in a context evidently receptive to "its gentle satire of the British Raj."[9] *The New York Times Book Review* continued, "it makes delightful reading and often its barbs strike home" (Bicknell). By contrast, as Susheila Nasta and others have observed, although Menen and his contemporary G. V. Desani were well received in Britain[10] as specifically Anglo-Indian or Indian phenomena, they did not form the subject of serious critical scrutiny.[11] This is particularly true of Menen's critique of Empire. Indeed, the contemporary British reviews of *The Prevalence of Witches* focused on the portrayal of the "backward" Indian State of Limbo and its "strange" superstitious "natives," even though the text complicates this representation, when it becomes increasingly clear that the inhabitants feign ignorance to their rulers and educators. Far from being devout believers in witchcraft, the villagers ask a woman to pretend to be a witch when they do not want to "disappoint" the misguided American missionary Reverend Cuff Small (he expresses an interest in seeing a witch). The text insistently draws parallels between the villagers' spells and prayers or "digging spells" in more conventional religions, and is a critique of the fundamentalisms of all religions.

---

[9] This advance and the sales in Europe and the US influenced Menen to abandon a lucrative post at JWT advertising company in Bombay to become a full-time writer and enabled him to move to Sicily where he took up residence.

[10] The first printing of 5,000 copies of Menen's *The Prevalence of Witches* sold out within the first four months in Britain. Translation rights were sold in Spain, Denmark, and Italy.

[11] See Nasta 46-48 and Innes 227-32.

The reviews ignore the satire in the representation of the villagers' view of the English residents. An example of this is the Headman, who is convinced that he cannot tell his story plainly to the English: "It would be much too gross for these delicate (and he was beginning to suspect, not very keen-witted) persons." He had to "make the whole thing sound whimsical and gay" and so recounts his story in a hilarious parody that begins: "we were all laughing and joking and playing games with one another in the cool of a very pleasant evening" (Menen 49). Early British reviews identify an exchange between the narrator, the local Education Officer, and the Political Agent Catullus as setting the tone of the whole novel:

> "Limbo seems to make nonsense of a lot of things".
> "That", said Catullus, "is because they have a different sense of right and wrong: or, rather, no sense of wrong at all, because they think that evil is all due to witches. You will find it very confusing at first". (44)

These reviews paid little attention to Menen's light yet caustic satire on imperialism, chiefly articulated in the portrayal of the garrulous Catullus, the British governor of the province or King of Limbo, "who always wanted to possess a country of [his] own, beautifully round as it was blank" (Menen 1). He bases his "sentences on the moral principle that [he] holds the arquebus [gun] and the Limbodians don't" (43). Revelling in a quibble in a treaty that gives the village chiefs the land, but secures the valuable teak for the British administration, he carelessly admits: "For sixty years we've been chuckling busily over our bargain as we cut down their trees, and we've had not time to build" a hospital (36). Similarly he exults in "the chiefs spending money received from the Durbar buying alcohol from the government pub" and "putting it back in our pockets" (27).

Catullus's observations underscore the collusion between Christianity and imperialism:

11. Rao's Kanthapura *and Menen's* The Prevalence of Witches

> We got an uncomfortably large slice of our Empire not by being good soldiers but by being quick at languages. First we sent the missionaries to make grammars and translations of the Bible, then we sent the Civil Servants to use the grammars to write our treaties. The Americans got the Red Indians drunk on gin: we got *our* Indians fuddled with words. (30)

Nor is the narrator spared when the novel skewers the vanity of the Limbodians' would-be educator, who on hearing of another missionary school feels disappointed that "nobody but myself had ever tired to educate the inhabitants" of Limbo, and is then relieved to hear no-one had learnt anything at this school (80). Furthermore he is disconcerted to find his "expectations of primitive people to be halting in their speech and to say only simple things" challenged (32).

Preferring to focus on British eccentricities rather than its callousness, *The Daily Mail* interpreted Menen's portrayal of the European colony as "a queer but agreeable lot [who] sit talking, talking and talking" (Quennel). Although this reviewer observes that the object of satire constantly shifts in the text, the target remains unclear to him: "*The Prevalence of Witches* is a diverting squib. I must confess I was not always quite sure whom or what it is aimed at; but the general effect was to leave me vaguely stimulated." In a similar vein, Webster Evans in *John O' London's Weekly* insisted that "Aubrey Menen's first novel *The Prevalence of Witches* is not meant to be taken seriously at all" adding that "this book is foolish [. . .] but it's fun." *The Birmingham Post* also describes the novel as "vastly entertaining nonsense" (Crosbie).

Menen's exuberant, boisterous satire stands out against his forerunners' Anand's and Rao's construction of "Indian-ness" and desire to "write India" in their early novels. The dominant atmosphere evoked in *The Prevalence of Witches* is that of a conversation over "a strawberry-tea on the lawn of an Oxford college" (Menen 68). Nevertheless, his publishers supply a different framework of reference to accompany the subsequent interpretation of the text to its putative British readers by presenting the writer as a native informant who can tell us the secrets of his otherwise obscure native culture. The blurb on the cover of the first edition of *The Prevalence of Witches*, for example, presents the Indo-Irish author as an informed mediator between two widely divergent, incompatible cultures and accentuates the anthropological, referential content of his fictional text:

> The author puts to good use a considerable first hand knowledge of India. *The Prevalence of Witches* is in some ways a novel of fantasy; but it is firmly tied to real human beings, and throws a sharp light on the gulf between European and Oriental morality and ways of thinking.

The *Times Literary Supplement* review reinforced this reading in its suggestion that "among Menen's strong qualities is an insight into the primitive mind" (Richardson). *The Birmingham Post* went on to further suggest that "like the natives of Limbo, a primitive district of India, where witches are thought to be the root of all evil, Menen is ingeniously puzzled by certain Occidental notions of right and wrong" (Crosbie). The *Sunday Times* regretted the "clever if sadly bogus Swami" was imported from Britain (Straus).

A thoroughly Westernised Menen wryly distanced himself from such constructions in his semi-autobiographical essays, *Dead Man in a Silver Market: An Autobiographical Essay on National Prides* (1954) and in his private correspondence to his publishers, Chatto and Windus:

> On the whole, I prefer not to be called "Indian". I am <u>not Indian</u>; I don't speak a word of any Indian language (except achcha). I am not Hindu or Muslim and I don't kill people who are [he converted to Catholicism in 1949]. I am by birth,

language and inclinations English, in fact so English that I do not like embarrassing other Englishmen by saying so.[12]

Menen was well aware of European predilections for stereotyped versions of India. With reference to publicity for the forthcoming book, he wrote in the same letter that "journalists will be disappointed if you don't assure them that I write my books sitting on a bed of nails." *The Prevalence of Witches* satirises such attitudes in its depiction of the Governor of Limbo, who instructs the native community to create specifically crude drawings in order to establish a trade in primitive artefacts.

Sensitivity to the particular tastes of the target British reading constituency may explain Chatto and Windus's construction of Menen's identity on the book jacket in these terms. It suggests that European literary antecedents notwithstanding, Menen's assimilation equally depended on the assertion of a particular form and degree of difference: one that did not challenge existing Western reading practices we saw in relation to Rao. Indian authors were encouraged not only to embody foreignness and describe the colonies in this way, but also to provide "alien" perspectives on British culture, largely, though not exclusively, for the majority population. An example of this is the criticism of D. F. Karaka's *Oh you English!* (1935). The reviewer noted that Karaka's assessment of English customs, morals, and institutions are not "formulated from a *novel* angle" but "might emanate from *any of the unnumbered young English writers* who are trying out their pens in malcontent journalism" (rev. of *Oh you English!*; emphasis mine). Part of Menen's appeal (in contrast to Rao's reception) appeared to be the way this text provided this "alien" perspective, while conforming to traditional Western narrative rules. The *Manchester Guardian* review observed that Menen exposed absurdities by employing a comic, satiric mode that drew upon the eighteenth-century

---

[12] Menen, letter to Peter Cochcrane, 16 October 1947, file Aubrey Menen, 1947-48, Chatto and Windus Archive (qtd. in Ranasinha 69).

literary tradition of bringing foreigners to record impressions of Europe, or sending a European to an imaginary country (as in Swift's *Gulliver's Travels*); Menen he observed, "sends us to Lilliput, or somewhere like that, to give us a refreshing inside-out view of too familiar circumstances" (Bloomfield). And indeed, Menen relies on the traveller's tale and the bizarre in his novel, which is paramount to its sketchy plot construction, particularly evident in its hurried denouement in the somewhat weaker second half of the story.

While the majority of critical assessments reinscribe the terms in which the publisher presented *The Prevalence of Witches*, one reviewer in *The Observer*, alive to Menen's conception of Limbo as a "contrived intellectual fun-fair," challenged Chatto and Windus's blurb to ask whether it was "a study in Oriental v. European morality, as its publishers suggest? I counter-suggest that all the novel has in common with India is its affinity with the Indian rope-trick – a spun yarn producing an entertaining illusion" (Hale). Significantly, the entire content of this favourable review is reprinted on the cover of the first edition of the novel, apart from this perceptive observation which is excised.

In different ways then, both Menen's and Rao's contrasting reception highlights how it was much more difficult for South Asian Anglophone writers to be taken seriously as writers of fiction than as social historians, in the British context at this historical juncture. My reading of the British reception and publication history of Rao's novel *Kanthapura* (and of the reception of other novels published by Indian authors in the late 1930s) delineates the emergence of a critical apparatus that in grappling to evaluate these challenging, "different" fictional texts, tended to interpret experimentation as inexperience with the European novel form and literary traditions. My analysis also identifies a reading public not prepared to engage with cultural difference, or only on specific terms, exemplified in the warm response to Aubrey Menen's novel with its exotic setting, but easily recognisable European provenance. Ironically, this same quality has perhaps con-

11. Rao's Kanthapura *and Menen's* The Prevalence of Witches

tributed to the relative neglect of *The Prevalence of Witches* in contemporary postcolonial studies. While Menen's deployment of mainstream European literary forms undoubtedly contributed to its wide acclaim, his publishers simultaneously chose to present the author as a native informant: his "insight into the primitive mind" is duly reinscribed and prized by most reviewers, although the parallel scrutiny and satire of the British in India is conveniently disregarded as frothy, inconsequential nonsense. In this regard, we can see the extent to which publishers and reviewers not only selected which narratives would be published and assessed, but also attempted to shape how they would be promoted and received in the predominantly metropolitan stronghold of English language publishing.

Works Cited

Ali, Ahmed. *Twilight in Delhi*. London: Hogarth, 1940.

Anand, Mulk Raj. Rev. of *Twilight in Delhi*, by Ahmed Ali, and novels by Louis Bromfield. *Indian Writing* 1.3 (Mar. 1941): 175-77.

___. *Two Leaves and a Bud*. 1937. Bombay, Kutub, 1946.

Bloomfield, Paul. Rev. of *The Prevalence of Witches*, by Aubrey Menen. *Manchester Guardian* 25 Nov. 1947: n. pag.

Bicknell, John. "The Raj and the Demon." Rev. of *The Prevalence of Witches*, by Aubrey Menen. *New York Times Book Review* 12 Feb. 1948: 12.

Bromfield, Louis. *Night in Bombay*. London: Cassell, 1940.

___. *The Rains Came: A Novel of Modern India*. London: Cassell, 1937.

Charques, R. D. "Tales of Indians." Rev. of *Twilight in Delhi*, by Ahmed Ali. *Times Literary Supplement* 12 July 1940: 619.

Coomaraswamy, Ananda K. *The Deeper Meaning of the Struggle between Englishmen and Indians*. N.p., Essex House, 1907.

___. *Suttee: A Vindication of the Hindu Woman*. London: London Sociological Society, 1912.

Crosbie, Mary. Rev. of *The Prevalence of Witches*, by Aubrey Menen. *Birmingham Post* 20 Nov. 1947: n. pag.

Editorial. *John O' London's Weekly* 4 Mar. 1938: 4.

Evans, Webster. Rev. of *The Prevalence of Witches*, by Aubrey Menen. *John O'London's Weekly* 28 Nov. 1947: n. pag.

Forbes, Geraldine. *Indian Women and the Freedom Movement: A Historian's Perspective*. Bombay: Research Centre for Women's Studies, 1997.

Fyzee-Rahamin, S. *Gilded India*. London: Michael Joseph, 1938.

Hale, Lionel. "Rope Trick." Rev. of *The Prevalence of Witches*, by Aubrey Menen. *Observer* 16 Nov. 1947: 3.

Innes, C. L. *A History of Black and Asian Writing in Britain: 1700-2000*. Cambridge: Cambridge University Press, 2002.

Karak, D. F. *I Go West*. London: Michael Joseph, 1938.

Katrak, Ketu. "Indian Nationalism, Gandhian Satyagraha and Representations of Female Sexuality." *Nationalisms and Sexualities*. Ed. Andrew Parker et al. London: Routledge, 1992. 395-406.

Menen, Aubrey. *Dead Man in a Silver Market: An Autobiographical Essay on National Prides*. London: Chatto and Windus, 1954.

___. *The Prevalence of Witches*. London: Chatto and Windus, 1947.

Moloney, John. Rev. of *Two Leaves and a Bud*, by Mulk Raj Anand. *Times Literary Supplement* 15 May 1937: 379.

Naik, M. K. *Raja Rao*. New York: Twayne, 1972.

Narasimhaiah, C. D. *Raja Rao*. New Delhi: Arnold-Heinemann, 1968.

Narayan, Shyamala. "Raja Rao." *Dictionary of Literary Biography: South Asian Writers in English*. Ed. Fakrul Alam. Columbia SC: Bruccoli Clark Layman, 2006. 296-304.

Nasta, Susheila. *Home Truths: Fictions of the South Asian Diaspora in Britain*. Basingstoke: Palgrave, 2002.

"Novels in Translation." *Times Literary Supplement* 26 Mar. 1938, 222.

Quennel, Peter. Rev. of *The Prevalence of Witches*, by Aubrey Menen. *Daily Mail* 22 Nov. 1947: n. pag.

11. Rao's Kanthapura *and Menen's* The Prevalence of Witches

Ranasinha, Ruvani. *South Asian Writers in Twentieth-Century Britain: Culture in Translation*. Oxford: Oxford University Press, 2007.

Rao, Raja. *Kanthapura*. 1938. Delhi: Delhi Orient Paperbacks, 1992.

Rao, Raja, and Iqbal Singh. Preface. *Changing India*. Ed. Rao and Singh. London: Allen and Unwin, 1939. 9-14.

Rev. of *I Go West!*, by D. F. Karaka. *Times Literary Supplement* 4 March, 1938. n.p

Rev. of *Oh You English*, by D. F. Karaka. *Times Literary Supplement* 18 July 1935: 468.

Richardson, Maurice. "Tribal Affairs." Rev. of *The Prevalence of Witches*, by Aubrey Menen. *Times Literary Supplement* 6 Dec. 1947: 625.

Russ, R. P. *Hussein: An Entertainment* Oxford: Oxford University Press, 1938.

Sethi, Rumina. *Myths of the Nation: National Identity and Literary Representation*. Oxford: Clarendon, 1999.

Straus, Ralph. Rev. of *The Prevalence of Witches*, by Aubrey Menen. *Sunday Times* 16 Nov. 1947: n. pag.

12. Casualty of War, Casualty of Empire: Mulk Raj Anand in England

Kristin Bluemel
Monmouth University

Mulk Raj Anand died in India on 28 September 2004, aged 98. In Anand's obituary for the *Guardian*, Jai Kumar and Haresh Pandya recall Anand's fame as a "founding father" of the Indo-English novel, noting that he was "one of the most prominent Indian novelists writing in English," and "a staunch Marxist and Gandhian." With this kind of legacy, it is obvious that Anand was not a casualty of war or casualty of Empire in the sense that combatant poets Wilfred Owen, Keith Douglas, or Alun Lewis were. He is a casualty insofar as he was *casually* (by chance or accidentally) erased from the literary traditions to which he contributed: British modernism and what I elsewhere call "intermodernism," the realist prose tradition of the 1930s and 1940s.[1] At the time of Anand's death late in 2004, I could find limited discussion of his contributions to the literature of British India or Indian Literature in English, only passing references to his name in discussions of 1930s or 1940s British leftists, a few listings of his novels on websites of booksellers, and only one essay by a postcolonial critic that attended to Anand's colonial-era anti-imperialist polemics. However, several years later, there are signs that Anand's casualty may not have been fatal. With the upsurge of interest in transnational modernisms, diasporic, postcolonial writing in English, and what Evelyn Nien-Ming Ch'ien calls "weird English," there is increasing evidence that Anand is finally gaining widespread recognition for his contributions to diverse literary traditions and his potential impact on contemporary literary theory.

---

[1] See my *George Orwell and the Radical Eccentrics: Intermodernism in Literary London*.

Taking encouragement from the modest signs of Anand's revival, this chapter argues that Anand is necessary to critical discussions of the literature of British Empire, the literature of colonial resistance, and British traditions of twentieth-century war (and anti-war) writing. At the very least, his novel *Across the Black Waters* deserves our close attention because it brings all these concerns together. Published in London in 1940, *Across the Black Waters* follows a group of Indian peasant soldiers who are transported with their regiment from northern India to fight in France during World War I. It exposes the hypocrisy, incompetence, deception, racism, and arrogance of a fictionalised imperial British military leadership and government at a time when England was in reality fighting for its survival in the face of Nazi Germany's global imperialism.

Across the Black Waters is about Empire, about war, about all the idiosyncratic details of character and community that get lost in such wide-sweeping nouns. But it is also and perhaps above all about the English language. Or rather, it is about English languages. English in the novel is an "Indo-Anglian" English, the Indian English that Anand defends brilliantly in his 1948 manifesto *The King-Emperor's English* as "a kind of regional branch of English literature" that is yet "a part of the Indian cultural development and has its value, if only as an interpretive literature of the most vital character" (16). This "hybrid" English that Anand defends against those Indian critics who want to "apply a kind of 'Quit India' resolution against the English language" (3) is on wonderful display for Western and especially British audiences in *Across the Black Waters*. But the novel is also "against" language, the jingoistic, idealistic, patriotic, lying language that is (by chance, in this case), English. In other words, in *Across the Black Waters*, Anand makes the *English* of the British authorities and their Indian military agents a casualty of war and Empire.

In this chapter, I argue that Anand's experiments with English transform or "translate" the distinct and familiar modernism of Britain's World-War-I prose literature into forms fit for the wartime culture of

12. Mulk Raj Anand in England

the early 1940s. They require us, with eyes open to representations of the Empire's others, to create an alternative English twentieth-century literary history, one which disrupts neat divisions between modernist and realist traditions, aesthetic and political imperatives, elitist and populist audiences and takes into consideration the literature of British India. Regarding *Across the Black Waters* as emblematic, we discover that many of the familiar conventions of celebrated World-War-I narratives, which usually harness the writer's disillusion on behalf of a new realism of masculine despair and redefinition of national aspiration, have been transformed by Anand's hybrid English. Anand artfully interlards Hindustani words into English sentences that also contain translations of Punjabi peasant idiom – proverbs, curses, superstitions, prayers, misinterpretations. The result is a remarkable, weird kind of writing made up of difficult, complex, colourful, critical, self-questioning English sentences.

Ch'ien provides one of the more playful, interesting accounts of this weird kind of writing. In her study on contemporary immigrant and postcolonial writers, she considers not only the weird forms of English found in literary texts – the difficult, complex, colourful, critical, self-questioning English sentences that are in many ways like Anand's – but also the social and linguistic contexts influencing them (3). She emphasises that

> weird English writers denormalize English out of resistance to it, and form their own language by combining English with their original language [...]
>
> Because weird English possesses the extra dimension of a foreign language, it requires not only interpretation but also translation. Weird English revives the aesthetic experiential potential of English; we see through the eyes of foreign speakers and hear through their transcriptions of English a different way of reproducing meaning. (6)

Instead of directing us toward the compliant, Western-sympathising English that other critics have found in Anand's fiction, Ch'ien encourages us to think of new alliances, intentions, and traditions, thereby breathing fresh life into a reputation in need of resuscitation. Past efforts to burnish that reputation through association with Britain's modernists have started Anand on his posthumous way to increased visibility, but his intentions and contexts are unlike those of the modernists, and his language, with its "extra dimension of a foreign language," is also unlike the modernists: "a mixture of two rather than an experiment with one" (Ch'ien 288).[2]

The sentences in Anand's mixed English are translations in literal and metaphorical senses. Evidence for understanding them as literal translations appears in *The King-Emperor's English*, written when debates about an official language for India were at their most intense. Anand announces that

> I for one, would plump for the vernacular and, though continuing to write in English, would like also to write in Punjabi and then render it into English more realistically and adequately than I do at present, for now I literally translate all the dialogue in my novels from my mother tongue and think out the narrative mostly the same way. (23)

For him, translation describes a peculiar composition process that is both fruitful and onerous. I argue that the difficulty of this mode of composition-as-translation (one Anand experiences at the level of production) results in a similarly fruitful, unique difficulty at the level of consumption. One of the most important effects of Anand's novels is a productive disorientation of the English-speaking, and especially British-identified, reader. In particular, the Englishes of *Across the Black Waters* challenge relations of power and traditions of domi-

---

[2] For two recent studies that read Anand in relation to British modernism, see Marcus and Berman.

12. Mulk Raj Anand in England

nance between literatures of East and West, even as they record the more violent disorientation of Indian colonial subjects acting within the Western history of war and genre of the novel.

Four decades after *Across the Black Waters* was published in London and *The King-Emperor's English* was published in Bombay, Anand labeled his distinctive literary language "pigeon Indian" in an essay by that name. He identified its sources in a vital "Indian-English language" that grew out of a cynical British-governed Indian university system, and in the "higgledy-piggledy spoken English of our country," which he distinguishes with the term 'pidgin English' ("Pigeon" 328). He speculates about the relation of these two Englishes, one "high," one "low," noting that they freely borrow from each other, their speakers ignoring the boundaries that racist British authorities or self-doubting "babus" would have set up between them (328). His purpose in distinguishing these Indian Englishes and describing their "intermixing" is to protect from attack exactly the kind of Indian English language on display in *Across the Black Waters*.

When Anand published his essay on "Pigeon Indian" in 1982, he still felt it necessary to defend "the introduction of original metaphor and imagery from our mother tongues into the English language" (327). Yet only twenty years later, critic Leela Gandhi would single out Anand's "effort to render into English the exuberant dialects of northern India" for special praise, concluding that "although awkward, Anand's exposition of 'pidgin-English' prepares the way for the subsequent linguistic and cultural translations of Indian-English writers" (179). What Gandhi calls awkward and Ch'ien calls weird, I call disorienting. Measuring the implied difference in value of these terms as they are used in their respective arguments is one of the primary aims of this chapter; I want to show how Anand's pigeon, hybrid English distinguishes him as a writer of unique value for diverse, but intersecting, literary traditions.

1910s: World-War-I France

Anand adopts the narrative perspective of India's others to wage his campaign of disorientation against British readers who encounter his novel in the last years of British rule. Using an omniscient narrator, Anand favours the points of view of the colonised Indians, whether the sepoys Lal Singh, a raw recruit, or the older, more seasoned foot soldiers, Daddy Dhanoo and Uncle Kirpu, or the Indian officer Jemadar Subah Singh. Describing war from the perspectives of these characters, Anand turns English, French, and other Europeans into exotic figures – "others" – who inspire wonder, fear, or good-humored contempt in the Indians. Anand's narrator captures the sense of awe felt by Indian mercenaries upon embarkation in Marseille, illustrating how their lives as colonial subjects had trained them to fear "the exalted life that the Europeans lived" (30). Little by little, these seemingly hopelessly submissive soldiers begin to develop a critical social consciousness. Even the cynical, seasoned sepoy Uncle Kirpu observes hopefully, "There are no untouchables in this country. [. . .] and there is no consideration of pollution" (31). Amid the new freedoms of France, the mystical aura of whiteness begins to dissipate. Seeing Englishmen acting within a polyglot but predominantly white society, they begin to understand the unreality of the racial superiority preserved through the "thick hedges outside the Sahibs' bungalows in India" (30). They also begin to understand the real motives for British imperial conquest in India. This process of disillusionment and demystification, one that Anand (as a Marxist Indian Nationalist) considered vital for India's transition to a free state, is exemplified by a chance encounter of the sepoys with a colossal statue of Joan of Arc in Orléans. Lalu, the youngest soldier whose consciousness dominates the narrative, is semi-literate and able to read "Jean d'Arc" on the inscription of the statue:

12. Mulk Raj Anand in England

> In a flash the last clue to Orleans returned to his memory from the story of Joan of Arc in the *Highroads of History* which he had read at the Church Mission School at Sherkot.
> "Who is it supposed to be?" one sepoy asked.
> "What a gigantic statue!" another exclaimed.
> "Who is it anyhow?" queried Uncle Kirpu walking up with an abounding curiosity. [. . .]" (34)

Recalling his reading, Lalu explains

> "In the fourteenth century there was a hundred years' war in which the English were fighting the French. . .
> "Then, do you mean to say, that the Angrezi Sahib and the Francisis were enemies at one time" one of the sepoys asked rather shocked. [. . .]
> "A girl Jarnel who drove out the Angrezi army!" commented a third.
> And the maid seemed to become a heroine like the Rani of Jhansi. Lalu felt the blood coursing in his veins with the ambition to follow her on the path of glory. (34)

Lalu's attempt to comprehend the possibility of English military defeat by comparing the French rebel heroine to the more familiar Indian heroine, Rani of Jhansi, shows how he orients himself in the unknown culture and geography of France. France is an "other," exotic; India is known, familiar. However, the effect of the statue is the same as the memory of Rani of Jansi; both inspire Lalu with a desire to follow "the path of glory." At this early point in the novel, Lalu is willing to seek that glory for his British masters, but once Lalu and his friends are in the trenches and find themselves being used as cannon fodder, they cease to believe in either the path or the glory. The novel ends with Lalu captured by German soldiers, his friends having already suffered ignominious deaths at the front; this ending leads Graham Parry to compare Anand to "all writers about the Great War" because he "permits us to know a small number of men well, [. . .] then one by one they are killed off so that we can share in the protracted misery of the war" (35). Yet unlike other Great War narratives, Anand wants our participation in this protracted misery to lead to real social and geopolitical change; "our," in this case, being the British and Indian novel-reading public who might be motivated to press for Indian independence. Anand's next novel in the Lalu trilogy shows us what we can expect as an alternative to the legal, organised dismemberment of British India. *The Sword and the Sickle* begins with Lalu's return to India where he is accused by the British of defecting to the Germans; instead of a hero's welcome and reward, he is treated as a traitor. This betrayal inspires him to become a Marxist revolutionary.

In addition to showing poor and illiterate Indians the possibility of successful resistance to English domination, the sepoys' encounter with the Joan of Arc statue also invites Anand's readers to see radical political goals through Modernist irony (something more typically associated with novels of the "Red Decade" of the 1930s). Mimicking dozens of earlier World-War-I narratives, the familiar irony of *Across the Black Waters* is put to new, anti-imperialist uses by Anand's adoption of Indian characters, geographical and cultural references, and "Indo-Anglian" English. The anti-imperialist force of Anand's irony emerges from the gap between the narrator's and readers' shared understanding about World War I (or even fourteenth-century France) and the political ignorance of the naïvely awestruck sepoys. Deprived of the whole story of Joan of Arc, the semi-literate Lalu can only appreciate the statue's crude symbolism (a girl chasing away the Angrezi army); his ignorance of Joan's demise (Western readers would have seen this as foreshadowing the betrayal of the Indians) means that readers more literate than Lalu will discover an instructive irony in the scene.

Another kind of instructive irony arises from the gap between the narrator's and soldiers' comfort with Anand's language, and the discomfort of the English readers who struggle to keep up with the

12. Mulk Raj Anand in England

novel's unfamiliar vocabulary, epigrams, curses, allusions, prayers and jokes. It is telling that I feel no obligation to footnote Anand's references to Joan of Arc or the Hundred Years' War, but I am tempted to provide a glossary of Indo-Anglian vocabulary and feel compelled to include a footnote indicating who the Rani of Jhansi was, and what she did.[3] These are signs of the "normal" disorientation English readers experience as they struggle to understand a known history of European conflict in terms of a history of Empire in India. It is an effect that Anand, a radical anti-imperialist and Indian nationalist, achieved through the deployment of particular narrative and linguistic strategies.

Anand's language, his translated "Indo-Anglian," is a vital tool in enacting imperial dissent through narrative disorientation. First, his language grants the primary consciousness of the novel to working-class Indians whose unfamiliar metaphors and comparisons routinely defamiliarise European material and human relations. For example, the following translations of curse words appear liberally throughout the narrative: brother-in-law, rape daughter, illegally-begotten, son of negation, rape-mother, Burnt up people! Owls! (36). Another example can be found in the sepoys' responses to the natural environment of Orléans:

> Look at their rivers – not bigger than our small nullahs. Their whole land can be crossed in a night's journey, when it takes two nights and days from the frontier to my village in the dis-

---

[3] Rani Lakshmi Bai, widow of the Raja of Jhansi (who died without a male heir in 1853). The British annexed Jhansi despite her protestations that, contrary to custom, she had not been allowed to adopt a successor. When rebellion broke out in 1857, the Rani led a successful defense of Jhansi from invading armies of neighboring rajas. In March 1858, the British Army laid siege to her city and captured it. She fled in disguise but was later killed on her horse in a skirmish with British forces. She has come to be known as the "Joan of India" (Wolpert 227).

trict of Kangra. Their rain is like the pissing of a child. And their storms are a mere breeze in the tall grass. (31)

Comparing foreign territory unfavourably to the familiar sights of home is of course, tourist bluster; but the speaker's sites of reference are also foreign to Anand's non-Indian readers, and the result is a metaphor that functions for the character as a reassuring, stabilising source, while the supposedly secure, ironic, or knowing European reader has his or her sense of superiority upset by the intrusion of foreign words, places, and comparisons on a familiar landscape.

Anand's technique of defamiliarising Europe for British readers by comparing its sights and sounds to Indian commonplaces, of exoticising or "orientalising" the West, is put to more dramatic use later in the novel when Lalu and his friends are sent to the front. While all writers of World-War-I combat narratives struggled to "translate" the horrific, unworldly sensations of trench warfare for civilians, Anand engages in a kind of double translation, making sense of (or translating) the sepoys' experience for British civilian readers by focusing on the Indian sepoys efforts to make sense of (or translate) the completely alien conditions of this European war. A good example of this process is evident in Anand's description of a barrage of machine gun fire as

> an impatient insistent threat which became the ferocious growling of a hundred fire-tongued lions, of a thousand flaming tigers, of a million roaring elephants, bursting upon the world from the jungle. [. . .] But as primitive men learned to live, and prowl about in the midst of the jungle, to brave the dangers of the dark, and to breathe its precarious air, as if it were the free air of an inhabited world, so the sepoys settled down. (106)

Comparing the noises of guns to Indian animals signals to British readers the "Indian-ness" of the novel they are reading, and reminds them of their distance from the sepoys the narrative asks them to imaginatively identify with. But the adjectives describing these animals, "fire-tongued," "thousand flaming," "million roaring," turn the metaphors into something more, a kind of myth populated by demons. Assuming the narrator is here speaking for the sepoys, that his metaphors are theirs, we realise that they too must stretch their imaginations to find some way of understanding and ultimately "settl[ing] down" in the midst of the horrifying sounds that encircle them. Unlike the sepoy who was able to tame the unfamiliar landscape of Europe through comparisons of rivers to small nullahs, the sepoys cited above cannot translate the experience of battle into familiar Indian sights and sounds. Instead, they must resort to fantastic figures out of folklore. The anti-colonial politics of the doubled translation implicit within this passage are made more explicit in Anand's comparison of the "inhabited world" of France to a jungle. The sepoys are turned into "primitive men" through the process of entering the "jungle" of European landscape. Anand's "Indo-Anglian" English metaphors create an untamed, beastly darkness in the heart of Europe, undercutting colonial hierarchies of race and Empire at the very moment Churchill was asking Indians to fight on behalf of the Empire that claimed them for its own.

Such an argument shows Anand's enduring commitment to what English readers would recognise as 1930s-style radical politics. A second way such politics are attached to disorienting effects is through Anand's use of military vocabulary. Anand was the son of an officer in the British Indian Army, Subedar Lal Chand Anand, M. S. M. 2/17th Dogra; *Across the Black Waters* is dedicated to him. The novel's realism is cemented through Anand's intimate use of the military argot that structured rank, race, and social status in the Indian Army; this language denies English civilian readers mastery over the representations of the very institution that insured British imperial rule in India. A reader with no knowledge of military hierarchies might find Anand's references to subedars, subedar majors, jemardars, lance-naiks, and sepoys completely bewildering, suggesting once again his ability to discomfort his readers.

While Anand's novel informs civilian readers about the Indian Army, it never specifies the sizes of military units that organise the soldiers' institutional positions and roles; David Omissi's *The Sepoy and the Raj* and *Indian Voices of the Great War* does just that. Omissi defines the titles and position of Indian officers, and describes the relations between them and their men. Indian officers, like the irresponsible Jemardar Subah Singh or the vindictive, power-hungry Lance-Naik Lok Nath, granted advancement to their sepoys either through personal connections or through recognition of loyalty and hard work.[4]

For readers seeking to understand the force and forms of *Across the Black Waters*'s social protest, it is important to understand the Army's structures which institutionalised racism *vis-à-vis* British officers, Indian NCOs, and Indian troops. Omissi explains that there was no British equivalent to the status of Indian officers, who served under commissions of the Viceroy (but not the King) and were thus known as VCOs: "they had the right of command over Indian troops, but not over British; and they were subordinate to all officers who held the King's Commission (who were almost invariably British until well after the war)" (*Indian Voices* xxi). Omissi describes the VCOs like Subah or his father Subedar Major Arbel Singh as "the link" between British officers and Indian NCOs and the sepoys. An officer at the top of the hierarchy was expected to inform his CO "on all matters concerning the religion and customs of the men under his command," in

---

[4] Omissi defines a naik as "An Indian infantry NCO, corresponding to a corporal," a havildar as "An Indian infantry NCO, corresponding to a sergeant," jemadar as "An Indian company officer, immediately junior to a subedar, and corresponding to a lieutenant," a subedar as "the chief Indian officer of an infantry company, ranking immediately superior to a Jemadar," and a subedar-major as "the senior Indian officer of an infantry regiment" (*Indian Voices* xiii).

other words, to "translate" the culture of the supposedly alien and inferior men of his regiment for the British. These men were typically of "class" or "class-company type" which meant they were selected to serve in regiments or companies composed of the same caste and religion. The 69th Rifles, which Lalu joins after his rebellion against orthodox Sikh social and religious beliefs in *The Village* (the first novel in the Lalu trilogy), is a class-company Dogra regiment of Hindus and Muslims.[5]

In addition to reproducing army terminology, Anand was attentive to the details of time and service regarding the Indian Army's engagement in France and Belgium. Comparison of *Across the Black Waters* to Omissi's brief chronology of events in 1914 shows Anand's scrupulous attention to history, including such details as the 12 November visit of Lord Roberts, known as "General Roberts Sahib" in *Across the Black Waters*, and his ignominious death three days later from what Uncle Kirpu mockingly describes as "a mere cold" (198). Anand's fidelity to factual events in *Across the Black Waters* is in stark contrast to his silence about that other valuable component of realism: place names. Anand's readers, like his soldiers, are not able to immediately place themselves; they quite literally cannot read the signs of Europe. The novel begins with three simple disorientating exclamations:

> "Marsels!"
> "We have reached Marsels!"
> "Hip Hip Hurrah!"
> The sepoys were shouting excitedly on deck.
> Lalu got up from where he sat watching a game of cards and went to see Marseilles. (7)

---

[5] A Dogra was "A high-caste soldier from Kangra, a Himalayan province" (*Indian Voices* x).

Only with the narrator's intrusion do we understand that Marsels is the Indians' pronunciation of Marseilles and that our novel begins with an approach over the waters to the French port; this narrative destabilisation is deliberate and effective. Secure in his readers' identifications with the Indian soldiers, the narrator later thematises the sense of disorientation experienced at the start. Anand mocks our desire for spatial certainty in a scene that highlights Lalu's habitual, almost neurotic need for a map, for something with which he can locate himself in space. Confronted for the first time with the smells and sights of combat death in the form of a hospital train that pulls in from the front, Lalu unconsciously seeks to displace the feelings of physical disgust and horror with the certainties of geographical knowledge:

> He wished he had a map of France. He had wanted to buy one at the shops in Marseilles and Orleans but he didn't know the French word for map. . . Havildar Lachman Singh and even Babu Khushi Rama didn't seem to know where they were bound for either. Nobody knew. . . nobody knew anything. . . (64-65).

Left like Lalu without a map, the reader has a hard time predicting the route to the end of the novel (even if a habit of reading World War I narratives makes it easy to predict the kind of ending he or she will find). Anand's deviations from standard English prose and conventions of realism (in a sense, modernist experimentation) create feelings in the reader mimicking those of the Indian characters in France (disoriented by language, religion, social customs, weather, trench conditions and mechanised warfare). The reader's sense of discomfort when reading *Across the Black Waters* is integral to his or her understanding of the hero's emotional state, and thus of our political education in imperial dissent.

12. Mulk Raj Anand in England

1920s: Britain between the wars

Great-War narratives began to flood the British book market during the late 1920s. *Across the Black Waters* shows off Anand's thorough knowledge of what was, by 1940, a well-worn territory. Anand's novel shares many of the standard ingredients that Paul Edwards identifies with World-War-I memoirs – "the chaos of battle, with pointless or mistaken orders arriving from the staff, advantageous military positions wasted, men killed by their own side's artillery, instances of comradeship and instances of selfish indifference" (16). However, unlike the writers Edwards cites, Anand was not remembering warfront experiences, but inventing them. Anand arrived in England in 1924 as an aspiring PhD candidate in philosophy, and never saw active combat. As a chronicler of the Great War, he drew on his childhood memories of the cantonments of northern India and more recent experiences of modern warfare from his months as a journalist covering the Spanish Civil War (Parry 37).

Anand succeeded as a chronicler of the Great War, but success is always relative. *Across the Black Waters* was never a commercial success; it was only ever a success of the historical and political imagination. Looking back at the "Indo-Anglian" English sentences produced by that imagination from the perspective of the postcolonial twenty-first century, it is hard to understand the significance of the linguistic details that insured its unpopular difference from the English war memoirs and novels with which it had so much in common. Linguistic difference, in Anand's case, is inseparable from political difference, especially the politics of class.

Surveying the paradigmatic British combat novel of World War I, David Trotter concludes that

> most British war novels were written by middle-class writers who fully intended to do justice to the point of view either of the officer and gentleman or of the gentleman-ranker [. . .] the implicit investment these novels all make, with or without

enthusiasm, is in the durability of the class-system. The class-system goes to war, and survives, even if its individual representatives do not. (35)

While Anand could be described as middle-class (based on his education and social position in interwar England), his novel takes up the point of view of neither officers nor gentlemen. His explicit aim is to put the subaltern sepoy on the map of Europe, to reclaim his experience, sacrifice and language for literature, and politically, to bring about the end of British rule in India. This included the end of the British class-system in India and specifically, that in the Indian Army.

The radical class politics of Anand's novel are thrown into sharper relief if we read it in terms of Trotter's statement that "this [World War I] was indeed, as the title of Charles Carrington's memoir has it, *A Subaltern's War*" (42-43). Trotter's subaltern is an "embryonic officer," an eighteen-year-old graduate of the Royal Military College in Kitchener's non-professional army; he notes that almost every Great War combat novel has one sympathetic junior officer who epitomises the "new army paternalism" that "entailed, inexorably, a literal and figurative *self-lowering*. The subaltern knelt at his men's feet" (44).

True to form, *Across the Black Waters* features a good, paternalistic British officer. Ajitan Sahib or Captain Owen, the adjutant to the 69th Rifles, is unlike the novel's other senior officers (British or Indian), because he cares more about his men than his standing in the Army. While he doesn't kneel at the sepoys' feet, he does speak their language fluently. Significantly, Anand gives him more complete and untranslated speeches in Hindustani than the Indian characters. During the march from Ypres to Festubert, Owen Sahib watches his soldiers file past, accepting their salutes, silent and spoken:

> "Salaam, *Huzoor*," Lalu offered a specially informal address.
> "Ah, Lal Singh, *acha hai?*" the Sahib said, patting him.
> "*Huzoor!*" returned Lalu.

12. Mulk Raj Anand in England

> "Where are the other companies gone, *Huzoor*?" a sepoy taking advantage of the adjutant's informal exchange with Lalu to put a query which was really a grievance.
> "*Bohat mushkil hai*," said Captain Owen, without putting on any of the airs and graces of authority in Hindustani. (133)

Owen Sahib's fluent Hindustani contrasts strikingly with the broken Hindustani of other British authorities; for example, when the ill-fated Lord Roberts addresses the assembled troops during his ceremonial visit to the front on 12 November, his sense of racial as well as military superiority is symbolised by his "speech in the broken Sahib's Hindustani" (192). The "meaningless snatches" of this speech that reach Lalu's ears appear in *Across the Black Waters* as fragmented English phrases. These fragments are meaningless as the breaks in Roberts's sentences cannot be imaginatively mended and more importantly, because the conditions of trench warfare have turned Roberts's platitudes about "loyalty to Empire and King. . .Law, liberty Europe" (sic) into empty rhetoric (192).

In contrast, Captain Owen's fluent Hindustani coupled with his willingness to tell the men where they are, demonstrates his humanity and his function as an agent of classed resistance – in this context, resistance to the classification of human beings in the Indian and British Army. The Indian Army, Omissi observes, was even more intensely and insidiously hierarchical ("classed") than the British Army, because more criteria (race, religion, caste, ethnicity) were used to determine any soldier's position. The subalterns we care most about in *Across the Black Waters* are not Owen Sahib or other junior British officers (Trotter's and Carrington's subalterns), but the common Indian sepoys who are the protagonists in the narrative. Their presence in the ranks of World War I narratives ironises Trotter's description of the paradigmatic combat novel as a middle-class subaltern's war, and provides a rare example of a war novel that deviates from "the story of damage, of middle-class suffering" (41).

In Trotter's strong reading, the combat novel is intensely conservative, committed to renewing a class system even as it insists on the extraordinary damage done to individuals who maintain it (36). On the surface, the deaths of the primary characters in *Across the Black Waters* seem to ally the novel with this conservative narrative pattern. Much like the gentleman-rankers tracked by Trotter, the upwardly mobile sepoys Uncle Kirpu and Riki Ram are killed off before the narrative's end. It is worth asking how the classed resistance represented by Owen Sahib's bilingualism is maintained in the face of the deaths of the Indian subalterns; did Anand's public commitment to socialism and anti-imperialism survive the conservative politics of Great War narrative form?

Uncle Kirpu's case is exemplary. An uneducated peasant and lifelong soldier, he is the canniest and most resilient of the sepoys, sidestepping the debilitating effects of institutionalised race and class prejudice through humour. From the first pages of the novel, he, rather than Lalu, is granted the most colourful idioms, curses, and metaphors. Apart from Owen Sahib, he is granted the only self-consciously class-resistant language, which mocks the trappings of authority, whether British or Indian. After the company's first failed offensive of 26 October (during which Daddy Dhanoo drowns in a shell hole), it is Kirpu who dares suggest that the British have inferior artillery. When Lalu tentatively asks, "Where were our guns?", Kirpu rails, "Where are our guns? Where are our guns? – We haven't got any guns! [. . .] this bitch of a Sarkar hasn't got as many big guns as the Germans" (121). The company's respected Havildar, Lachman Singh, does not deny Kirpu's rumour, but tries to soothe Lalu by saying, "Don't mind Kirpu clown, Holdara" (122). Attempting to reduce the bitterness of Kirpu's words by reminding his listeners of his habitual clowning, Lachman may have put to rest some of the sepoys' doubts about the

12. Mulk Raj Anand in England

Sarkar, but not those of the reader, privy to the narrator's confirmation of Kirpu's suspicions several pages later (128).[6]

The clowning, which has functioned for Kirpu on behalf of class solidarity and against the Indian Army's class system, is not powerful enough to save him. The status-conscious Lok Nath is Kirpu's undoing; he cannot tolerate this combination of subversive humour and the stripe of Lance-Naik on his sleeve. Antagonised by Kirpu's informal address, he has him arrested, and before Lalu and others can gain his release, Kirpu commits suicide in jail by putting the barrel of a rifle in his mouth and pulling the trigger. Readers become acutely aware that the primary enemy in *Across the Black Waters* is not the Germans who are trying to kill the Sepoys, or the British officers whose arrogance and racism leave the sepoys undergunned, but the Indian officers who exhibit a venomous pride of position and devotion to enforcing the codes of the Sarkar.

Kirpu's defeat by Indian agents of the system raises questions about whether the conservative politics of Great War narrative form have extracted collaborationist class politics out of an overtly anti-establishment, Marxist novelist. In other words, it raises the question of Indian collaboration with the British Empire that lies at the heart of the Indian Army, Anand's representation of it, and for some, the English literature of British India. Omissi reminds us that the Indian Army, staffed mainly by Indians, was an institution caught in a deeply ambivalent political and social space, as both the strongest defense of Empire and its greatest threat (*Sepoy* xviii). When reading *Across the Black Waters* it is important to remember that Anand's characters are based on men who had agency; they were not simply victims of Empire but individuals who made choices about their lives including the choice to serve the Sarkar (Omissi, *Sepoy* 47). Postcolonial critics of

---

[6] Omissi confirms Kirpu's suspicions: "Indian troops arrived in France equipped only for a colonial war. Little money had been spent on Field Army support units: there was no mechanical transport, and the artillery – all British – could be made up only by denuding other divisions" (*Indian Voices* 2).

Empire might not like to confront the fact that such agency sustained the British Indian Army, but Anand, with his dedication to his Subedar father and to Congress politics, is able to make room for the more complex reality of individual resistance within institutional collaboration.[7]

The doomed Kirpu, the most heroically resistant individual in the novel, is clever, funny and illiterate. When Lalu goes to visit him in prison, he is told there is a message for him from Kirpu. Expecting a transcribed, private note, Lalu is completely unprepared for the contents of the "Regimental Orders, 69th Rifles" which are publicly posted: *"Lance-Naik Kirpa Ram of Number 2 company committed suicide last night at 2:20 a.m. while he was detained in the guard room for insubordination to a superior officer on duty"* (207). This shocking, devastating message, which consigns the true story of Kirpu's arrest to an Orwellian memory hole and leaves instead a permanent stain on Kirpu's reputation, seems an affirmation of the stability of the class system within the social world of the novel. Yet even at this moment of defeat the novel manages to depart from Trotter's depressing "same story" of narrative compliance; *Across the Black Water's* difference and hope lie in Anand's Indian English or pigeon Indian. The Regimental Orders announcing Kirpu's suicide appear late in the novel, and by this point we have learned to ask of Anand's Indian English sentences, "What language does this represent in the world of the novel?" We read English words, know those words communicate the authoritative voice of the Sarkar, but don't know whether they are to be read as English or as Hindustani translated into English (for us and the narrator) by Lalu. Lalu's bilingualism means that the exact lan-

---

[7] Omissi is critical of one group of scholars who could be expected to take an interest in the sepoy, The Subaltern Studies Project, because aside from David Arnold, their bias towards "moments of resistance and protest has not encouraged them to study the peasant-soldier groups who voted with their feet in favour of colonial power – as if peasants ceased to be subordinate, or conscious, or potentially dissident once they had enlisted" (*Sepoy* xix).

guage we imagine on the public notice board (and the kind of authority and collaboration it represents) remains unknown.

As a semi-literate, semi-bilingual sepoy who survives the novel to become a Marxist revolutionary, Lalu is a liminal character: his linguistic facility earns him social mobility. His movement is not facilitated by the British military authorities through promotion to higher established ranks, but by the narrator and reader who observe his "intermixing" of groups and categories stratified by institutional rule and social habit. His mobility represents the vulnerability of the class system that Anand wants to overthrow. What Anand's novels give us that history can't take into account is the flexibility of Indian English, with all its ambiguity of metaphorical and literal translation. At the end of *Across the Black Waters*, the Indian Army's class system is intact, but the novel suggests its instability. Its language (and thus its structures) have been dislocated in the process of Anand's fictional translations. The reader experiences this dislocation as a politically meaningful disorientation or awkwardness. The novel's dislocated, disorienting language encourages readers to move between different languages and literacies (Lalu, Owen Sahib, the narrator, etc.), presenting opportunities for multiple orientations amid disorientation.[8] Encouraging us to move between positions, to repeatedly reorient ourselves, the novel achieves a fluidity of effect that resists its apparent conformity of content. What the novel *does* to readers, challenges and arguably overwhelms what the novel *says* to readers. The sepoys may not escape the class-system of the typical Great War narrative, but thankfully, Anand's language, his Indian English, discourages us from renewing our commitment to its oppressive structures.

---

[8] I want to thank Prabhjot Parmar for helping me see this possibility during our discussion following the 2005 MLA Panel titled "Caught by the Empire at War: Representing Britain's Others in World Wars I and II," at which I delivered an early version of this paper.

1940s: World-War-II London

Elsewhere I have traced the ways that Anand himself was disoriented by his rejection in the 1930s and 1940s by British leftists who were unable to accept his radical, critical interventions in the discourse of Empire at a time of total war with fascist-imperialist Germany and heated conflict with pacifist-anti-imperialist Gandhi. The timing of *Across the Black Waters*'s publication was both perfect and disastrous. A note from the author on the novel's copyright page reads, "This book was sketched out in a rough draft in Barcelona, Madrid, during January and April 1937, and entirely rewritten in Chinnor, Oxon, between July and December, 1939." Encountering these words in 1940, the British public resented Anand's reminder of the too-recent betrayals and failures of the first anti-fascist war in the twentieth century, the Spanish Civil War. Valentine Cunningham, in his classic *British Writers of the Thirties*, judges that "[t]he most positive result of Spain, the period's renewed perception of the destructive element's destructiveness, the relearning of Owen's First War lessons, was heavy with negativity and the denial of a period's aspirations" (462). Such negativity reduced the number of the "old leftist guard" to a few stalwart holdouts; Anand was among them, joining Charlotte Haldane, Pat Sloan, John Sommerfield, Randall Swingler, Sylvia Townsend Warner, and Alic West in signing Poetry and the People's appeal for funds in February 1940 (Cunningham 462). This was during the phoney war, when Britons waited for the invasion that never materialised. When *Across the Black Waters* appeared in London later that same year, so did the German bombers. English readers were even less inclined to forgive a novel or novelist that wove together the bitter memories of Spain with those of World War I and dared compare the casualties suffered by the British at Barcelona and Ypres with those of Indian subjects, who suffered the bloody consequences of imperialism at home and abroad. When Anand's implicit call for an end to British colonialism in *Across the Black Waters* became explicit in his 1942 non-

12. Mulk Raj Anand in England

fictional *Letters on India*, he suffered what must have been his most painful rejection by any English literary figure. Accepting an invitation to write an introduction to *Letters on India*, the socialist Leonard Woolf, Anand's one-time employer at the Hogarth Press, contested Anand's research and arguments and publicly dismissed him as a Congress Party extremist (Woolf vii).

Anand had not started out as a despised alien in London's literary-political culture. In the thirties he had been friends or colleagues with some of England's most prominent writers and publishers. In addition to Leonard Woolf, he was acquainted with Louis MacNeice, Virginia Woolf, T. S. Eliot, William Empson, George Orwell, E. M. Forster, Herbert Read, and Stevie Smith, and was loudly and widely acclaimed for his polemical novels *Untouchable* (1935) and *Coolie* (1936) (Cowasjee 27). Comparing Anand to Orwell, Parry comments that both men wrote books "powered by a need to show their middle-class readership what it is really like to be at the bottom of the social pile" (31). He adds, "Although the subject matter of Anand's novels is intensely Indian, the social concerns belong very much to England in the 1930s" (31). Anand's sense of "belonging very much to England in the 1930s" changed when Britain went to war with the Axis powers and India became a vital support for the British war treasury, as well as a dominion vulnerable to both Japanese invasion and revolution. In this context, Anand's decision to publish *Across the Black Waters* was politically brave though professionally unwise. It seemed to seal his fate as a literary casualty of war and Empire. Faced with such opposition in England and tempted by the new possibilities of Gandhi's campaign for a free India, Anand moved to India permanently in 1945 where he lived as a hopeful Marxist-humanist advocate and sometime friend of India's new rulers, writing novels, stories and treatises for Indian readers on behalf of the illiterate poor.

In *Weird English*, Ch'ien compares immigrant and postcolonial writers to the poets of World War I, noting that both war poets and immigrant writers faced "redescription of their worlds in a language which did not have all the vocabulary they required," and both sought "reembodiment" of and through language (18). *Across the Black Waters*, situated at the intersection of war literature, British modernism, and the literature of Empire, is haunted by the "ghosts and shadow warriors" that Ch'ien associates with weird English literature (18). The ghost of Daddy Dhanoo, "still going round the trenches demanding the ceremonial rites" (128), symbolises the past and its languages, while the living sepoys are described as "ghosts from another, warmer world, transplanted into the creeping wet, cold autumnal underworld of 'Franceville'" (129).

Yet for Anand, the ghosts of a vernacular language do not have to remain in the past or be assimilated into the weird English present, since India, with its languages and politics, becomes his future. Beyond the ending of *Across the Black Waters*, this future may have sealed his fate as a casualty of war and Empire in the eyes of his London compatriots. From the perspective of postcolonial readers and writers, Anand's trajectory is a sign of his potential for recovery and renewal. Situated on the cusp of Independence, *Across the Black Waters* looks both ways: it memorialises the Indian sepoys who helped maintain the British Empire during World War I, and anticipates their liberation through a post-World War II negotiated freedom. Moving like Lalu between cultures, languages, and traditions, Anand offers an exemplary text of literary and linguistic reorientation. *Across the Black Waters* contributes equally to the literature of British India and the beginnings of a postcolonial literature of Independence, thereby generating a mobile, fluid English language and literary history.

Works Cited

Anand, Mulk Raj. *Across the Black Waters*. 1940. New Delhi: Vision, 1978.

___. *Coolie*. 1936. London: Wishart, 1975.

———. *The King-Emperor's English, or The Role of the English Language in the Free India.* Bombay: Hind Kitabs, 1948.

———. *Letters on India.* London: Wishart, 1942.

———. "Pigeon Indian: Some Notes on Indian-English Writing." *World Literature Written in English* 21 (1982): 325-36.

———. *The Sword and the Sickle.* New Delhi: Arnold-Heinemann, 1942.

———. *Untouchable.* London: Lawrence and Wishart, 1935.

———. *The Village.* London: Cape, 1939.

Berman, Jessica. "Comparative Colonialisms: Joyce, Anand, and the Question of Engagement." *Modernism/Modernity* 13 (2006): 465-85.

Bluemel, Kristin. *George Orwell and the Radical Eccentrics: Intermodernism in Literary London.* New York: Palgrave, 2004.

Ch'ien, Evelyn Nien-Ming. *Weird English.* Cambridge, MA: Harvard University Press, 2004.

Cowasjee, Saros. *So Many Freedoms: A Study of the Major Fictions of Mulk Raj Anand.* Delhi: Oxford University Press, 1977.

Cunningham, Valentine. *British Writers of the Thirties.* Oxford and New York: Oxford University Press, 1988.

Edwards, Paul. "British War Memoirs." *The Cambridge Companion to the Literature of the First World War.* Ed. Vincent Sherry. Cambridge and New York: Cambridge University Press, 2005. 15-33.

Gandhi, Leela. "Novelists of the 1930s and 1940s." *A History of Indian Literature in English.* Ed. Arvind Krishna Mehrotra. New York: Columbia University Press, 2003. 168-92.

Kumar, Jai, and Haresh Pandya. "Obituary: Mulk Raj Anand." *Guardian* 29 Sept. 2004. *Guardian Unlimited.* 26 May 2007 <http://books.guardian.co.uk/obituaries/story/0,,1315235,00.htm>.

Marcus, Jane. *Hearts of Darkness: White Women Write Race.* New Brunswick: Rutgers University Press, 2004.

Omissi, David, ed. and introd. *Indian Voices of the Great War: Soldiers' Letters, 1914-18.* London: Macmillan, 1999.

Omissi, David. *The Sepoy and the Raj: The Indian Army, 1860-1940.* London: Macmillan, 1994.

Parry, Graham. "Anand, Orwell, and the War." *The Novels of Mulk Raj Anand.* Ed. R. K. Dhawan. New Delhi: Prestige, 1992. 30-38.

Trotter, David. "The British Novel and the War." *The Cambridge Companion to the Literature of the First World War.* Ed. Vincent Sherry. Cambridge and New York: Cambridge University Press, 2005. 34-56.

Wolpert, Stanley. *A New History of India.* 4th ed. Oxford and New York: Oxford University Press, 1993.

Woolf, Leonard. Introduction. *Letters on India.* By Mulk Raj Anand. London: Labour Book Service, 1942. vii-ix.

Contributors

Viqar Atiya is a Documentation Officer / Assistant Librarian at the Centre for Women's Studies, Maulana Azad National Urdu University (MANUU), Hyderabad, India. Her area of interest is Indian minority women's issues.

Prodosh Bhattacharya is Reader in English at Jadavpur University, Kolkata. His recent publications include analyses of Old English poetry and prose, as well as a study of two Marie Corelli novels from the viewpoint of Orientalism. He has recently submitted his doctoral thesis on Marie Corelli as well, in addition to having completed a Minor Research Project entitled "The Popularity of Marie Corelli in Britain and India." His forthcoming publications include a study of two Old English and one Early Middle English poems, a study of two Bengali transformations of Sherlock Holmes narratives, and two further studies of Marie Corelli.

K. C. Bindu is Research Fellow at the Centre for Women's Studies at Maulana Azad National Urdu University (MANUU). Her work comes under the broad rubric of Culture Studies and focuses on the question of identities and their relationship to power in society. Her publications have dealt with both gender and community identities and their interconnectedness.

Kristin Bluemel is Professor of English at Monmouth University in West Long Branch, New Jersey, where she edits the interdisciplinary journal, *The Space Between: Literature and Culture, 1914-1945*. She is author of *George Orwell and the Radical Eccentrics: Intermodernism in Literary London* (Palgrave 2004) and *Experimenting on the Borders of Modernism: Dorothy Richardson's "Pilgrimage"* (Georgia 1997). Her work in progress includes an edited anthology of critical essays titled *Intermodernism: Writing and Culture in Interwar and Wartime Britain*, forthcoming from Edinburgh University Press.

Marianna D'Ezio completed a PhD in English Literature at the University of Rome "La Sapienza." She lives and works in Italy, where she teaches Italian at the University of California (Rome Study Center) and English at the University of Perugia, where she is Adjunct Professor of English. Her research interests focus on late eighteenth-century literature, with special attention to women writers. She has published many articles on eighteenth-century women travelling to Italy and is currently preparing a monograph on Hester Lynch Piozzi for the University of Toronto Press.

Nira Gupta-Casale is Associate Professor in the English Department at Kean University, New Jersey. She has published articles on gender and Indian cinema and is currently working on eighteenth-century British women travellers and the rhetoric of commerce and desire.

Angma Dey Jhala recently completed her doctorate in Modern History at Christ Church, Oxford, where she was a Clarendon scholar. She will begin teaching in the History Department at Tufts University in September 2007. Her dissertation on courtly women in late Imperial India is to be published by Pickering and Chatto Press in 2008. She received undergraduate and graduate degrees from Harvard, focusing on comparative religions, gender, and culture. Jhala is also a published fiction writer and is at present working on a novel.

Pia Mukherji has a PhD in English Literature from the Graduate Center of the City University of New York. She has been a lecturer in English at Tufts University in Medford, Massachusetts, for the past three years. At present, she is working on a book-length project that studies connections between the British-Indian colonial archive and the modern British novel. She anticipates her first electronic book publication – *An Introduction to Post-Modernism* – forthcoming in Fall 2007 from the Humanities ebook Series.

Rekha Pande is a faculty member in the Department of History, University of Hyderabad. Earlier she has worked as a director, Centre for Women's Studies, at Maulana Azad National Urdu University (MANUU). She works in the interdisciplinary area of women's studies and history. She is the author of four books and a large number of papers in national and international journals on women's studies and history. She has received three international visiting fellowships (University of Bristol, England; Maison des Sciences de l'Homme, Paris; University of Buffalo, USA). She is the editor of two international journals: *International Feminist Journal of Politics* (Routledge) and *Foreign Policy Analysis* (Blackwell).

Masood Ashraf Raja is Assistant Professor of Postcolonial Literature and Theory at Kent State University. He specialises in literatures of South Asia, the Caribbean, and Africa with a special emphasis on responses to the neoliberal globalisation. His essays have appeared in *Interactions*, *Mosaic*, *Digest of Middle East Studies*, *Muslim Public Affairs Journal*, *South Asian Review*, and *Caribbean Studies*. Raja has also contributed book chapters to several anthologies. He is currently working on a book entitled *Islam and the Nation-State*.

Ruvani Ranasinha is Senior Lecturer in English at King's College, London and author of *Hanif Kureishi* (Northcote House, Writers and their Works series, 2002) and *South Asian Writers in Twentieth-Century Britain: Culture in Translation* (Oxford University Press, 2007), and a joint editor of *Interventions: International Journal in Postcolonial Studies*.

Andrew Rudd is a literary critic based in London. He holds a PhD from Trinity College, Cambridge, and was George B. Cooper Fellow at the Lewis Walpole Library, Yale University. He writes regularly on Romantic literature and Orientalism, and is a contributor to the *Times Literary Supplement*, the *Church Times*, and the *Journal of Imperial and Commonwealth History*.

Nandini Sengupta is a doctoral student in the Department of English at Syracuse University, USA. She is currently researching and writing her thesis tentatively titled "Representations of Interracial Mixing in the Literature and Culture of British India: 1835-1885," in which she examines the various manifestations and implications of interracial intimacy in relationships established between Indians and British in the "contact zone."

Shafquat Towheed was educated at University College London and Corpus Christi College, Cambridge. He is Lecturer in Literature at the Open University and the editor of *The Correspondence of Edith Wharton and Macmillan, 1901-1930* (Palgrave 2007), of a forthcoming Broadview edition of Arthur Conan Doyle's *The Sign of Four*, and co-editor (with Mary Hammond) of *Publishing in the First World War: Essays in Book History* (Palgrave 2007). He is project supervisor for "The Reading Experience Database, 1450-1945 (RED)" <http://www.open.ac.uk/Arts/RED>.

STUDIES IN ENGLISH LITERATURES

Edited by Koray Melikoğlu

ISSN 1614-4651

1   *Özden Sözalan*
    The Staged Encounter
    Contemporary Feminism and Women's Drama
    2nd, revised editon
    ISBN 3-89821-367-6

2   *Paul Fox (ed.)*
    Decadences
    Morality and Aesthetics in British Literature
    ISBN 3-89821-573-3

3   *Daniel M. Shea*
    James Joyce and the Mythology of Modernism
    ISBN 3-89821-574-1

4   *Paul Fox and Koray Melikoğlu (eds.)*
    Formal Investigations
    Aesthetic Style in Late-Victorian and Edwardian Detective Fiction
    ISBN 978-3-89821-593-0

5   *David Ellis*
    Writing Home
    Black Writing in Britain Since the War
    ISBN 978-3-89821-591-6

6   *Wei H. Kao*
    The Formation of an Irish Literary Canon in the Mid-Twentieth Century
    ISBN 978-3-89821-545-9

7   *Bianca Del Villano*
    Ghostly Alterities
    Spectrality and Contemporary Literatures in English
    ISBN 978-3-89821-714-9

8   *Melanie Ann Hanson*
    Decapitation and Disgorgement
    The Female Body's Text in Early Modern English Drama and Poetry
    ISBN 978-3-89821-605-5

9   *Shafquat Towheed (ed.)*
    New Readings in the Literature of British India, c.1780-1947
    ISBN 978-3-89821-673-9

FORTHCOMING (MANUSCRIPT WORKING TITLES)

Lance Weldy
Seeking a Felicitous Space
The Dialectics of Women and Frontier Space in *Giants in the Earth*, *Little House on the Prairie*, and *My Antonia*
ISBN 3-89821-535-0

Paola Baseotto
Spenserian Views of Death
ISBN 3-89821-567-9

Kevin Cole
Levity's Rainbow
Menippean Poetics in Swift, Fielding, and Sterne
ISBN 3-89821-654-3

Series Subscription

Please enter my subscription to the series **Studies in English Literatures**, ISSN 1614-4651, as follows:

- ❏ complete series   OR   ❏ English-language titles
- ❏ German-language titles

starting with
- ❏ volume # 1
- ❏ volume # ___
  - ❏ please also include the following volumes: #___, ___, ___, ___, ___, ___,

- ❏ the next volume being published
  - ❏ please also include the following volumes: #___, ___, ___, ___, ___, ___,

- ❏ 1 copy per volume   OR   ❏ ___ copies per volume

Subscription within Germany:

You will receive every title on 1st publication at the regular bookseller's price incl. s & h and VAT.

Payment:
❏ Please bill me for every volume.
❏ Lastschriftverfahren: Ich/wir ermächtige(n) Sie hiermit widerruflich, den Rechnungsbetrag je Band von meinem/unserem folgendem Konto einzuziehen.

Kontoinhaber: _____ Kreditinstitut: _____
Kontonummer: _____ Bankleitzahl: _____

International Subscription:

Payment (incl. s & h and VAT) in advance for
- ❏ 10 volumes/copies (€ 319.80)   ❏ 20 volumes/copies (€ 599.80)
- ❏ 40 volumes/copies (€ 1,099.80)

Please send my books to:

NAME _____ DEPARTMENT _____
ADDRESS _____
POST/ZIP CODE _____ COUNTRY _____
TELEPHONE _____ EMAIL _____

date/signature _____

Please fax to: **0511 / 262 2201 (+49 511 262 2201)**
or mail to: *ibidem*-Verlag, Julius-Leber-Weg 11, D-30457 Hannover, Germany
or send an e-mail: ibidem@ibidem-verlag.de

ibidem-Verlag
Melchiorstr. 15
D-70439 Stuttgart

info@ibidem-verlag.de

www.ibidem-verlag.de
www.edition-noema.de
www.autorenbetreuung.de

Zeitfracht Medien GmbH
Ferdinand-Jühlke-Straße 7,
99095 - DE, Erfurt
produktsicherheit@zeitfracht.de